Praise from the Experts

Tanya Dominick, after appearing on the Oprah Winfrey Show, wrote this book that hits the Alternative Dispute Resolution Career nail right on the head in her brilliant and realistic book, *How to Make it Big Resolving Disputes.* She leads you by the hand from total darkness to revelation of this exciting field. Her book reveals jealously guarded secrets of making money in mediation, arbitration, training, consulting and much, much more.

I highly recommend that you follow her road map to your success.

Martina S. Moore, President & Licensed Counselor
Moore Counseling and Mediation

How To Make It Big Resolving Disputes is a "must have" for any mediator's bookshelf. In her book, Tanya Dominick makes it easy to find mediation resources and contacts in every state to enhance your practice. And the best part is the resources are all at your fingertips in one book, *How To Make It Big Resolving Disputes.* Tanya offers sage advice on finding the perfect mediation career for you from writing and consulting to arbitration and training. She also offers valuable tips and resources for starting a mediation practice, from phone services to setting up a virtual office.

I particularly enjoyed the positive flavor in which this book is written. The myth that you have to be an expert to mediate is dispelled by Tanya and is replaced by a positive yes-you-can message. At first, I felt intimidated entering the field of mediation. Between the book and Tanya's expertise in her online mediation training, I gained the confidence I needed to not only know that I can mediate, but mediate well without a law degree.

Kathy S. Garber, R.N., B.S.N., M.A.
Certified Anger Management Facilitator
Certified Online Instructor
Certified Parenting Instructor
Author of *Stop Anger, Be Happy*

How to Make It Big Resolving Disputes

How to Make It Big Resolving Disputes

A Step-by-Step Guide to Making Serious Money in *Conflict Resolution*

Tanya L. Dominick

Second Edition

Brooklyn, NY

How To Make It Big Resolving Disputes
by Tanya L. Dominick

ISBN-13: 978-0-9722088-3-3
ISBN-10: 0-9722088-3-6

Printed in the United States of America.

American Center for Conflict Resolution Institute
45 Main Street, Suite #309-70
Brooklyn, NY 11201

http://www.accri.org

Dedication

To all of the people who have served as lights along my path:

My mother—*the woman who continues to birth me daily*
My father—*the man who taught me the joy of loving myself*
My grandmothers—*the women who taught me about unconditional love*
My grandfathers—*the men who taught me how to sow*
My aunts—*the women who taught me how to laugh*
My uncle—*the man who implanted the joy of being an entrepreneur*
My cousins—*the men and women who taught me how to fight and play*
My sister–*the woman who teaches me about God's love*
My brother—*the man who provided a new direction in life*
My daughter—*the woman who freely shares her wisdom and heart with me*
My friends (Nekole, Tina, Mitch, Willa, Barbara, Martina, April and Lisa)—*the men and women who teach me how to unselfishly love others*
My students—*who instill within me the desire to learn more*
My pastor—*the man who taught me to value relationship with God over religion*
My husband—*a best friend who has helped me to realize my God-given potential*
Dr Phil and Oprah—*two great people that gave me courage to make it happen*
My Savior, Jesus Christ—*the one that always cares for me*

Contents

Introduction

This is a book for anyone who wants to learn how to make real money in the Alternative Dispute Resolution profession, but may have little or no experience in this field. It is also designed as a resource for those who wish to help others (individuals or businesses) resolve their differences through mediation, arbitration, facilitation, etc. I affectionately refer to these individuals as peacemakers.

There is a myth floating around among many "experts." The myth is that one must be an attorney or have numerous years of work experience before being able to succeed in this field. This is just plain untrue. I know because I shot the myth down and so have countless others. I was always taught that there is no such word as "can't."

Let me digress for a moment. In high school, a high school counselor told me that I couldn't go to college because I wasn't college material. But I did go to college. After becoming a single mother right before entering college, I was told that I would never finish and I'd be a professional college student, but I graduated from college in the honors program. In law school, I was told that perhaps I should consider another field since everyone is not meant

1

to become a lawyer; however, I graduated from law school. After successfully completing dispute resolution education, I was told that I could not prosper in this field unless I had five years of work experience in law or another field, but I have become successful even without five years of experience in any field. Now I help other individuals with all sorts of educational backgrounds do the same, from factory employees to CEOs.

Currently, I am President and Founder of the American Center for Conflict Resolution Institute, a graduate of Pepperdine School of Law and Straus Institute for Dispute Resolution, a provider/trainer of dispute resolution education, a mediator, an arbitrator, a public speaker, and a consultant. I have extensive knowledge and experience in this field. Please do not let my education or experience convince you that you need the same or similar background to succeed in this field. Some of the most successful, effective conflict resolution professionals have little more than a high school education. This also does not mean that I have all the answers about every single area in the field. However, it does mean that I have a number of suggestions that will assist you in your career as a peacemaker.

This invaluable guidebook is designed to help peacemakers find rewarding careers in dispute resolution and, I pray, make a good living. This book covers:

- ♦ Getting Alternative Dispute Resolution training
- ♦ Choosing your area(s) of specialization, such as:
  - mediation
  - arbitration
  - training
  - writing
  - consulting
  - other
- ♦ Finding resources for peacemakers
- ♦ Joining professional associations and acquiring insurance
- ♦ Obtaining grant money for peacemakers
- ♦ Using the power of networking

As you see, whether you're an amateur or a pro, this book provides information not found in any other single source. This book's ultimate goal is to help you prosper and advance in the field of Alternative Dispute Resolution; hence, this book should assist you in finding a true secret of happiness in life and in business.

How to Use
This Book

This book is designed for individuals desiring to enter the Alternative Dispute Resolution field, whether in one specialty area or several. I suggest that all individuals read, then follow, the success checklist on the next page and then study the subsequent chapters according to their desired area(s) of choice.

Since there is very little instruction out in the world from an insider's view into this wonderful profession, this book will serve as a step-by-step guide to help you avoid the trials and tribulations of finding the path to your dreams. While some may wish to enter this occupation as a means to supplement or earn a living, there is a basic characteristic that all who are successful, both financially and emotionally, in this field hold: the desire to serve others.

Congratulations!

You are on your way to a rewarding and satisfying career that will help you obtain financial freedom! You should be proud of yourself. You will accomplish the following items on your success checklist by implementing the instructions in this book.

Success Checklist

☐ You will learn important definitions in Alternative Dispute Resolution (ADR)

☐ You will choose an ADR specialty or several specialties to pursue (check those you have chosen to pursue):

☐ ADR Consultant
☐ ADR Trainer
☐ ADR Author
☐ Mediator
☐ Arbitrator
☐ Consultant
☐ Faith-Based Organization
You will apply for grant money from ⎯⎯⎯⎯⎯⎯⎯⎯
☐ ADR Job
☐ You will review the 60 sample job titles and send your resume to at least 100 institutions.

☐ You will complete the necessary training for each specialty you plan to pursue

☐ You will join at least one professional organization

☐ You will contact your state's ADR offices to get information about ADR opportunities to begin networking

☐ You will read at least one article daily about how to increase your marketability

☐ You will talk to, email, or write at least one successful person per day in the ADR profession to network about available opportunities

☐ You will keep fresh in your mind daily that this profession is all about serving others

Please send a note about your success to be displayed in future publications to: support@breakupfights.com.

What Is Alternative Dispute Resolution?

Objective
To provide a background of
Alternative Dispute Resolution.

Introduction

The field of law has explored various ways of solving disputes. For centuries the most effective and popular way of solving disputes was going to court and having a formal trial. As time went by, scholars continued to study methods other than litigation that could be effective and justified in solving disputes. Such methods were closely examined by the American Bar Association at its annual convention on Hawaii in 1989. The convention was devoted to "Resolving Disputes in Pacific Ways" and attracted many visitors. More than fifteen years after the convention, "Alternative Dispute Resolution" or "Appropriate Dispute Resolution" (hereafter referred to as ADR) became an important substitute for litigation. For many years it has been explored and debated. It gained a significant place in the reports concerning new ways of dispute resolution all over the United States.

Alternative Dispute Resolution comprises more than ten methods, referred to as "alternatives to litigation as a means of dispute resolution." A person who decides to forgo a formal trial but refers to ADR companies always has a choice concerning which method of solving the dispute to use. Usually, ADR costs less than pursuing litigation; thus, it appears to be more attractive to people than participating in a full and formal trial. Despite the fact that ADR is less formal than litigation, it does result in some form of negotiation between the parties. ADR is confidential and offers a level of self-determination for every client.

This chapter was designed to explore the essence of Alternative Dispute Resolution and its peculiarities and advantages as compared to other methods of dispute resolution. It will focus on various types of ADR—including mediation, negotiation, conciliation, arbitration, and others—which are used to resolve disputes. Pros and cons of every type of ADR also will be discussed.

Recent Recognition

ADR is rapidly growing across America. It currently exists in every state. More than 600 of the largest corporations in the United States have agreed to sign a pledge to seek to resolve disputes out of court before filing lawsuits against each other.

The rise of ADR is highly attributable to the overload of litigation thrown upon the American court system. Additionally, stresses of modern society and confrontation make ADR a growth opportunity.

In 1990, Congress enacted the Administrative Dispute Resolution Act, which mandates that agencies explore the development of Alternative Dispute Resolution programs. In addition, many court systems have also begun to utilize ADR to pare down their dockets.

The Essence of Alternative Dispute Resolution

Due to the increasing costs of paying for litigation and the growth of court congestion, individuals as well as whole companies slowly but steadily are starting to turn to Alternative Dispute Resolution in order to solve their disputes. The acronym ADR stands for the set of methods by means of which legal conflicts and various disputes are solved outside the courtroom. Usually, ADR is less formal than litigation but does include the presence of a third party to preside over the hearing between the two disputing parties. It is also less expensive and time-consuming. The specialists working at the Center for Effective Dispute Resolution (CEDR) gave the following definition of the term ADR: "A body of dispute resolution techniques which avoid the inflexibility of litigation and arbitration, and focus instead on enabling the parties to achieve a better or similar result, with the minimum of direct and indirect cost." As mentioned above, there are different methods used in ADR, and each of them possesses certain characteristics. However, it is possible to identify certain characteristics that are peculiar to the whole process of ADR.

The first characteristic feature of ADR is that it deals with all disputes confidentially, meaning that the process of dispute resolution and its outcomes are usually kept in secret unless disclosure is mandated by a special law or mandatory reporting obligation. For example, most mediators are considered to be mandatory reporters, and the law compels them to report child abuse or elder abuse if it is revealed during a mediation session.

ADR is more flexible than usual litigation. It leaves room for creativity and cooperation to come to a common solution and to meet the requirements of both parties. This is mainly due to the fact that it is less formal than litigation. ADR gives an opportunity to gain more control over the process of dispute resolution.

ADR involves personal communication among all parties, who might be working or living together after the process ends. Thus, it maintains the existing relationship by using methods that encourage people to cooperate in order to reach an agreement. Often ADR leads to the improvement of the relationship and elimination of further conflicts. This is the reason that many families and businesses have come to rely on this type of conflict management, since employees and family members usually have long-term relationships, that require preservation.

ADR establishes certain rules that govern the process of solving disputes. Methods of ADR involve the presence of a third party, termed neutrals or peacemakers. These individuals are normally chosen because they do not advocate for one disputant but rather manage the process. Generally, the process of ADR is not as expensive in comparison with litigation, along with being more expeditious and less complex.

ADR affords disputants the possibility of personal satisfaction, as they take a more active part in the process and can decide for themselves which method of ADR to use. Normally, in a court setting there is a "winner" and a "loser;" however, with this form of resolution the parties can enter into a mutually satisfactory agreement through the use of collaboration. ADR helps to reach the compromise between the parties, while litigation results in the satisfaction of only one party.

The last characteristic is: by means of ADR, it is possible to get to the root of a problem due to the use of personal approach. In ADR the decision-making is the responsibility of the disputing parties or the neutral.

Though ADR has many obvious advantages compared to usual litigation, there are some disputes that cannot be solved by means of ADR. For example, cases of violence—when courts are able to provide better protection for victims of violence—or cases when one of the parties possesses too much power. Also, ADR is improper when one of the parties wants the issue in dispute to become public knowledge or wants the outcome to set precedent. Such a desire goes against standard practice. ADR cannot be used as the means of dispute resolution when the outcome may influence a great number of people, for example where a definite and broadly applicable solution is required. Court proceedings are more effective for the above-mentioned cases.

Advantages of ADR

Below is a summary of the benefits of ADR.

ADR **saves money.** It is less expensive than litigation. According to ADR experts, the cost is often 10–50 times less expensive than going through the court system.

ADR **saves time.** Typically, there is little or no need for case preparation. Additionally, one may participate in an ADR process almost immediately—unlike litigation, where it may take months or years to present a case before the court.

ADR **is private.** ADR proceedings are usually confidential; therefore ADR protects the reputation of the participants and there is no public record of the proceedings.

ADR **is convenient.** Scheduling can be done at a time and place that is amenable to all parties involved.

ADR **prevents litigation.** The use of ADR is a consensual process that provides a non-adversarial way to resolve a dispute.

ADR **is creative.** It allows the parties involved in the dispute to "think outside the box." This usually gives rise to results not available in typical court settings.

Types of ADR and Their Peculiarities

There is a great variety of disputes as well as a great variety of methods to handle them. Legal practice has shown that usual forensic methods of solving disputes are not always the best. ADR offers a whole range of methods, out of which the most suitable one can be chosen. Thus, the expanded definition of ADR has slightly changed, and the word "alternative"—for which the letter "A" stands—was changed to "appropriate." Indeed, methods used in ADR are appropriate for various disputes, including family, business, governmental, and other disputes.

Having described the essence of ADR and its peculiarities, I will now explore various types of ADR, including: ombudsmen, conciliation, negotiation, mediation, arbitration, adjudication, early neutral evaluation, expert determination, med-arb, and med-rec.

Ombudsmen

Ombudsmen are specialists who are trained to examine the case and help the parties solve complaints concerning public and private matters. Ombudsmen may use a number of methods to facilitate dispute resolution, among which are counseling, mediating, conciliating, and fact-finding. After receiving a complaint, an ombudsman interviews the parties and possibly examines the files; however, ombudsmen do not pronounce judgment or determine a solution. All ombudsmen are neutral parties in the dispute. In some organizations, an external ombudsman will not consider a complaint unless the organization or company has first been given a chance to deal with it through its own internal complaints procedure. Ombudsmen do not have the power to impose a solution; however, they may have an ability to persuade the parties to accept their recommendations. Services of ombudsmen may be limited, requiring the disputing parties to reach an agreement with a fixed period of time (six – twelve months) or perhaps permanently. Initially, an ombudsman would try to help the parties resolve the conflict informally. Otherwise, the ombudsman may refer the disputants to an internal organizational investigation process in order to conduct an investigation which may result in the issuance of a report with a conclusion.

Conciliation

Conciliation is the process during which a conciliator (a third party or a neutral) builds positive relationships between the disputing parties in order to solve the dispute. "A conciliator may assist parties by helping to establish communication, clarifying misconceptions, dealing with strong emotions, and building the trust necessary for cooperative problem-solving." (http://www.ADRnow.org.uk/go/SubSection_15.html, accessed September 17, 2006).

Conciliators may choose a neutral place for meeting, carry messages between the parties, and assure parties that they are able to communicate and work together. Conciliation helps the disputing parties start a dialogue, build a positive attitude towards each other, and enhance mutual trust. There are two characteristic features concerning conciliation. First, this process is totally voluntary. Second, it is absolutely private and confidential. After conciliation the parties may or may not agree on the resolution. In his turn, a conciliator may meet with each of the parties together or separately, or may not meet with them at all and announce the resolution by phone or other means of communication.

Negotiation

Negotiation is probably the most fundamental method of solving any dispute and is used more often than others. However, that does not mean this method is the most effective. It all depends on the type of dispute. If the parties are willing to communicate, this method will definitely work; if not, other methods may be chosen. Negotiation can also be the quickest and the cheapest way to resolve a dispute. As a means of ADR, negotiation can be done directly between the parties or with the help of their representatives. The main goal of negotiation is to reach an agreement. There are two types of negotiation: facilitated negotiation, when a neutral is chosen; and non-facilitated negotiation, when the parties seek a solution themselves.

Negotiation involves communication among people in an effort to reach an agreement or new understanding. This process involves consenting disputants who seek to resolve their differences without the intervention of a third-party facilitator. The disputants may or may not choose to have legal representation.

The parties usually meet face-to-face, through written/electronic communication, or by representatives of their respective viewpoints who are often—but not necessarily—attorneys. If the parties decide to settle their dispute without representatives, they can completely control the process. This is the most consensual and informal process in dispute resolution. The results are less expensive to the disputants in the form of time, money, and efficiency. An example of this process might be going next door to talk to your neighbor about shrubs he/she is growing on your property line and to resolve this matter through a mutually satisfactory verbal agreement.

Mediation

Mediation is facilitated negotiation. Mediation is a process of resolving a dispute by means of third-party intervention. A mediator (a neutral or a third party) works with a single objective: to help the parties reach an agreement. Mediation works effectively in "highly-polarized disputes where the parties have either been unable to initiate a productive dialogue, or where the parties have been talking and have reached a seemingly insurmountable impasse." ("Alternative Dispute Resolution." http://www .opm.gov/er/ADRguide/Section1-a.asp, accessed September 17, 2006).

A mediator is not authorized to make any decisions or impose solutions; however, he/she may suggest how to improve the relationship between the parties. Sometimes, mediators work with each party separately.

There are several distinguishing features of mediation. Mediation is absolutely voluntary. No parties are under obligation to take part in mediation. As with any other type of ADR, mediation is private and confidential. It is up to the parties—not a mediator—to make the decision and resolve the dispute. The most important feature is that a mediator should be impartial and independent with no personal interest in the outcome. Mediation is often used to solve disputes over divorce and separation, business claims, consumer disputes, small claims, and others. Eighty percent of mediated disputes end in a mutually satisfactory agreement between the parties. Despite the fact that mediation is a rather effective method, there are some cases when other methods of solving disputes need to be used.

Since mediation is facilitated negotiation, the parties of a dispute design their own resolution with the help of a trained neutral to bring the parties to agreement. The mediator has no independent authority and does not render a decision. The parties of the dispute must reach the decision. This process usually ends with an agreement, which is signed by the parties of the dispute. This process usually has five stages, according to Professor Peter Robinson and Professor Randy Lowry at the Straus Institute for Dispute Resolution at Pepperdine School of Law: convening, opening, communication, negotiation, and closing.

1. Convening. The convening stage consists of getting the parties to the table. This process may be accomplished by telephone, letter, or in person.

2. Opening. In my experience, this is one of the crucial stages of the mediation process. The purpose of this stage is to create safety and hope for the disputants. This is a period when the mediator educates the disputants about the mediation process; sets the ground rules; informs the disputants about the mediator's role and the disputants' roles, the agenda, time constraints, caucus, confidentiality, impartiality, neutrality, and mediator credentials.

3. Communication. Mediators explore each party's positions and underlying interests. According to Ury and Fischer in the book *Getting* *to Yes*, a position is what a party wants and interests are why they want it. For example, the position of a disputant may be "I want money for my damages," but she may want the money because she felt a loss of respect. This loss of respect would be the disputant's interest. By knowing the underlying interest, a mediator may be able to help the parties focus their dispute on satisfying the interests, thus allowing for more creative solutions to the problem. For example, an apology could be a powerful resolution to this particular situation.

This is where training and experience are needed to be an effective mediator. (See more about obtaining training in Chapter Two.) Mediators will need to use skills such as information gathering, active communication, validation, summarization, mutualizing, normalizing, reframing, power balancing, recognition, and empowerment during this stage. (For more information about these skills there is a great book titled the *Fundamentals of Family Mediation* by John Haynes.)

When we communicate, it is usually about feelings or substance. We have two ways we usually communicate: active and passive. Passive communication implies that the listener understands. This is usually accomplished through nodding, silence, or minimal prompts (uh-huh, I see, OK, etc.). On the other hand, active communication clearly communicates understanding. One of the most powerful ways of accomplishing this is through validation. According to Professor Peter Robinson of the Straus Institute of Dispute Resolution at Pepperdine School of Law, when a person feels validated he is more willing to share the components of his reality with the mediator. Validation does not mean that the mediator has to agree with the party, but that the person must feel accepted. This validation can be accomplished through "You feel (emotion) because (situation)." An example would be: "You feel upset because you did not get the raise you expected." A mediator must make sure to communicate the correct feeling and to display understanding of a situation. These statements clearly convey to a party that you are relating to what they are feeling.

4. Negotiation. This is the stage when the parties generate options and brainstorm about possible solutions to their particular dispute. Negotiation can be collaborative or competitive in nature. Competitive negotiation is where the ultimate goal is to win a share of limited resources. On the other hand, collaborative negotiation seeks a win-win resolution for all parties of the dispute. Collaborative negotiation is the heart of the mediation process.

There are also two types of bargaining in this part of the process: distributive bargaining and integrative bargaining. Distributive bargaining assumes a relatively "fixed pie" and the focus is generally a finite resource such as the purchase of a car. Fixed pie means that the negotiator assumes that there is only a fixed amount to be negotiated and, in order for one person to win, the other must lose. Integrative bargaining goes beyond this zero-sum exchange and allows for the creative generation of options. Negotiations usually involve both integrative and distributive bargaining.

5. Closing. This is the stage where the parties draft the agreement or terminate the mediation process. The drafted agreement should use the words of the participants and is usually signed only by the parties to the dispute. The mediator will need training to ensure that the agreement is durable, able to be carried out, and mutually satisfactory to the parties.

Arbitration

Arbitration is a "private dispute resolution process where disputing parties agree that one or several individuals can make a decision about the dispute after receiving evidence and hearing arguments." (http://www.mediate.ca/arbitration.htm accessed September 17, 2006).

A simple definition of arbitration is a process in which a dispute is submitted to a third party or neutral (or possibly a panel of three arbitrators) to hear arguments, review evidence, and render a decision. It is obvious that arbitration differs from the other types of ADR discussed above, as it involves the decision-making process conducted by the third party. Generally speaking, arbitration is similar to a formal trial. Both parties present their statements, then the arbitrator examines evidence and announces the decision. However, arbitration is done more rapidly and informally than a trial. When the arbitrator announces the award, he/she may or may not also give the reasons for such a decision. As with any other type of ADR, arbitration is private and confidential. Before the arbitration starts, both parties must agree to participate. Usually the process is legally binding (binding arbitration), meaning that the decision is obligatory to both parties according to the law. Arbitration hearings are less formal than trials, and sometimes hearings are not even necessary, as the dispute can be resolved with the help of documents only. An arbitrator may be a lawyer, a lay person, or an expert in a specific area. In some cases where the parties cannot choose an arbitrator, one can be chosen by a competent company. All arbitrators should be neutral and have no interest in the outcome of the dispute.

There are usually six stages involved in this process: initiation, preparation, pre-hearing, hearing, decision-making, and award.

1. Initiation. In this stage of the arbitration process there are two sub-stages: initiation of the proceeding and selection of the arbitrator. Arbitration proceedings may be initiated either by submission, demand, or notice of a court ruling by court order.

Both parties must sign a submission if there is no previous agreement to arbitrate. This submission usually names the arbitrator (or method of appointment) and contains considerable details regarding the arbitrator's authority, the procedure to be used at the hearing, a statement of the matter in dispute, the amount of money in controversy, the remedy sought, and other matters.

However, where the description of the dispute is contained in an agreement and the parties have agreed in advance to arbitrate, arbitration may be initiated unilaterally by one party serving a written demand or notice to arbitrate. It is important to note that even where the agreement contains a demand or notice clause, parties sometimes also choose to execute a submission after the dispute has materialized.

There are multiple types of panels, and methods of selecting membership, available to parties who wish to arbitrate. Parties may choose between the use of a temporary or permanent arbitrator. They can also choose to have single or multiple arbitrators. Since success of the arbitration process often depends on the expertise of the panel, parties usually try to select a panel whose members possess impartiality, integrity, ability, and experience in the field in which the dispute arises.

2. Preparation. It is important for parties to thoroughly prepare their arbitration cases. Each party must communicate their case effectively to the arbitrator. Depending on the nature of the case, pre-hearing discovery may be necessary, and this is usually determined by the arbitrator(s). Discovery is defined as an act, process, or instance of gaining knowledge of, or ascertaining the existence of, something previously unknown or unrecognized.

During this stage the parties may enter into stipulations. Stipulations are agreements between the parties about how the arbitration proceedings will be conducted.

Most of the arbitrator's knowledge and understanding of the case is based upon evidence and arguments presented at the arbitration hearing; however, the arbitrator does have some preparation functions. Generally—where there is no panel—an arbitrator, upon accepting the office, designates the time and place of the hearing by mutual agreement of the parties. The arbitrator also signs an oath, if required, and determines whether the parties will have legal representation during the hearing.

3. Pre-Hearing. Depending on the complexity of the matter involved, the arbitrator has the option of scheduling a pre-conference hearing, which is usually administrative in nature. If necessary, briefing schedules are set on motions attacking the validity of the claims of the proceeding. But, generally, briefing is minimized to preserve the efficiency of the process. Discussion of the underlying merits of claims or defenses of the parties are avoided during a pre-hearing conference. Ex parte conferences between the arbitrator and either party are not permitted. An ex parte conference is a meeting with one side in the absence of, and often without notice to, the other party.

4. Hearing. Parties may decide not to have an oral hearing but to have the controversy determined on the basis of documents only. However, an evidentiary-type hearing in the presence of the arbitrator is usually necessary in all cases. Since arbitration is a private proceeding, the hearing is not open to the public as a general rule, but all persons having a direct interest in the case are ordinarily entitled to attend.

A formal record of the hearing is not always necessary. Use of a formal reporter is the exception rather than the general practice. A party requiring an interpreter has the duty to arrange for one. Witnesses testifying at the hearing may also be required by law to appear, if ordered by the arbitrator, or on the demand of any party. These witnesses must normally sign an oath for the information that they will present.

Opening statements are made orally by each party in a brief, generalized format. They are designed to acquaint the arbitrator with each party's view of what the dispute is about and what the parties expect to prove by evidence. Sometimes an arbitrator will request that each party provide a short, written opening statement and a brief prior to the hearing.

There is no set order by which parties present their cases in arbitration, although in practice the complaining party normally presents the evidence first. The parties may offer any evidence they choose, including personal testimony and affidavits of witnesses. They may be required to produce additional evidence the arbitrator deems necessary to determine the dispute. The arbitrator, when authorized by law, may subpoena a witness or document on his or her own initiative or by a request of a party. The arbitrator also decides relevancy and materiality of evidence offered. Conformity to the legal rules of evidence is not necessary. Additionally, the arbitrator has the right to make a physical inspection of a particular location in order to fairly arrive at his/her decision.

The parties make closing arguments, usually limited in duration. Occasionally, the arbitrator requests post-hearing briefs. When this occurs, the parties usually waive oral closing arguments.

5. Decision-Making. When the issues are not complex, an arbitrator may render an immediate decision. However, when there is a large amount of evidence to be reviewed or the members of the arbitration panel need time to confer, it might require several weeks to make a decision.

6. Award. The award is the arbitrator's decision. It may be given orally, but it is normally written and signed by the arbitrator(s). Awards are usually short, definite, certain, and final for all matters under submission. Occasionally, they are accompanied by a short, well-reasoned opinion. This award is issued no later than 30 days from the closing date of the hearing. When a party fails to appear, default may be entered. Depending on the nature of the award, it may be judicially enforceable and reviewable. However, most arbitration awards are not overturned when appealed to court.

Adjudication

Adjudication is a type of ADR that involves the judge or a specially trained third party who considers the opinions of both parties, examines the facts, and makes the decision concerning how best to resolve a dispute. Adjudication is similar to other types of ADR in terms of the third party's neutrality and independence. However, unlike other types of ADR, adjudication is "an involuntary, adversarial process." (Spangler, Brad 2003, "Adjudication," http://www.beyondintractability .org/essay/adjudication/, accessed September 17, 2006)

The decision made by the third party is binding for every party; thus, adjudication is very close to a trial, as opposed to mediation or negotiation. Usually, after adjudication—as well as arbitration—there is one party who has won the dispute and another one who has lost it.

Early Neutral Evaluation

Early neutral evaluation is another type of ADR used to provide the parties with more information concerning their dispute. For this reason, an impartial third party or neutral is chosen to examine the peculiarities of the case by studying written statements of both parties. A third party evaluates the situation and announces strong and weak sides of the case. Sometimes oral presentations are done by the disputing parties in order to highlight positions of each party. Early neutral evaluation helps to avoid going to court and having a formal trial. It is used "when the parties disagree significantly about the value of their cases and when the top decision makers of one or more of the parties could be better informed about the real strengths and weaknesses of their cases." ("Alternative Dispute Resolution," http://www.opm.gov/er/ADRguide/Section1-a.asp, accessed September 17, 2006).

Early neutral evaluation is also a good way to avoid the large expenses of litigation.

Expert Determination

Expert determination is used to resolve uncomplicated disputes when both parties agree to choose an expert to assist. The expert (a third party) in his turn agrees to follow certain rules, including: to "adopt procedures suitable to the circumstances of the particular case, avoiding unnecessary delay and expense, so as to provide an expeditious cost-effective and fair means of determining the dispute;" (*Information about Expert Determination*, http://www.iama.org.au/expert.htm, accessed September 17, 2006); to be impartial and fair; to keep the process confidential; and to allow both parties to take part in the process. Before the expert starts to work, the parties have to agree that the expert's decision will be binding for all parties.

Med-Arb

Med-arb is one of the mixed processes used in ADR, a combination of mediation and arbitration. At first the parties take part in mediation, with the mediator trying to solve the dispute and guiding the parties until they come to a common decision. In cases when the parties are unable to reach an agreement, the mediator changes to an arbitration process and becomes an arbitrator. Parties may agree to continue the process or may wish to select another arbitrator to continue. The biggest advantage of med-arb is that a mediator can perform the function of arbitrator better than another neutral, as he/she is already aware of the particulars of the dispute. Med-arb is especially effective for conflicts between employers and employees.

Med-Rec

The last type of ADR presented is med-rec, a mixture of mediation and recommendation. The process of resolving a dispute starts as a mediation. However, if the parties do not reach an agreement, the mediator "makes a recommendation to the court or other decision-maker as to a recommended resolution." ("ADR Options," http://www.directionservice.org/cADRe/other .cfm, accessed September 17, 2006).

Career Outlook in the Field of ADR

According to the Bureau of Labor Statistics, U.S. Department of Labor, *Occupational Outlook Handbook, 2006–07 Edition, Judges, Magistrates, and Other Judicial Workers* (which can be found on the Internet at http://www.bls.gov/oco/ocos272.htm), employment of arbitrators, mediators, and conciliators is expected to grow about as fast as the average for these occupations through 2014. (Average means that between now and 2014 the field will increase 9–17 percent.) Many individuals and businesses try to avoid litigation, which can involve lengthy delays, high costs, unwanted publicity, and ill will. Arbitration and other alternatives to litigation usually are faster, less expensive, and more conclusive, spurring demand for the services of arbitrators, mediators, and conciliators. The handbook also reported that arbitrators, mediators, and conciliators earned a median income of $54,760.

In speaking about career outlook in the field of ADR, it is necessary to emphasize that it is becoming widely accepted and popular to use ADR methods instead of going to court. Thus, this field is an excellent area where new specialists in law can find good jobs and new opportunities. This is a result of the constantly growing costs of litigation such that parties prefer to choose an alternative to going to court, paying large sums of money, and waiting until the process ends after an extended period of time.

ADR is already supported by the government, so there are vacancies not only at private companies but also at state courts. There is a growing need for mediation among the population due to the growing number of divorces and small disputes between parties. ADR is a developing area of business and, like any other business, requires a high quality of judging, competence, and persistence. If a person possesses certain skills in working with people and solving disputes and is knowledgeable about relevant points of law as well as human psychology and sociology, that person is highly likely to become a successful mediator or conciliator by establishing a reputation that will attract clients. This training is normally provided through educational organizations specializing in mediation education.

Conclusion

As it can be seen from the information provided in this chapter, there are various methods used to resolve disputes between people. Court proceedings are very time-consuming and expensive, which compels individuals to seek an alternative. Alternative Dispute Resolution is an effective means of resolving disputes, and its methods are less expensive, confidential and more expeditious. They get much closer to the root of problems that need to be solved. Besides, the main goal of the majority of types of ADR is to improve the relationship between the disputing parties to help them reach an agreement. Hence, many peacemakers find great satisfaction in being appreciated for their service to others. This is what distinguishes ADR methods from litigation. There can be only one winning party after a court trial, while after conciliation, mediation, or negotiation all parties can be considered as winning, since the end result may be a mutually satisfactory agreement.

Choosing a Specialty

Objective
To help you identify your areas of interest
in the Alternative Dispute Resolution field.

Introduction

When I first completed my dispute resolution education, I moved to a city in the Midwest where mediation was not prevalent. As a matter of fact, my own mother asked me "What is mediation?" and "Can you make any money doing that?" I had also never practiced law and I was fresh out of my master's program. I had, however, done several volunteer mediations in the municipal court in California.

When I looked up the heading "Mediator" in the yellow pages, there were only 16 mediators listed and half of those had no business address. I immediately knew that this was going to be another challenge in my life. So I began to pray for direction and obtained a job as a substitute teacher until I could make the appropriate connections in the city.

I called every mediation program in town and asked each program for a referral to other programs. This became my first experience with networking in the field, a skill that would prove to be greatly valuable in the future. In cities where alternative dispute resolution does not have strong roots, networking will probably be your most useful tool for finding out about opportunities. This is because these positions are rarely advertised publicly. Networking can increase your marketability as others get to know what you can do for them, and it can also increase your capability to deliver services by letting you know others who can help you. According to Marsha D. Lewin, in the book *The Overnight Consultant*, networking also allows you to find out what's happening with competitors, find out what's happening in your client-based industry, get new ideas by interacting to and with others, and learn more about the market trends.

In addition, I called my state's Dispute Resolution Office to get advice on other dispute resolution opportunities in the state. I have provided a list of organizations and state Dispute Resolution Offices in the appendix. You may also want to consult the professional organizations listed in Chapter Six.

Once I made these connections, I sent each program my resumé even when I was told by some programs that they were not looking for anyone. I also called these programs every two weeks and spoke to the director. My calls paid off when I landed my first independent contractor mediator assignment at the juvenile court in my city, for which they paid me $50 per hour to mediate custody and visitation disputes. Although I had many hours of training from Pepperdine University, I had to repeat a basic mediation training course for their particular program. From my experience this is the norm, because each mediation program wants you to learn to do mediation their way. In addition, each program has different forms that have to be completed.

Next, due to my own persistence, the U.S. Postal Service called me for their new company mediation program. I participated in their free two-day training. My fee of $400 per case was then approved. I began to do Equal Employment Opportunity (EEO) mediations at the U.S. Postal Service. I received about two to four of these mediations cases per month.

I then found out that the Better Business Bureau had received new grant funding for mediation, and once again I sent them my resume. They called and asked me to participate in their $250 basic mediation training to do their custody, visitation, delinquency, unruly, and business cases. I completed the training and started receiving $75 per hour for mediating these cases.

After this successful experience, I was invited to participate in the defective product (lemon law) arbitration training. The training was three days with an exam at the end; 75% of the participants passed this exam. I was one of them and became a certified arbitrator. I began to arbitrate these cases on a voluntary basis, but now receive $100 per case. I do approximately two to four of these cases per month. The experience is priceless because of the great networking opportunities.

Other attorney friends of mine, as well as my mother, wanted to learn mediation, and I knew that God had blessed me with the gift of teaching. So I contacted my state's Dispute Resolution Office once again. They sent me an application to become a certified trainer. Since I had already attended a training program at Rockland College for professional trainers/speakers, and I was certified, I knew that I could now teach adults. I applied for this certification, and it was granted. This began an unexpected turn in the income for my business. The training industry is a 200-billion-dollar industry, according to Don Schrello, author of *How to Market Training and Information* (book available by calling 1-800-ENROLLX). I now do training in 10 states across the country and charge $449 for a two-day Basic Mediation Training Course, $999 for a five-day Advanced Mediation Training Course, and $449 for a Basic Arbitration Training Course. There are usually 10–25 attendees in each class, and the overhead is fairly low, except advertising and brochures. For more information on marketing, see Chapter Four.

I then began to advertise to professionals and the general public about the mediation services my firm provides. A lot of education was required in the beginning, because no one in the city really knew what mediation was. However, now I have personally mediated well over 400 cases, and most of my cases come from referral. I charge $150 per hour for my services and most of my cases last for about three to five hours, with about 50 cases per month.

Last, I consult with businesses and government entities about setting up dispute resolution systems or conflict prevention programs in their organizations. I generally charge $1,000 for an eight-hour, all-day session or $500 for a half-day session. I chose to include consulting after reading an article in the September 1998 issue of *Black Enterprise Magazine,* which featured a dispute resolution consulting company that made over 2.1 million dollars in its second year in operation. This consulting company specialized in showing companies how to save money and time by setting up dispute resolution mechanisms as a part of their corporate structure.

You may be saying now, what does all of this have to do with me? Well, it is important for you to develop a personal strategic plan in pursuing the ADR field. It is often said a goal without a plan is nothing but a dream. Melanie Gray in her article "Success is

Planned, So is Failure," states that in order to achieve what 95% of the population has not you must be willing to do what most people are not willing to do. Build and encourage yourself. Turn a deaf ear to nay-sayers. A strategic plan is a road map to help guide you in your career decision-making processes while simultaneously serving as a mechanism of encouragement. This document can be used to align your budget structure with career priorities, missions, and objectives. This strategic plan should include (1) a mission statement, (2) a description of the individual's long-term goals and objectives, and (3) strategies or means the individual plans to use to achieve these general goals and objectives.

To develop your mission statement you must know your strengths and your weaknesses so that you select the particular ADR field or fields that most naturally complement your personality. To accomplish this you will want to assess your personality traits. A free way to accomplish this is to visit http://www.advisorteam.org/, then click on the button labeled "The Keirsey Temperament Sorter-II #1 Online Personality Instrument." This is a powerful 70-question personality instrument that helps individuals discover their personality type. The KTS-II is based on Dr. David Keirsey's Temperament Theory and has helped over 30 million people worldwide gain insight into themselves and the people around them. This insight is useful when selecting a career or choosing a work environment. This instrument has enabled companies, academic institutions, and counseling professionals to increase team effectiveness and productivity, match individuals to career interests, improve employee communication, reduce workplace conflict, and help employees to better understand themselves and others.

According to Keirsey's Temperament Theory, people can be sorted into four temperament groups. These groups are referred to as Artisans, Guardians, Rationals, and Idealists. Within each of the four temperaments, there are four temperament variants, which Keirsey calls "character types." Upon completion of the instrument, you will receive a free report like the one presented below (this happens to be my report) displaying your particular personality type.

Of course there are other instruments, such as Myers Briggs and countless others, that you may seek. Hence, it does not matter whether you select a particular instrument but rather that you choose at least one as an important first step prior to preparing your mission statement.

Free Report for Tanya

Your Temperament Is
Idealist

Idealists, as a temperament, are passionately concerned with personal growth and development. Idealists strive to discover who they are and how they can become their best possible self--always this quest for self-knowledge and self-improvement drives their imagination. And they want to help others make the journey. Idealists are naturally drawn to working with people, and whether in education or counseling, in social services or personnel work, in journalism or the ministry, they are gifted at helping others find their way in life, often inspiring them to grow as individuals and to fulfill their potential.

Idealists are sure that friendly cooperation is the best way for people to achieve their goals. Conflict and confrontation upset them because they seem to put up angry barriers between people. Idealists dream of creating harmonious, even caring personal relations, and they have a unique talent for helping people get along with each other and work together for the good of all. Such interpersonal harmony might be a romantic ideal, but then Idealists are incurable romantics who prefer to focus on what might be, rather than what is. The real, practical world is only a starting place for Idealists; they believe that life is filled with possibilities waiting to be realized, rich with meanings calling out to be understood. This idea of a mystical or spiritual dimension to life, the "not visible" or the "not yet" that can only be known through intuition or by a leap of faith, is far more important to Idealists than the world of material things.

Highly ethical in their actions, Idealists hold themselves to a strict standard of personal integrity. They must be true to themselves and to others, and they can be quite hard on themselves when they are dishonest, or when they are false or insincere. More often, however, Idealists are the very soul of kindness. Particularly in their personal relationships, Idealists are without question filled with love and good will. They believe in giving of themselves to help others; they cherish a few warm, sensitive friendships; they strive for a special rapport with their children; and in marriage they wish to find a "soulmate," someone with whom they can bond emotionally and spiritually, sharing their deepest feelings and their complex inner worlds.

Idealists are rare, making up between 20 and 25 percent of the population. But their ability to inspire people with their enthusiasm and their idealism has given them influence far beyond their numbers.

Mission Statement

Writing a personal mission statement offers the opportunity to establish what's important, and perhaps make a decision to stick to it before you even start a career. The first rule of thumb is to keep your career mission statement limited to no more than two sentences and no more than thirty words. Begin your statement with the words "My personal career mission is…" and finish with qualifying words and phrases to describe your mission. In addition, your personal mission statement should be focused toward the first three to five years of your ADR career. Following are some examples:

> My personal career mission is to become a world-class mediator in the entertainment industry.

> My personal career mission is to gain experience in the alternative dispute resolution field toward earning my professional mediation certification.

A mental conception of your personal career mission statement is not enough. You must write it down on paper and, ideally, put it up on your wall where you can see it every day. If it needs to be changed or modified over time, make sure to produce the necessary changes. But keep your career mission statement sharply focused in your mind. As you focus in on your larger goal, your short-term goals will also become clearer.

Developing Your Goals

Chris Joscelyne in her article "Setting Personal Goals" states that "without personal goals life can be an aimless journey lacking positive direction and achievement. If your life is to follow a Positive Path you need a plan, and to establish a plan personal goals are necessary." Think about your priorities in life and the goals you have for yourself. Then make a list of your personal career goals, both short-term (up to three years) and long-term (beyond three years). Ask yourself some other questions like: What is my chosen vocation? What level do I want to reach in my career, and by when? Are my goals realistic? What is my time-line to achieve them? Are there different time-lines for different goals?

Strategies to Achieve Goals

You must first be able to visualize your goal. As Jesse Jackson has often stated, "If you can conceive it and believe it then you can achieve it." You must give your subconscious mind a detailed set of instructions to work on. The more information you give it, the more clear the final outcome becomes. The more precise the outcome, the more efficient your subconscious mind can become.

Second, you will need to identify your biggest fear and develop ways to manage it. Fear is a natural reaction to danger or the threat of injury. If suddenly confronted with a dangerous animal, most everyone would turn and run. Likewise, if you are given a choice of doing something you perceive as harmful, you will usually avoid the danger. The problem occurs when the danger is not real or the fears are not rational. You can overcome fears by gaining confidence in your ability to do such tasks. That is usually done by doing something difficult or dangerous and seeing that the consequences of failure are not so awful or that the chances of failure are not so great.

Setting Boundaries

A boundary is defined as something which serves to mark the limits of something; the limit itself, a dividing line. Lifestyle makeover expert Cheryl Richardson says that creating stronger boundaries is the number one way for most people to improve their lives. We are bombarded daily with requests for our time.While helping others can be very rewarding, at the same time we can feel distraught about constantly obligating ourselves to others while not fulfilling our own needs.Make sure that you have enough time to dedicate to your personal strategic plan. Learning to say no is one of the most powerful ways to establish boundaries, yet it is difficult for most of us to do.

Most people feel ashamed or guilty if they say no. A simple and direct "no, I am not able to help you with that" is the best solution. If you feel the need to give an explanation you should keep it simple: "No, I have already made another appointment for this time" or "No, sorry, I am afraid I have to decline because I have no spare time."

Build a Support System

The right people can inspire you to achieve your goals, too. Timothy Gallwey—a leading motivational coach in sports, health, business, and education and author of *The Inner Game of Work: Focus, Learning, Pleasure, and Mobility in the Workplace* (Random House, 2001)—identifies several essentials for such a support group. "First, find people who can really share in the journey," Gallwey says. "You need people who will hold you to your agreements." These people need to be knowledgeable, he says, and you have to get some joy out of being with them. Miller found all of these things through her online (and, eventually, offline) network.

Conclusion

In order to identify your areas of interest in the Alternative Dispute Resolution field, you must develop your personal mission statement, your goals, and a strategic plan for reaching those goals. If you can conceive it, believe that you can achieve it through surrounding yourself with the appropriate support system while setting healthy boundaries.

3

Life as a Dispute Resolution Consultant

Objective
To provide instruction for those wishing to become dispute resolution consultants.

How to Become a Professional Consultant

The chapter will describe how to become a professional dispute resolution consultant, the spheres in which professional consultancy is appropriate and most profitable, and the marketing tools for independent consultants and sample documents necessary for work.

Introduction

As long as businesses have people problems (and they always will), consultants in the dispute resolution field will enjoy a never-ending supply of corporate clients, both large and small. People-problem prevention programs could include teaching employees how to get along with others, demonstrate mutual respect, and even prevent violence in the workplace. In 1997, U.S. businesses spent just over $12 billion on consulting. Consulting is a growing industry dominated by home businesses. Home-based entrepreneurs who desire greater work flexibility and have the initiative to aggressively sell their expertise are finding consulting work to be a financially rewarding opportunity.

A consultant works with the management of a business to improve the profitability of the business. Working with top management, the consultant is a very highly paid individual. Some consultants charge $100 per hour. Others charge $1,500 per day for their services, and still others work on an annual retainer fee of $12,000 to over $30,000 from any number of large corporations. Because a dispute resolution consulting career is so lucrative, an individual selecting this as a niche in the vast field of Alternative Dispute Resolution could end money worries forever.

Until a few years ago, the consultant title was more or less limited to retired diplomats and top corporate officers. In other words, until recently, the consultant's position was more honorary than actual. But that has all changed dramatically in the past few years.

The number of consultants for almost any problem in life has increased by tenfold or more during the past ten years! And the field of consultants is continuing to grow. In fact, independent consulting is one of the fastest growing businesses in the country today!

A consultant is an expert at recognizing problems and shaping solutions to those problems. The need for business problem solvers—among large and small businesses worldwide—has never been greater. The ever-changing moods of the buyer plus the myriad of crisis situations businessmen face almost daily, have created this "seller's market" for the alert consultant.

Reaching for a consultant when problems arise is as natural as looking for the sun to come up every morning. When you're not feeling well, you call for the services of a doctor. If your car isn't running right, you take it to a mechanic. And so it is with a business owner or manager when he or she encounters a problem—whether it be in the field of accounting, law, sales, or customer relations.

As stated by Consulting Ready Works, these are the top nine reasons companies hire consultants to:

- ♦ Provide objective, independent viewpoints
- ♦ Complete short-term projects without adding to staff
- ♦ Provide specialized expertise for specific needs
- ♦ Provide imaginative solutions for company problems
- ♦ Prevent political problems within the client company
- ♦ Train client personnel
- ♦ Provide sources of capital
- ♦ Deal with federal, state or local government laws and regulations
- ♦ Act as a catalyst between internal groups

The dispute resolution consulting services industry offers excellent opportunities for self-employment. Because capital requirements are low, highly experienced workers can start their own businesses fairly easily and cheaply; indeed, every year, thousands of workers in this industry go into business for themselves. Some of these workers come from established management, scientific, and technical consulting services firms, whereas others leave industry, government, or academic jobs to start their own businesses. Still others remain employed in their primary organizations, but have their own consulting jobs on the side.

It is not necessary for you to have owned or operated a successful business to become a successful business consultant. Nor is it imperative that you have been in management or have held a titled position. You will, however, need the ability to sell yourself, and an up-to-date understanding of the conflict resolution field in which you intend to assist others. However, to start a career as a dispute resolution consultant, it is first of all necessary to understand who a consultant is.

How to Start a Consulting Business

In fact, it is stated that a consultant is an independent contractor, who sells his professional knowledge and expertise in some specific field. The main aim of any consultant is to assess any situation, represented by the client, to analyze it and to propose certain actions to change (or to use) said proposed actions in the existing situation to promote changes for the better. (http://www.coker.com.au/~russell/consultant/how-do-i.html) After the prospective client agrees to the actions and solutions, proposed by the consultant, these actions are performed by this consultant for some set fee.

A consultant is also an adviser who may work full-time or is hired only for the solution of some specific problem in the sphere of their expertise. However, for small businesses, which may not have an opportunity to hire a full-time specialist, hiring an independent contractor may become the best time- and cost-saving choice.

In the desire to become a consultant, one should weigh all of the pros and cons carefully. To become a consultant it is necessary to have some level of knowledge of a particular area (that is, the skills, which will become the product you sell to your clients). For purposes of this book, the area is the acquisition of dispute resolution or ADR knowledge and experience.

The first step is to make an honest evaluation of your own training and experience. Just about everyone has had special training or experience in a certain line of work, which can be utilized in some form of consulting. So, why shouldn't a woman who has worked 20 years as a waitress represent herself as a consultant for training waitresses within a restaurant organization? A shipping and receiving clerk would be a natural for setting up efficient operations and solving problems for businesses just beginning or expanding their production output.

The point is most people don't realize how much expertise they really have, or the probable marketability of their training, knowledge, and experience. The important thing is to look over your educational strengths, combine that with any special training or on-the-job experience, and then offer your expertise to help others with their problems in the areas you know best.

Career Outlook

According to the Bureau of Labor Statistics, U.S. Department of Labor (*Career Guide to Industries, 2006–07 Edition: Management, Scientific, and Technical Consulting Services*—available at http://www.bls.gov/oco/cg/cgs037.htm), between 2004 and 2014 wage and salary employment in the consulting services industry is expected to grow by 60, much faster than the 14% growth projected for all industries, ranking the industry as the fifth fastest growing industry in the economy. All areas of consulting should experience strong growth.

According to a 2004 survey conducted by Abbot, Langer, and Associates, the median annual total cash compensation for junior consultants was $40,000; for consultants, $61,000; for senior consultants, $80,250; and for principal consultants, $107,000. However, the salary of an independent contractor will certainly depend on the way he sells his services, the methods of promotion he uses, the quality of his services, and the amount of time he wants to devote to consultancy. These factors are extremely important in the wish to achieve high results and satisfactory salary. In relation to the consultants who work for a company, the structure of the salary will also depend on the level of the consultant's education and experience. The salary of a consultant working in a consulting company and contracted out will also depend on the quality of consultations he provides to management. The salary of the specialist may depend on the number of clients, with whom he was able to set stable business relationships and who usually pay for his/her services. (http://www.cbsc.org/servlet/ContentServer?cid=1106739780776&pagename=CBSC_FE%2Fdisplay&lang=en&c=GuideHowto)

Many dispute resolution consultants migrate from former employment positions. For example, a professional with a background in the business, management, customer service, human resources, ministry, law,communications, mental health counseling, etc coupled with practical experience may easily come into dispute resolution consultancy. Such individuals may consider combining both professions, thus providing himself with stable and dependable sources of income.

It is also expected that, in the near future, employment opportunities for both independent and staff consultants will increase, as more and more companies understand the importance of hiring a well-qualified specialist who will provide wonderful solutions for the problems and complicated situations arising in any type of business activity.

Establishing Expertise

How do you establish expertise as a consultant? Is there any opportunity for the professional consultant to acquire higher fees and to have more consumers of his services? When the professional ADR consultant acquires the status of expert, all this will become possible as explained below. Once this status is achieved it allows one to earn more money, since mentioning this newly obtained expert status in various marketing and advertising materials surely attracts more customers; it also allows one to change markets from the small firms to larger businesses. It is also quite possible to achieve an expert status without having a huge list of publications—or being a specialist in some specific area of interest . Self-promotion is is not the right choice in setting one's own expertise. Therefore it is necessary for a professional ADR consultant to be recognized by a reputable third party source. This is accomplished by providing high quality answers for your client's problems. If a professional ADR consultant provides his clients with the solution and advice they need, they will for sure return to this specialist. (http://www.workz.com/content/view_content .html?section_id=465&content_id=5675)

Obtaining Training

Management and leadership classes and seminars are available throughout the United States. Some are hosted by volunteer senior executives and management experts representing a variety of businesses and industries. A number of large firms invest a great deal of time and money in training programs, educating new hires in formal classroom settings over several weeks or even months, and some even have separate training facilities. Small firms often combine formal and on-the-job training.

The Institute of Management Consultants USA, Inc., (IMC USA) offers a wide range of professional development programs and resources, such as meetings and workshops, that can be helpful for management consultants. The IMC USA also offers the certified management consultant (CMC) designation to those who meet minimum levels of education and experience, submit reviews from clients, and pass an interview and exam covering the IMC USA's code of ethics. Management consultants with a CMC designation must be recertified every 3three years. For more information, visit their website at http://www.imcusa.org/ or call them at (800) 221-2557.

On June 15, 2007, the American Center for Conflict Resolution Institute, a not-for-profit conflict resolution training organization, announced that it will begin offering a certification course specifically designed for those individuals seeking specialized training and designation as a dispute resolution consultant (DRC). This program will increase the value and recognition of your credentials. To receive more information about this program, please visit the website at http://www.accri.org/ or call (216) 255-6722.

The International Guild of Professional Consultants (IGPC) offers a three-day Certified Professional Consultant (CPC) Certification Course. Graduates of this Certified Professional Consultant Course will be immediately recognized by the International Guild of Professional Consultants (IGPC) as Provisional Certified Professional Consultants (CPC) and will receive a provisional certificate from IGPC. Certified consultants are then able to use the designation CPC following their name and display the CPC/IGPC logo on business materials. This is the contact information for this organization:

> International Guild of Professional Consultants (IGPC)
> 5703 Red Bug Lake Road, #403
> Winter Springs, FL 32708
> Phone: 407-678-7928
> Fax: 407-678-8173
> Email: info@igpc.org
> Website: http://www.igpc.org/seminars/cpc.shtml

Other Consulting/Trainer/Public Speaking Training Programs

Start your own Consulting/Training Business. This program offers a weekend training program to start your own consulting/training business. The topics include marketing, personal and professional development, business etiquette, customer service, etc. For more information call: (312) 642-4449 or (312) 409-8372.

The Mediation Training Institute offers "train-the-trainers" courses. Upon completion, successful participants receive a certificate suitable for framing. This program promises to help market your services and maintain a web page on your behalf. You may contact them by calling (913) 341-2899 or write them at:

> Mediation Training Institute International
> 5700 West 79th Street
> Prairie Village, KS 66208-4604

Determining Options

In a desire to become a professional consultant, there should be defined options, among which are the options to work either part-time or full-time, and working for oneself versus a consulting firm.

You don't need a big, fancy, executive-type office to get started, especially if you start your consulting business on a part-time basis. A spare bedroom, a section of the basement, or even a corner of the dining room will do very nicely. If you handle your own bookkeeping and filing, you will need a ledger of some kind and a file cabinet or two. You will need a computer if you plan to do your own correspondence. An alternative is to write all letters, etc. by hand and hire someone to type them in final form for you. Check the local high school or college. They may be happy to post your ad for a young person looking for part-time work.

Instead of going to the expense of paying for a business phone, which can cost hundreds of dollars each month for one line through your local telephone company, consultants may choose a virtual office and/or Voice over Internet Protocol (VoIP) system. A virtual office service allows a small business to have a voice and fax communications system that functions just like systems Fortune 500 companies use costing thousands of dollars to purchase and maintain. Virtual office fees range in price starting at $9.95 per month from companies like http://www.gotvmail com/. The virtual office usually works with any phone—including your cell phone, home office phone, even VoIP phones and PDAs—from anywhere, yet requires no additional equipment or software. VoIP is a great new way to make and receive phone calls using your broadband Internet connection instead of your standard phone line. This system converts your phone calls into data that zips through your high-speed Internet connection just like email. It comes out the other end just like a regular phone call. Your callers will never detect any difference since it sounds just like a regular phone call. Companies such as Vonage (http://www.vonage.com/) and Sun Rocket (http://www.sunrocket com/) offer these services for as little as $9.95 per month.

In making the right choice between working for oneself or working for some company, keep in mind that being an independent consultant and working as an independent contractor is similar to running one's own business. If the person is not sure if he is able to run such a business, it is better to start by working for a consulting company that specializes in the sphere of consultancy of interest, thus allowing one to acquire the experience necessary for running an independent business in the future.

Marketing and Selling Your Services

Once you've decided that dispute resolution consulting is the field for you, and you have your office or working space set up, the next thing is to let people know you're available for work. Definitely use some common sense and applied knowledge before spending any money on advertising. Generally speaking, you will pick up some customers, regardless of the problem area in which you specialize, by advertising in your area's most popular newspaper. However, I do not recommend placing much more than a small ad in the Sunday editions.

Check with your chamber of commerce for a list of trade and specialized business publishers in your area. Either pick up a sample copy of the business journal at the local newsstand or write to the publisher and ask for a sample. Look through those catering to the type of business you want to serve. Check the editorial styles and types of advertising they carry, then select the one that corresponds with your needs. Unless a publication reaches the people you are trying to sell to, don't advertise in it regardless of style, quality, or advertising rates.

Radio or television would probably be a complete waste of advertising dollars. However, the best time for any broadcast advertising, in order to reach your best prospects, seems to be in the evening hours after the late-night news, when these people are either still laboring over their special projects or relaxing before going to bed. If you do use broadcast advertising, the commercial is very important. Really concentrate on this, and use a lot of common sense in writing the message. Even if you engage the services of an experienced broadcast copywriter, make sure the message speaks to your potential customers and convinces them that you can help solve their problems or improve the profit picture of their business.

Finally, you need to determine where to advertise. Since the invention of the Internet, companies such as eWork bring companies and consultants together through the use of the world wide web. This company assists consultants looking for the best way to find new projects. There are over 200,000 business members, including 465 of the Fortune 500, that have successfully used eWork Markets for services sourcing. eWork Markets services are free of charge to client members looking to hire a consultant. Consulting firms who qualify as affiliated suppliers pay an initial setup fee plus commissions on projects won through the eWork. They can be found at: http://www .eworkmarkets.com/index.cfm.

Another good choice may be a quarter-page ad in the yellow pages of your telephone directory. The space sales representative will help you with the ad, but—remember—you want it to catch the eye of your particular client and offer a promise of an end to his problems. Always talk to your kind of people, emphasizing the benefits of your services. It's not good practice to quote or even discuss prices in either your advertising or on the phone when people respond. Always get name, address, and telephone number, then explain your services in general. Set up an appointment to look over their operation, analyze their needs, and make a written proposal to solve their problems.

As in any business, marketing is the key to success if the consultant decides to work independently. The correct choice of marketing tools and marketing strategies may result in a drastic increase in the number of clients. The following are among the most successful and appropriate marketing methods:

1. Registering in various business directories and resource lists
2. Contacting various consulting firms and other similar companies, which are known to receive consultancy contracts, for cooperation
3. Joining professional organizations for meeting clients and colleagues in the specific area
4. Developing a website
5. Developing brochures and newsletters and sending them to proposals, as well as distributing them at various seminars and presentations (http://www.cbsc.org/servlet/ContentServer?cid =1106739780776&pagename=CBSC_FE%2Fdisplay&lang= en&c=GuideHowto)

Developing the Business Plan

However, the intention to become an independent professional consultant requires the development of a business plan that notes each step of the business's development, accounting for the cost of expenses and the possible returns. A business plan should be thorough and take into account all aspects of the consultancy work. It should include all necessary chapters: executive suwmmary, business description, marketing strategies, competitive analysis, design and development plan, operations and management plan, and financial components. (http://www .myownbusiness.org/s2/)

1. Executive Summary
1.0 Executive Summary
ABC Dispute Resolution Consultants is a full service company that provides complete dispute resolution consulting services for companies. Our consultants are experienced and dedicated professionals with many years of management experience. ABC is unique in that we give our clients our undivided attention. We listen to their needs and work with them to create a plan for their particular concerns. Our clients' wishes become our commands. So whether our client wants training or workplace mediation services, we can help.

1.1 Objectives
Whether this is our client's first conflict or an ongoing conflict, we want every detail of their concern to be both professional and customized. Therefore, we offer a host of packages and services specifically tailored to the needs of each organization. We are confident that this business venture will be a success and we estimate that our net income will increase more than 10% by the second year.

1.2 Mission
Our vision is to be the natural choice for companies for support in resolving conflicts at work. We will work in partnership with our customers and engage with them in finding creative solutions to conflict and disputes. We will enable clients to create strategies, policies, and procedures to build robust and respectful organizations.

Their managers and staff will improve their ability and confidence in managing conflicts and resolving disputes at work. We will give colleagues the tools to rebuild working relationships, so that they will be more able to sustain and cope with change, and adapt to working environments characterized by diversity. As a result our clients will be better able to refocus employees on their core objectives in a supported environment and achieve their corporate missions.

1.3 Keys to Success

The keys to our success are as follows:

◊ Depth and length of experience—reflected in our client list and the background of our practitioners

◊ Ability to target our approach to each client, each training group, and each individual with whom we work

◊ Tried-and-tested approach, using a new model of managing and resolving disputes—Content Interaction and Process (CIP), which is showcased in the directors' book, *Mediation for Managers* (NB Books, 2002)

◊ Understanding of, and a commitment to, working with diversity and issues of equality

2.0 Company Summary

ABC Dispute Resolution Consultants is a start-up company that provides workplace mediation and dispute resolution training and services across the United States and in Canada. ABC has become the natural choice for organizations wanting to improve how they manage the inevitable conflict that arises within the workplace.

The factors which make us the natural choice are our highly specific offerings and capabilities. We are recognized as a pioneering and values-driven organization which focuses its expertise solely in the arena of managing and resolving conflicts at work. We gear our skills and experience to meet the needs of each client, and we establish ongoing relationships which endure and enable us to continue to meet their changing requirements.

2.1 Company Ownership

This business will start out as a simple partnership owned by its founders, Jane and John Doe. As the operation grows, the owners will consider re-registering as a limited liability company or as a corporation, whichever will better suit the business's future needs.

2.2 Start-up Summary

The company founders, Jane and John Doe, will handle day-to-day operations of the plan and will work collaboratively to ensure that this business venture is a success.

We estimate that our start-up costs will be $3,000 (including legal costs, logo design, advertising, direct mail, and related expenses). An additional $5,000 will be required in the bank account as operating capital for the first two months of operation. The start-up costs are to be financed in equal portions by the owners' personal funds (i.e., Jane and John Doe are investing $4,000 each).

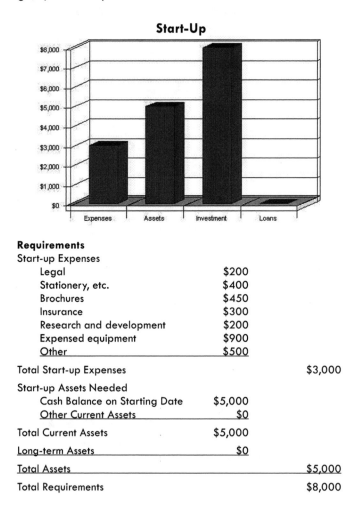

Start-Up

Requirements

Start-up Expenses

Legal	$200
Stationery, etc.	$400
Brochures	$450
Insurance	$300
Research and development	$200
Expensed equipment	$900
Other	$500

Total Start-up Expenses	$3,000

Start-up Assets Needed

Cash Balance on Starting Date	$5,000
Other Current Assets	$0

Total Current Assets	$5,000
Long-term Assets	$0
Total Assets	$5,000
Total Requirements	$8,000

Funding

Investment

Jane Doe	$4,000	
John Doe	$4,000	
Total Investment		$8,000

Current Liabilities

Accounts Payable	$0	
Current Borrowing	$0	
Other Current Liabilities	$0	
Total Current Liabilities		$0
Long-term Liabilities		$0
Total Liabilities		$0
Loss at Start-up		($3,000)
Total Capital		$5,000
Total Capital and Liabilities		$5,000

2.3 Company Locations and Facilities

Initially, this will be a home-based business; however, by 2008, we intend to expand our facilities into a well-equipped and operational office.

3.0 Services

We are a full-service workplace dispute resolution consultant group and provide the following services: training and workplace mediation.

4.0 Market Analysis Summary

Nearly $12 billion dollars are spent every year on consulting services. ABC Dispute Resolution Consultants is a full-service workplace consultant company that offers a variety of services to our clients. We pride ourselves on being professional and courteous at all times, and we have packages to suit every company's needs.

4.1 Market Segmentation

ABC will target companies with 10–500 employees. It is ABC's goal to be recognized for providing high-quality dispute resolution services and outstanding customer service for this size client, who is often overlooked in the market place.

The ratio currently used today to substantiate the size of a human resources (HR) department is one HR professional per

100 employees. As a company grows, the HR department should also grow proportionately. However, most smaller companies are charged with complying with the federal and state employment and discrimination laws no matter their size. Human resources departments are responsible for this compliance. Therefore, the level of expertise of a personnel clerk twenty or so years ago does not equal the expertise one would need today. There are many companies with 500 employees or less who are faced with laws that only existed in the last 10 or so years.

In summary, companies now have many more human resource-related rules and regulations with which to comply, and adding more overhead personnel is very costly. By outsourcing these administrative functions, companies are paying for a service and are not burdened by more overhead costs.

4.2.1 Market Needs

The outsourcing of a business function such as dispute resolution can truly benefit any size or type of company. It is estimated by SAP, a major HR technical company, that human resources transactions will increase by 224% by 2006. And, as predicted by the Industrial Democracy Commission (IDC), the amount spent on human resources outsourcing is expected to reach $10.2 billion by 2003. These estimates include all types of industry and all sizes of companies.

The following quote is taken from the book *Outsourcing Human Resources Functions* by Mary Cook: "If you think HR outsourcing is a trend that will dissipate with time, think again. Outsourcing is a serious and permanent new development. When done properly, outsourcing can deliver radically improved services and significant bottom-line savings—benefits that are too attractive to be ignored."

Human resource professionals need to become a strategic partner and assist their companies in becoming and staying an employer of choice. Dispute resolution functions are increasing at an astronomical rate and, even though automation can help to some extent, employees still need the personal service of an HR department. As the HR departments become overwhelmed with the amount of dispute resolution issues, ABC can provide this personal service to their employees.

4.1.1 Market Trends

The trend today is for human resource professionals to assist their companies in basic survival and growth. Unemployment fluctuates with the times, and companies need to be recruiting, hiring, and retaining the right people. HR is the key. Once the employee is hired, HR needs to work on staying competitive—keeping their companies on the leading edge of work and life issues in order to sustain the workforce. Employees are looking for more than just base pay to keep them at a job. Addressing employee concerns and complaints needs to be done quickly and proficiently—not just major concerns. Employee retention is one of the most visible ways a human resources department can substantiate a return on investment. When these departments become overwhelmed with the day-to-day conflicts, other more important functions fall through the cracks. Outsourcing this dispute resolution service is the answer for many companies.

4.1.3 Market Growth

Companies are discovering the strategic value that HR professionals can have on their business—it is imperative that human resources attract, obtain, and retain the workforce.

With an estimated increase of employee complaints of over 200%, the strategic value of HR is in jeopardy. It is very difficult for any HR department to demonstrate a good return on investment (ROI) for the company, especially when their time is eaten up by dispute resolution and labor relations concerns. Therefore, requesting more headcount to help with this administration is not a good option.

A labor relations representative in the Any Town area has an average annual base salary of $45,000. In addition, a company will need to pay benefits and taxes on that amount for an estimated total of $63,000. For a company with 250 employees, ABC could handle basic dispute resolution and labor relations for $36,000. As companies become aware of administrative outsourcing options, and the amount of money and time to be saved, outsourcing will grow.

4.2 Competition and Buying Patterns

The dispute resolution consulting business is not based on industry seasonality.

5.0 Strategy and Implementation Summary

ABC will initially focus on employers with 10 to 500 employees within the local counties. Dispute resolution prevention training will be the main focus, for this is an area in which companies can already begin to see the need for outsourcing services.

5.1 Value Proposition

By outsourcing labor relation functions, a company can save in two very important areas: time and money. This is the basic goal of outsourcing.

By contracting with ABC, companies can use their current human resource professionals in other strategic areas. For example, if the company is growing, it will need to hire qualified people—and keep them. The company needs their HR department to focus on these issues—not just attracting and interviewing the employees, but making certain the employees stay once they are hired. Turnover and retraining are so expensive. If the company outsources the labor relations training and mediation, they would then be able to save the time and use their current staff to help with all of these more important issues. As the company grows and decides it needs to add HR staff, it does not have to add a labor relations manager—for they have outsourced that function. They can then use that budget for additional HR staff to hire a more strategic position—such as a full-time recruiter or compensation manager.

As stated previously in Section 4.1.3, in the Any Town region the average salary of a labor relations manager is about $45,000 annually plus benefits. For an average small company of 250 employees, ABC can administer training and mediation services for approximately $36,000 annually plus a start up fee of $2,000.

5.2 Competitive Edge

Most of the competitors will shy away from offering a call center to answer employee questions. This gives ABC a definite advantage—called Customer Service.

When a client contracts with ABC, we represent two clients. One is the company, and the second is the company's employees. The call center is a priceless customer service tool to both clients. By providing a call center, ABC saves the client the time that the labor relations manager would normally spend on the phone with employees, plus it is a valuable service to the employees as their questions are answered on a timely basis.

The next edge is the expertise of the two principals. Both have held labor relations and administration positions and are aware of the laws, responsibilities, and customer service needed to excel. Competitors lack this advantage.

5.3 Marketing Strategy
The initial push for marketing will be the employer size, under 500 employees. The business line of the company truly doesn't matter.

Networking and keeping a mailing database is crucial. Both principals are members of human resources professional organizations which meet monthly—each attending approximately four meetings per month. At certain times, ABC will sponsor these meetings to present their services; however, these affiliations will be used as networking tools, and word-of-mouth marketing.

In conjunction with this, ABC will also build a database with information obtained through the small business resources at the county library. Informational packets and brochures will be sent out to the members of the database, with follow-up phone calls within two weeks of mailing.

The company website will be linked to other popular sites, as well as advertised on small-business service sites. By linking with these sites, ABC will be able to market its services over the Internet.

5.3.1 Pricing Strategy
Each level of service will be priced separately; the all-inclusive option will be discounted. Pricing will follow the industry standard and be charged on a per-employee, per-month basis. Each

client will also be charged a start-up fee depending on the number of employees. Depending on the size of the client and the number of complaints per quarter, ABC may impose an additional charge for the call center operation. Each client will be charged a one-time start-up fee for transfer of employee data into employee management software.

5.3.2 Promotion Strategy

ABC's main focus on promotion will consist of speaking engagements at the professional associations, as well as networking with the members. Initially these engagements will be educational in nature, explaining the services and laws with which employers must comply. ABC will also show that, by offering a dispute resolution mechanism for employees, employers will be able to help their employees resolve their issues, which reduce the number of lawsuits. Smaller employers may need education on these items since they may not have the resources to employ the HR knowledge.

As previously stated, the website is also a very important part of the promotion strategy. The majority of businesses today use the Internet not only for information but also for comparing and pricing what is available. The website will house information about ABC, as well as educational information for companies. Direct mail will also be a small portion of the strategy—with follow-up calling.

5.3.3 Marketing Programs

The most important marketing program is the networking, and both principals will initially be involved in the speaking engagements and subsequent sales presentation.

The first speaking engagement is May 18, 2007, at the monthly luncheon meeting of the Any County Human Resources Association. The meeting will be attended by approximately 65 members.

ABC will sponsor this luncheon. Ms. Doe will speak about the outsourcing market and give a brief biography of both principals. Mr. Doe will speak about ABC's services. A table with promotional material will be set-up, and a raffle (from which ABC will keep business cards) will be held for a gift basket. Follow-up notes and thank you notes will be sent the following week.

The other key marketing tool, the website design is currently being handled by Ms. Doe, who will contract with a designer by the end of May. The budget for this project has not yet been decided. The direct mailings will be handled by both principals.

5.4 Sales Strategy

As stated previously, customer support for the clients' employees is key. If the employees are satisfied with the timely handling of their conflicts and concerns, the client will hear no complaints. However, it is also necessary to keep the client company satisfied as well. Along with customer service, bottom line savings will be stressed in the sales presentation.

Considering that ABC is starting out small, with just the two principals on staff, there is no question of accountability. Each principal is committed to customer service and keeping the client happy with the services provided. To make certain this happens, ABC will listen to the client and try to accommodate client needs with ABC services. ABC will provide clients with the services and reports that will make the clients' jobs easier. Internally, clients HR departments may be responsible for different reporting, and ABC will mold its services to fit those needs.

5.4.1 Sales Forecast

Projected sales figures are based on the two different services that labor relations provides.

1. Level One is conflict resolution training for clients with an average of 100 employees.
2. Level Two is workplace mediation services, including a call center, also for clients with an average of 100 employees.

The sales forecast is based on obtaining one client a month for conflict resolution training and one workplace mediation client for the first year, adding six new clients each calendar year (one per quarter, and two at the beginning of each year).

5.5 Strategic Alliances

ABC will depend on alliances with the following:

◊ EAP (employee assistance providers), which provide services to employers with less than 500 employees. These providers speak with clients daily and listen to their needs. Partnering with EAP providers is a great strategy, for they can market our services initially without our presence.

◊ Law firms—Many small to medium size companies use outside law firms to handle their legal transactions and case filings. By affiliating with these firms, ABC can obtain referrals if the law firms' clients are in need of the services we offer.

◊ Chambers of commerce and other business associations— These associations mainly deal with the same size client ABC is targeting. Speaking engagements and networking are very big marketing and sales tools.

In addition to the above strategic alliances, ABC will also be a referral source and advocate of these companies and associations.

5.6 Milestones

As described in the business plan's affiliated table, both principals have responsibilities with the milestones that have been set. Most of the initial milestones have been met, with the marketing and follow-up calls still to take place. Both principals are accountable for these milestones.

Milestones					
Milestone	Start Date	End Date	Budget	Manager	Department
Obtaining Office Space	3/1/2007	4/1/2007	$1,200	Jane Doe	Principal
Marketing Postcard Mailing	5/1/2007	5/14/2007	$75	Jane Doe	Principal
Bulk Mailing—Obtaining Leads	5/16/2007	6/1/2007	$0	John Doe	Principal
Bulk Mailing—Letter Draft	5/16/2007	6/1/2007	$0	John Doe	Principal
Bulk Mailing—Mail Merge & Mailing	6/1/2007	6/5/2007	$400	Jane Doe	Principal
Obtain SBA Loan	4/1/2007	6/30/2007	$1,000	Jane/John	Principals

Milestone	Start Date	End Date	Budget	Manager	Department
Speaking Engagement	5/18/2007	5/18/2007	$150	Jane/John	Principals
Follow-Up Calling	5/25/2007	6/1/2007	$0	Jane/John	Principals
Brochures	4/1/2007	5/16/2007	$500	John Doe	Principal
Office Furniture & Equipment	4/1/2007	4/2/2007	$500	John Doe	Principal
Supplies	4/1/2007	5/24/2007	$400	Jane/John	Principals
Business Plan	1/1/2007	4/1/2007	$150	Jane Doe	Principal
Success	4/1/2007	4/1/2007	$0	Jane/John	Principals

It should be noted that most of the milestones with commitment dates prior to the office opening in April 2007 have been omitted. The principals had been talking, planning, and preparing for this for almost a year.

6.0 Management Summary

The principals of ABC, Jane and John Doe, have over 25 years of experience in corporate employee relations, communications, and legal compliance. They have sat at the labor relations manager's desk and know the tasks that these HR professionals face everyday. In order to be successful, human resources professionals need not only to know the laws governing their labor relations but also how to communicate with both management and employees.

John Doe has been involved in human resources for over 18 years. During the past 15 years, he held several positions with one employer, most recently as Director of Labor Relations. He led the development of the Human Resources Department and was responsible for a wide range of activities including employee benefits, payroll, employee relations, and legal compliance.

Mr. Doe has extensive experience in contract negotiations with unions. His background includes supporting employees in multiple domestic locations, as well as in an international environment.

He is a graduate of the University of South Florida with a degree in Fine Arts with continued studies at the graduate level. He is a member of the Society for Human Resources

Management (SHRM), the County Human Resources Association (CHRA), as well as the Valley Human Resources Association (VHRA).

Jane Doe was most recently employed as a Senior Employee Trainer and Developer. She has held diverse HR positions since her career began in 1989. She began her HR career as an Employee Benefits Manager and was responsible for the design, implementation, and maintenance of all employee benefit plans. She has also held senior employee benefits positions at another high-tech firm, with very similar duties, from 1992 through 1996.

In 1995, Ms. Doe obtained her PHR (Professional in Human Resources) certification and expanded her HR focus to include generalist duties, compensation plan research, development and consulting, employee relations and diversity, and executive search. She is a member of the Society for Human Resource Management (SHRM), the Valley Human Resources Association (VHRA), and the County Human Resources Association (CHRA).

Mr. and Ms. Doe bring into this business venture not only a vast knowledge of the employee benefits field but also a focus on customer service and communication. This is a key factor, for not only are the clients their customers, but so are the clients' employees. They understand this and are committed to providing the highest level of customer support to both.

6.1 Management Team Gaps

The present management team, consisting of the two principals, Jane and John Doe, require professional support for accounting functions with an emphasis on filing company taxes. To date, an accounting firm has not been contracted.

The team is aware that, as the company obtains clients, they will need administrative and marketing support and have planned for that in the personnel plan. In order to compensate for this lack, both principals are doing their own administrative work and are attending coaching sessions on marketing and sales with the Enterprise Business Center, which offers entrepreneurial training, and the Service Corps of Retired Executives (SCORE), which is affiliated with the Small Business Association and offers mentoring of new businesses.

6.2 Personnel Plan

The two principals will initially staff ABC. In 2008, an administrative assistant will be hired in January, a marketer in July, and a labor relations coordinator in October.

It should be noted that both Mr. and Ms. Doe are committed to staffing their business with qualified people who have a background in human resources and/or customer service.

The Consultant's Resume

The next essential step is creating the consultant's resume, which will include the achievements of the consultant in his professional career. A resume should be a part of the successful strategy and should present the consultant in the best light. It should include all degrees and specialized training the consultant has acquired, with the description of his aims and goals, showcasing the best features that allow him to support stable relations with his clients. Three sample resumes follow, although not specific to ADR.

Promotional Packaging

The promotional package is usually created to be sent to the potential clients who will be able to consider the consultant as a future partner. In sending promo packages, it is necessary to be sure that only appropriate materials are included, often at various meetings and forums. The purpose of promo packages is to represent the consultant, showing who he is, what he is able to do, and what services he offers. However, the key to success lies in the following: in the first several years of a consultancy career the promo package will constantly change with various achievements; thus, there is no need to create a large issue. The only thing necessary is the number of promo packages to be at hand – their number should be reduced to minimal. The purpose of the brochure to attract clients through creative design and wording to compel them to look inside.

Sample Resume 1

Entry Level Management Consultant

Jane Doe
5555 Gardenside Avenue, Los Angeles, CA 90000
(415) 555-5555 ♦ mcr111@somedomain.com

Professional Goal
Contribute to a management consulting firm whose clients will benefit from my strengths in revenue enhancement, economic analysis, product development, governance system development, performance bench-marking, and other organizational enhancements.

Qualifications
Projects: Project management support pertinent to managed care delivery systems for HMOs, IPAs, medical groups, multihospital systems, and national health care providers.

Verbal: Client communications/interaction (medical directors, chief executives, administrators), interdisciplinary team collaboration, and management reporting.

Research: Data collection, organization, and analysis; investigative and interviewing skills.

Finance: Predictive models, financial impacts, budgeting, projections. Economics degree.

Bilingual: Fluency in Spanish language, business etiquette, and culture.

Computer: PowerPoint (multimedia presentations), Excel (financial modeling, budgeting), Word (report generation, business communications), and E-communications.

Experience
Medical Management Advisors, Los Angeles, California
9/97–Present
Associate Consultant for management consulting firm servicing market-leading health plans, integrated delivery systems, integrators, and providers throughout the U.S. Clients include Columbia-HCA, Cedars-Sinai Medical Center, U-Mass Memorial Health Care, UCSF Stanford Health Care, and others. Provide project support in strategy and business planning, network design operations and organization, and health care finance.

Sample Projects
Challenge: For New England regional health system—expand scope of services, create physician-linking mechanisms, foster medical group-hospital relationships, and optimize acquisitions position.

Sample Resume 1, cont.

Action: Developed and implemented instrument to conduct national survey; determined respondents' needs and interests in joining client's new institute that is designed to provide expertise in practice management, managed care administration, and population-based management.

Result: Proposed infrastructure model, regional sites, program content, and target groups to participate in unique think-tank/training institute; program will link physicians and senior management from key IPAs and medical groups, expand scope of services, and provide client with solid acquisition opportunities.

Challenge: For leading Midwestern health system—develop revenue enhancement opportunities.

Action: Collaborated with team to identify 12 major opportunities and was assigned to handle Medicare Select component. Conducted competitor research; prepared financial models (administrative and marketing budgets, hospital impacts, enrollment projections, annual growth rates); structured product benefits; developed story-lines, slides, and materials for client presentation.

Result: Client selected Medicare product as strongest growth opportunity with a projected revenue enhancement of $13 million.

Education
Bachelor of Arts, Economics; minor in Hispanic Studies, Scripps College, Claremont, CA (1997). Sigma Delta Pi. Economics, history, and literature courses (all conducted in Spanish), University of Salamanca, Spain (1995).

Sample Resume 2

Amy Smith
123 Main Street, Atlanta, Georgia 30339
Home: (555) 555-1234 ♦ Cell: (555) 555-1235
asmith@sample~resume.com

Objective
To assist in the development and guidance of establishing and increasing a high-tech business in today's competitive environment.

Notable Achievements
♦ Guest lecturer, Business Department, Ohio State University, 1999–2000.
♦ Frequent contributor, *Business Monthly*.
♦ Excellent communication, interpersonal and managerial skills

Sample Resume 2, cont.

Technical Expertise

Software—Microsoft Office (Word, Excel, PowerPoint, Access), WordPerfect, FrontPage, PhotoShop, PageMaker, Printmaster, Corel Paint 8.0, Microsoft Publisher, Harvard Graphics, Norton Utilities, Cleansweep, PC Anywhere, Close-Up, QuickBooks.

Code—Strong knowledge of html, java (script, applets, JDK *.*), asp, meta tags, keywords, graphics, animation, dynamic solution, online customer attention and direction, search engine placement, forms and database cookie development.

Other—Expert in online technology, strategy, management and application of internet business. Comprehensive knowledge of downloading/uploading and sharing.

Employment History

Edu-Tech, Columbus, OH
President and Chief Executive Officer, 1997–Present
Responsible for all operational aspects of award-winning internet based educational company. Developed yearly business plans and financial goals while providing leadership for a team of more than seventy employees. Formed key partnerships with Dell, IBM, and National Geographic. Built corporate revenues from $2M to $3.1M.

J.M. Edwards, Cleveland, OH
Vice President of National Development, 1993–1997
Built company revenues to $1.6M per year. Designed and implemented product tracking system that was adopted by seventeen major nutritional wholesale companies. Spearheaded the successful campaign to establish a corporate office in Mexico City, and a partnership with the Mexican communication's firm, Viven Inc.

Kent Western Systems, Inc., Houston, TX
Eastern Regional Project Manager, 1990–1993
Direct sales of custom Kent Systems technical solution within a ten state region. Won a contract with IBM worth $27M in annualized revenue, the largest sale in Kent history. Managed entire IBM project, in addition to another IBM project that involved sites throughout Eastern Europe and Asia. Traveled throughout China to coordinate and design production efforts with KWS customers. Top regional sales manager in 1993.

Education

1990, B.S. Economics, University of Michigan, Ann Arbor, MI
Bartels Research Scholar
Dean's List, 3.9 GPA

Professional Affiliations

- Advisor, Future Technological Leaders of America.
- Board of Directors, Infotech Corporation.
- Midwest States Business Ethics Council.

Sample Resume 3

Objective
Serve as a lead expert resource for strategic business initiatives, workforce development and analytics, human resource management, workplace best practices, organizational enhancement, project management, performance measurement, government relations, communications and other organizational consulting functions.

Relocate
DC FL GA IN LA TX

Dean A. Black, SPHR, CPC, CAPM
Management and Human Resources Professional
Strategic Business Partner
Senior Project Manager

Career Objective
Serve as a lead expert resource for strategic business initiatives, workforce development and analytics, human resource management, workplace best practices, organizational enhancement, project management, performance measurement, government relations, communications and other organizational consulting functions.

Fields Of Expertise
Growth Strategy Initiatives, Project/Program Management, Human Resources Management, Workforce Transformation, Budgeting - Financial Reporting, Compensation and Benefits, Operations Management, Management Development, Talent Management - Recruiting, Marketing and Development, Turnaround Leadership, Business Analysis - Auditing, Administration/Support Services, Progressive Management Practices, Community/Public Relations, Strategic Partnership Development, Senior Level Management and Leadership, Urban/Multicultural Programs, Statistical Process Control, Continual Improvement Processes, Benchmarking, Activity Based Costing.

Professional Experience
JustAskHR—Management and Human Resource Consulting
September 1996–Present
President and Managing Consultant: Serve as the chief executive officer of the company and responsible for the operation and administration of the firm. To provide leadership for the company's strategic direction and market penetration and play a key role in new product development, client relationships, and profitable corporate revenue growth. Responsible for creating and driving a winning corporate culture while building an outstanding senior executive team. Manage all corporate operations/functional roles/budgets as well as lead all future rounds of business development. Approve, execute, and administer all client contracts. Serve as Senior Consultant on all client assignments. Interface with clients. Lead teams in giving shape to extensive analyses of cutting-edge strategic issues. A sampling of client assignments are listed below:

Sample Resume 3, cont.

- *Usfilter Operating Services, Inc.—Veolia Water (Vivendi)*
  May 2000–Present
  Senior Management Consultant: Executive level involvement in the development and coordination of long-range strategies to achieve business growth and enhanced profitability in urban municipal markets. Project management for the development of Strategic Business Plans, coordinating activities of multiple departments utilizing project management techniques with full supervision of costs, methods and processes. Responsible for a $1.1 million dollar annual budget and leadership of project teams in excess of fifty professionals.

  Generated of over $1 billion dollars of backlog contracts. Guaranteed clients at least 30% reduction in operating costs. Enhanced positioning of Business Development strategies. Designed human resource transition, transformation and deployment strategies. Implemented performance monitoring. Established community, minority attainment and economic development programs.

  Human Resource Consultant: Led HR efforts in mergers, acquisitions and contact operations. Successfully managed the integration of a 50% increase in staff. Improved profit utilizing progressive management techniques, metric measurements and aggressive cost modeling. Developed and implemented workforce re-engineering programs. Dramatically increased employee satisfaction. Reduced turnover. Implemented strategies to achieve 'Employer of Choice' status. Designed and delivered public education programs.

- *United Water Services, Inc.—Suez International*
  February 1994–May 2000
  Senior Management Advisor—Human Resource Consultant—Business Development Strategist
  September 1996–May 2000
  Team Leader in the five largest public-private transfers of employees in the United States; Indianapolis Wastewater and Collection System, Milwaukee Metropolitan Sewerage District, Gary Sanitary District, Atlanta Water Supply System and Indianapolis Water. Request for Proposal Analysis, Due Diligence, Proposal Development, Employee Transition Management, Benefits and Compensation Analysis, Mobilization, Labor Contract Negotiations, Outplacement Management, Labor-Management Relations, On-Site Human Resource Management, Employee Training and Management Development Program design and facilitation, Community and Client Relations.

  Successfully transitioned more than 2,500 municipal employees into private sector employment, including labor contract negotiation. Complete organizational restructuring from private sector operations to private sector standards. Overall generation of nearly $100 million dollars in annual saving, Achieved an average of 30% cost savings through the implementation of Business Process Analysis, Activity Based Costing, Benchmarking, Process Improvement Plans, Metrics, Balanced Scorecards and Project Management techniques.

Sample Resume 3, cont.

♦ *United Water Services, Inc.—Suez International*
Vice President of Human Resources: (promoted from Director in 1995)
Directed human resource management activities within the organization to maximize the strategic use of human capital and maintain functions such as employee compensation, recruitment, personnel policies, and regulatory compliance. Responsible for all labor relations activities. Formulated policies and business strategies for the overall direction of the organization. Staff management providing services for 1,800 employees with a budget of $750,000.

Reduced grievances by 90 percent and work related accidents by 80%. Participation in more than fifty acquisition, marketing and proposal development efforts; including completion of full-scale labor, compensation and benefits analysis for each. Team leader for the development of Human Resources Standard Operating Procedures, Skill Based Training and Incentive Team-Based Pay Programs.

♦ *City Of Indianapolis—Mayor's Office*
June 1990–february 1994
Director of Personnel: Instrumental in the competitive bidding process for the City of Indianapolis, resulting in $48 millions dollars in annual savings and a 40% reduction in the non-public safety workforce. Lead Labor Relations negotiator. Designed a complete organizational restructuring. Formulated policies and provided overall direction of municipal government activities. Directed and coordinated operational activities at the highest level of management with the help of subordinate managers. Implemented employee adjustment and transition programs. Staff management with an annual budget of $2.4 million servicing just over 5,600 employees.

Education
Bachelor of Science
Business Management, Human Resources Concentration
Indiana State University—May 1987

Senior Certified Human Resource Professional (SPHR)
Society for Human Resource Management (SHRM)

Certified Associate in Project Management (CAPM)
Project Management Institute (PMI)

Certified Personnel Consultant (CPC)
National Association of Personnel Services (NAPS)

Stanley K. Lacy Executive Leadership Program
Indianapolis Chamber of Commerce

Sample Resume 3, cont.

Additional Training

Extraordinary Leaders and Unleashing Executive Talent, FrontLine Leadership, Project Management. Six (6) Sigma, DMAIC, Total Quality Management (TQM), Strategic Planning, Goal Setting, Return on Investment (ROI)

Willing to Relocate and/or Travel Extensively

Additional Information Available Upon Request

The Portfolio

A portfolio is another kind of marketing tool that must be used properly to benefit the consultant, especially if combined with the other marketing tools described. First of all, a portfolio is a collection of various items, which may be organized in different forms, and its aim is to present the skills and experience the consultant possesses in relation to the career. It may also be used by consultants that work for a firm. In this situation the portfolio is used for presenting qualifications to an employer when seeking full-time work immediately after graduation. The portfolio is typically used in the creative professions. It is one of the most appropriate ways of making your service or qualifications known among the target audience (either clients or potential employers) and is usually used during interviews and negotiations. Each item in the portfolio should be captioned. (http://careerservices.uvic .ca/tutorials/career-portfolio.html)

Setting Your Fees

There may be a number of factors involved in establishing your fees, but starting out with beginning and small businesses, and until you line up 50 regular clients, your best bet would be $50 per hour. Assuming two to three hours per client per day, devoting 10 days per month to work on each client's needs, you may earn about $1,000 to $1,500 per month from each client. Multiply that times 50 clients, and you'll be grossing $5,000 to $7,500 per month. As a one-man operation, you'll be plenty busy.

Insiders in this business say a person can leave his regular job on Friday, start a consulting business on Monday, and within six months, have an income of more than $100,000 per year. Realistically, a beginning business consultant should earn from $30,000 to $60,000 before taxes and office expenses, in his first year in the business.

It is also very difficult to define the level of fees for each kind of service in case one chooses to work as an independent contractor. On the one hand, low fees may attract clients, though they may simultaneously bring the thought that these services are not of high quality. On the other hand, too high prices surely won't attract the number of clients necessary to bring the planned return on investments. Consultancy fees must cover not only the time the consultant spends solving problems or creating projects; it must also cover the expenses (or the time spent) of marketing and various administrative procedures. The fees will also depend on factors such as the experience the consultant possesses, current market prices, and the urgency. Price usually serves as a screening method for finding high-quality consultants, thus the choice and determination of fees may create a negative impact on consultant's career. (http://www.entrepreneur.com/startingabusiness/businessideas/startupkits/article41384.html)

Your initial clients may be found through your current circle of acquaintances, who will later bring more and more clients through positive recommendations. Different internet search engines may also be used as a means of making your consultancy service popular. Two such search engines can found at http://www.overture.com/ and http://adwords.google .com/. However, the main means of attracting clients is of course high-quality service, which is indispensable in any kind of business activity.

Sample Forms

A consultant agreement is a contract through which allows an organization to hire a person or firm to obtain professional knowledge, skills or expertise. A sample consulting contract can be found at http://www .managementhelp.org/misc/smplcntr.htm. However, it does not mean that this contract should be used verbatim for any consultant services. It can be amended, though in the form presented in this chapter, it may be used for various types of consultancy services. Two other consultant contracts along with other useful forms follow on the next page.

EMPLOYMENT AGREEMENT WITH CONSULTANT
CONSULTING CONTRACT

THIS AGREEMENT is made as of _____[date] between _____("Client") and _____("Consultant").

In the event of a conflict in the provisions of any attachments hereto and the provisions set forth in this Agreement, the provisions of such attachments shall govern.

1. Services. Consultant agrees to perform for Client the services listed in the Scope of Services section in Exhibit A, attached hereto and executed by both Client and Consultant. Such services are hereinafter referred to as "Services." Client agrees that consultant shall have ready access to Client's staff and resources as necessary to perform the Consultant's services provided for by this contract.

2. Rate of Payment for Services. Client agrees to pay Consultant for Services in accordance with the schedule contained in Exhibit B attached hereto and executed by both Client and Consultant.

3. Invoicing. Client shall pay the amounts agreed to herein upon receipt of invoices which shall be sent by Consultant, and Client shall pay the amount of such invoices to Consultant.

4. Confidential Information. Each party hereto ("Such Party") shall hold in trust for the other party hereto ("Such Other Party"), and shall not disclose to any non-party to the Agreement, any confidential information of such Other Party. Confidential information is information which relates to Such Other Party's research, development, trade secrets or business affairs, but does not include information which is generally known or easily ascertainable by non-parties of ordinary skill in computer systems design and programming.

Consultant hereby acknowledges that during the performance of this contract, the Consultant may learn or receive confidential Client information and therefore Consultant hereby confirms that all such information relating to the client's business will be kept confidential by the Consultant, except to the extent that such information is required to be divulged to the consultant's clerical or support staff or associates in order to enable Consultant to perform Consultant's contract obligation.

5. Staff. Consultant is an independent contractor and neither Consultant nor Consultant's staff is or shall be deemed to be employed by Client. Client is hereby contracting with Consultant for the services described on Exhibit A and Consultant reserves the right to determine the method, manner and mean by which the services will be performed. Consultant is not required to perform the services during a fixed hourly or daily time and if the services are performed at the Client's premises, then Consultants time spent at the premises is to be at the discretion of

the Consultant; subject to the Client's normal business hours and security requirements. Consultant hereby confirms to Client that Client will not be required to furnish or provide any training to Consultant to enable Consultant to perform services required hereunder. The services shall be performed by Consultant or Consultant's staff, and Client shall not be required to hire, supervise or pay any assistants to help Consultant who performs the services under this agreement. Consultant shall not be required to devote Consultant's full time nor the full time of Consultant's staff to the performance of the services required hereunder, and it is acknowledged that Consultant has other Clients and Consultant offers services to the general public. The order or sequence in which the work is to be performed shall be under the control of Consultant. Except to the extent that the Consultant's work must be performed on or with Client's computers or Client's existing software, all materials used in providing the services shall be provided by Consultant. Consultant's services hereunder cannot be terminated or cancelled short of completion of the services agreed upon except for Consultant's failure to perform the contract's specification as required hereunder and conversely, subject to Client's obligation to make full and timely payment(s) for Consultant's services as set forth in Exhibit B, Consultant shall be obligated to complete the services agreed upon and shall be liable for non-performance of the services to the extent and as provided in Paragraph 10 hereof. Client shall not provide any insurance coverage of any kind for Consultant or Consultant's staff, and Client will not withhold any amount that would normally be withheld from an employee's pay. Consultant shall take appropriate measures to insure that Consultant's staff is competent and that they do not breach Section 4 hereof.

Each of the parties hereto agrees that, while performing Services under this Agreement, and for a period of six (6) months following the termination of this Agreement, neither party will, except with the other party's written approval, solicit or offer employment to the other party's employees or staff engaged in any efforts under this Agreement.

6. Use of Work Product. Except as specifically set forth in writing and signed by both Client and Consultant, Consultant shall have all copyright and patent rights with respect to all materials developed under this contract, and Client is hereby granted a non-exclusive license to use and employ such materials within the Client's business.

7. Client Representative. The following individual _____ shall represent the Client during the performance of this contract with respect to the services and deliverables as defined herein and has authority to execute written modifications or additions to this contract as defined in Section 14.

Sample Contract Form 2

1. Terrific Consulting (hereafter called Contractor) agrees to provide the following products and services to the Iceberg County Art Center (hereafter called Client):

A. Information gathering: Contractor will review the following information compiled by Client:

1) Information on attendance at past events

2). Samples of past promotional pieces and any recent press coverage

3). Samples of past membership flyers

4). Financial information from the past three or four years

Contractor will also inquire into the availability of any recent market studies on the Iceberg area done by the city government or other groups working on the Iceberg's economic development.

Contractor will also confer by phone with the part-time coordinator and two or three Client board members to get their view of the issues facing Client.

B. Member survey: Contractor will design a one-page membership survey. Client will be responsible for duplicating the survey, sending it out to the membership and tallying the responses.

C. Contractor will design a "community leader interview" format. Client's board members will call on community leaders and conduct interviews. Contractor will summarize the finding and merge them with the survey responses, giving Client a written report on how it is perceived by members and community, and what people think it should be doing.

D. Contractor will travel to Iceberg for a one-day stay to meet for half a day with Client's board to discuss:

1). the survey findings, Client's audiences or "publics", Client's "position" in the community, the "messages" that Client wants to communicate to people, past promotional efforts and possible changes to make in the future.

2). the management training needs of Client's staff, board and committee chairs. Contractor will present a format to use in writing job descriptions and teach Client how to use it. The group will also develop an organizational chart for Client, identifying the various committees, board officers, committee chairs and others with particular management responsibilities.

3). Client's fundraising needs and opportunities. Contractor will explore how much Client wants to raise, and what Client is willing to do to raise it, including Client's membership program, grant opportunities and the possibility of more individual fundraising.

E. Before leaving, Contractor will give some "homework" assignments to Client. They would likely include preparation of some job descriptions and a clear annual fundraising goal.

F. Contractor will write:

1) a regular promotional schedule based on the goals identified at the meeting above

2) a review of Client's job descriptions with suggested revisions

3) recommended management training opportunities

4) if feasible, an annual calendar of management tasks

5) recommendations for raising more contributions

This work will be completed no later than December 31, 1999, and will be conducted by Contractors' agent, Edmund E. Expert.

It is understood that circumstances arising during the consulting project may require the activities described above to be replaced with other activities of an equivalent value. Such changes will be based on mutual agreement of both parties, which may be recorded as an addendum to this agreement, or as a letter from one party to the other.

2. Client agrees to:

A. participate as requested in consulting activities. This includes calling meetings, providing meeting sites and amenities, and providing information requested by Contractor. Client's entire board will be involved in this process, not just the coordinator. Client will also be asked to duplicate, distribute and tally the results of a membership survey, to conduct communicate leader interviews and to complete the homework assignments.

B. Pay Contractor a fee not to exceed $1,405,000 plus expenses. Expenses to be billed include travel ($.25 per mile for auto travel), lodging and meals while in Iceberg, long-distance phone calls, and any copying and mailing services, outside of normal communication with Client. Lodging and meal expenses will be documented with receipts.

The payments will be made in three installments: $400,000 at the signing of this contract; $400,000 upon completion of the Iceberg meeting described above; and $605,000 upon completion of this project. The project will be considered complete when the written report described above is submitted.

C. Authorize Amy Administrator to approve Contractor's work and any expenses Contractor wishes to incur on behalf of Client.

3. Either Party may terminate this agreement with thirty days' written notice. If the agreement is terminated, Contractor will present Client with a statement of account showing all fees paid to that time, and itemizing work performed. If work performed exceeds fees paid to date, Client will pay Contractor for such work at the rate of $40,000 an hour. If fees paid exceed work performed to date, Contractor will return unearned fees to Client.

(http://www.managementhelp.org/misc/smplcntr.htm)

Sample Portfolio

A sample portfolio for a professional consultant may include the following.

Career focus: Dispute Resolution

Position type: Independent Contractor

Fees: According to the Rates

Education: Relevant Training or University Degree

Experience: Senior Adviser. Three years of experience in law consultancy, primarily focused on the civil law and civil litigation. Involved in all aspects of alternative dispute resolution. Invaluable for clients who need highly professional consultations in the area of training and workplace mediation. Maintaining philosophy of analyzing the situation and offering several possible solutions for the client who wants to have a choice. Positions held: mediator, trainer, manager, coming to work as an independent consultant.

Sample Rates

Sample rates for work of an independent consultant

First consultation (30-40 minutes): includes the description of the client's situation, with setting the time and terms of providing the consultancy service. $50 per consultation. Discounts for this kind of service are not offered.

Each subsequent consultation: $115 per hour. Discounts are offered for each 10th consultation and for permanent clients.

Written recommendations: $80 per page. Provided on the demand of the client, and according to the client's requirements. Discounts are offered for each document longer than 10 pages.

Sample testimonial letter

To whom it may concern.

I have been a client of ABC Consulting for three years before writing this letter and will remain its client for an unlimited period of time. During these three years I feel that our labor relations concerns surrounding conflict resolution have become clear and understandable to me. I have stopped investing time in these labor relations matters and have concentrated on the work I usually do—running a small company with 20 employees specializing in the field of medicine. ABC Consulting regularly provides me with wonderful guidelines that make my work easier and less time-consuming. The experience of those who work in ABC Consulting is not subjected to any doubt and the high quality of their service is always combined with excellent abilities to support business relations for reasonable pricing. I will refer my friends and colleagues to ABC Consulting and will continue to contract with them, as they have saved me several thousand dollars.

Sincerely,
Mike Hudson,
The President of MedAx & Co.

Do you prefer to work for a dispute resolution consulting firm? Here are just a few firms that provide dispute resolution consulting services, which may or may not be seeking to fill positions within their organizations:

Caras and Associates, Inc.
P.O. Box 230
Clarksville, MD 21029
Website: http://www.carasadr.com/index.html
Telephone: 301-854-9996
Fax: 301-854-2929

Kevin J. Fleming, Ph. D., P.C.
P.O. Box 11840
970 W. Broadway, Suite 212A
Jackson, WY 83002-9496
Website: http://www.effectiveexecutivecoaching.com/index.html
Telephone: 307-733-4580
Toll-Free: 888-833-4580
Fax: 307-733-4584

Conflict Management Plus Ltd
Low Farm
Bassingbourn, Royston
Herts, SG8 5NT
England
Website: www.conflictmanagementplus.com
Telephone: 01763 852225
Fax: 01763 853313
Email: info@conflictmanagementplus.com

Bear Wolf Consulting & Mediation Services, Inc.
Jo-Marie Lisa, President
3412 E. 123rd Avenue
Thornton, CO 80241
Website: http://www.bearwolfmediation.com/
Telephone: 303-469-8403
Fax: 303-439-0426

Center for Aggression Management, Inc.
Suite 144
605 Crescent Executive Court
Lake Mary, FL 32747
Telephone: 407-804-2434
Fax: 407-804-3826
Email: DrJohnByrnes@AggressionManagement.com

Federal Mediation and Conciliation Service
2100 K Street, NW
Washington, DC 20427
Telephone: 202-606-8100
Fax: 202-606-4251

Workplace Mediation Ltd.
Zenith House
210 Church Road
London E10 7JQ
England
Website: http://www.wpmed.org/aboutus.htm
Telephone: 020 8556 6200
Fax: 020 8556 5011
Email: admin@wpmed.org

PMR LTD
Nora Doherty & Associates
SkyCliff House
25 Woodland Avenue
Teignmouth TQ14 8UU
England
Website: http://www.workplacemediation.co.uk/
Telephone/Fax: 01626 776857
E-mail: admin@workplacemediation.co.uk

Workplace.calm, Inc.
1200 Bay Street, Suite 1202
Toronto, Ontario M5R 2A5
Canada
Website: http://workplace.calm.to/index.html
Telephone: 416-922-8838
Fax: 416-922-3188
Email: admin@workplace.calm.to

Interpeople Inc.
311 Great Road
Littleton, MA 01460
Website: www.interpeople-inc.com
Telephone: 978-486-3338
Toll-Free: 800-336-0956

Conclusion

To become a professional consultant working as an independent contractor, experience, expertise, and consulting skills are required. These can be gained from training programs and life experience. A consultant is an expert at recognizing problems and shaping solutions to those problems. The need for business problem-solvers—among large and small businesses worldwide—has never been greater. The ever-changing moods of the buyer, plus the myriad of crisis situations businesses face almost daily, have created a seller's market for the alert consultant.

Want To Be a Conflict Resolution Author?

Objective
To provide information for becoming
a conflict resolution author.

Becoming a Freelance Writer

You can turn your conflict resolution expertise into income by writing about it in magazines and books. This chapter will help you get started and point you to some of the best books for more information.

Words are a writer's livelihood, and a writer must learn to use them effectively. Among the many available grammar books is a tiny book, published originally in 1935, usually referred to as simply Strunk and White (*The Elements of Style* by William Strunk Jr. and E. B. White). A couple of hours with it will set you on the right track. For an updated approach, try Arthur Plotnik's *Spunk & Bite: A Writer's Guide to Punchier, More Engaging Language & Style* (Random House, 2005).

Every writer needs a good dictionary (e.g., *Merriam-Webster's Collegiate*) and a good thesaurus (e.g., *Roget's International Thesaurus*). These days, you really need a computer, since editors expect to receive manuscripts in common electronic formats. If you can't type, either learn or hire somebody to type your handwritten words into a computer.

Responsibilities of the Writer

To become a successful freelance writer, you must understand the standards expected of professional writers, which means doing some homework. The following books will help you learn the basics:

> *The ASJA Guide to Freelance Writing: A Professional Guide to the Business, for Nonfiction Writers of All Experience Levels,* edited by Timothy Harper (St. Martin's Griffin, 2003)

> *Formatting and Submitting Your Manuscript* by Cynthia Laufenberg (Writer's Digest Books, 2004)

Dealing With Editors

Editors are always harried, with more submissions than they can possibly read and another deadline just around the corner. They will reject your submission if it shows you failed to study their magazine or book list, look at their published writer's guidelines, or learn basic professional manuscript standards. To avoid summary rejections, learn to do it right. An excellent guide is Bonnie Hearn Hill's *The Freelancer's Rulebook: A Guide to Understanding, Working With and Winning Over Editors* (Story Line Press, 2001).

For magazines, the most efficient approach is to send a query letter before writing the entire article. For books, send a thorough proposal with a brief cover letter before writing the whole book. Sell your concept and expertise before writing something you may not be able to sell. That's how freelancers make a living.

Writing for Magazines

Writing for magazines can earn you some money or increase your professional standing, or both. Before submitting a query, read several issues and study the masthead page (the page listing the publisher, editors, columnists, and contributors) to find out the kinds of articles they publish, how much is written by staff and how much by freelancers (names listed on the masthead as "contributing editors" are usually free-lancers), typical article length and extras (sidebars, footnotes, references, etc.), and writing style (breezy and conversational or formal and academic). Review back issues (check your local libraries and the magazine's website) to ensure your idea has not been covered recently.

Next, select an editor's name to whom you can address your query letter, rather than sending it to a generic "submissions editor." The masthead typically lists editors, a managing editor, and one or more assistant editors. Assistant editors (usually entry-level jobs) frequently scour queries for a great idea or writer, hoping to prove their value and move up the hierarchy. If your target editor has written a recent article, mention it in your query letter. Even if your article is rejected, a well-crafted query may lead to an assigned article on a topic you may have overlooked.

Your query should clearly define your idea, its proposed length, why readers will care, and why you are best qualified to write it. Mention any previous—and relevant—published articles or books. When proposing a nonfiction piece do not mention your published short stories and novels. Keep the letter tightly focused and make sure there are no spelling or grammar errors (never rely on your word processing software's spell-checker). Always include a self-addressed, stamped envelope (SASE) for a response. There are many how-to books on query letters; one of the best is Lisa Collier Cool's *How to Write Irresistible Query Letters* (Writer's Digest Books, 2002).

Formatting and Submitting Manuscripts

Manuscripts must be double-spaced with at least one-inch margins on all sides. On the first page, include your name, mailing address, phone number, and email address, plus an approximate word count. Adding a copyright notice is amateurish, as every editor knows your work is copyrighted as soon as you commit it to paper or computer. For more on manuscript formats and other magazine standards, read the *Writer's Digest Handbook of Magazine Article Writing,* edited by Michelle Ruberg (Writer's Digest Books, 2005).

Typical Income

Pay rates for articles run from zero (usually with some free author's copies) to several dollars per word, with most averaging under 25 cents per word. You should always insist that the article include a short author's biographical note in which you list your professional qualifications, pertinent published books, and contact information (mailing address, telephone number, email address, etc.). This short note can be an important, although intangible, benefit.

Pay rates are frequently negotiable, and it never hurts to ask for more. Offer solid rationale why your article is worth more than the standard rates, such as years of related experience, available quotes from celebrities or other well-known people (don't promise this unless you absolutely know you can deliver them), or maybe well-targeted sidebars providing solid benefits to readers (e.g., "Five Ways to Stop Workplace Conflicts Now").

Don't worry that the editor will become annoyed and tell you to forget the whole thing. If you make your request in a professional manner and explain how valuable your article will be to readers, the response should be equally professional (maybe a counteroffer). If the editor does overreact, you have found an editor to avoid.

Writing Books

Writing nonfiction books requires more time, research, and dedication than articles. Marketing and selling that book is far more difficult and will require even more time, energy, and resources.

Before writing, research the competition. If you think you have no competition, you probably have not done enough research. You can use Internet search engines (like Google) with appropriate keywords or the world's largest online book retailer (Amazon.com) to browse your subject area, or visit local bookstores and libraries. Buy or borrow some of the most popular books and study them. How are they the same as, or different than, the book you want to write? What can you do to make your book stand out from the rest? How can you capitalize on your own qualifications and experience?

Next, write a detailed, chapter-by-chapter outline of your book, including your unique ideas and the specific benefits you can provide to readers. Remember, readers do not buy books, they buy benefits. Your book must answer the big question: Why would a browser want to read and/or buy your book rather than somebody else's?

Finally, you must decide how to publish your book—traditional publishing, subsidy publishing, or self-publishing. Before deciding, you must understand the differences.

Traditional publishing means you have a contract with a publishing company (e.g., Random House or Simon & Schuster), usually with some percentage of the book's profits (your royalties) and an up-front cash advance against the projected royalties. You will receive no royalties until total royalties exceed the advance (most books never do). These publishers do not ask you to pay for any portion of the publishing. Unfortunately, first-time authors have little chance of signing a publishing contract with a major publisher without a literary agent, and most successful agents are not interested in first-time authors unless they can prove they have, and know how to reach, a ready-made audience.

However, to get an agent or a traditional publishing contract, you must write an excellent book proposal. Neither publishers nor agents truly want to read your completed nonfiction manuscript; they prefer a thorough proposal stressing marketing and unique benefits. Either *Write the Perfect Book Proposal: 10 That Sold and Why* by Jeff Herman and Deborah Levine Herman (Wiley, 2001) or *How to Write a Book Proposal* by Michael Larsen (Writer's Digest Books, 2004) will show you how.

Subsidy (aka vanity) publishing has expanded along with the Internet. Subsidy publishers charge authors to publish books—either through large set-up fees or expensive per-copy costs or both. Many online subsidy publishers call themselves POD (print-on-demand) publishers or claim to offer self-publishing. Regardless of terminology, they profit from selling books and services to authors, not by selling books to bookstores or readers. If you search the Internet for book publishers, you will find these publishers: Infinity, iUniverse, PublishAmerica, Xlibris, AuthorHouse, Vantage Press, Lulu.com, etc. If you want your book reviewed in major publications or stocked in bookstores across the country, avoid them. Major reviewers will not consider books with those imprints, and bookstores typically will only special order them (except maybe local bookstores you contact directly).

Every service these publishers offer can be done cheaper by the author (personally or by contracting the work). Due to the high per-copy costs, subsidy books carry retail prices much higher than the market averages and, as a result, sales and profits suffer. Based on data published by subsidy publishers themselves, the average subsidy-published book sells less than 100 copies, most to the author and his friends and relatives.

Self-publishing is viable for those willing to assume full responsibility for all aspects of publishing, along with all the risks and, of course, all the profits. A self-publisher must learn as much as possible about the creative and business sides of the industry and may choose to contract for individual tasks or work with a book packager who can do it all.

If You Choose to Self-Publish

Successful self-publishing is both challenging and rewarding, requiring skills in editing, cover design, interior design and typesetting, indexing, and working with book printers. In addition, books require copyright registration, Advance Book Information submitted to R. R. Bowker's *Books in Print, and* acquisition of an International Standard Book Number (ISBN), a Library of Congress Control Number (LCCN), and a Bookland EAN (European—now International—Article Number) bar code for the back cover.

Although every writer should learn basic editing skills, self-editing of a final manuscript should only be attempted by those with considerable experience. Asking friends or relatives to edit your manuscript may work if they have editing experience and a penchant for bluntness. Professional editors, who understand the application of grammar and style rules, typically offer a range of services from light editing (primarily correcting spelling, grammar, capitalization, punctuation, and word usage) to heavy editing (involving fact-checking, rewriting for consistency and wordiness, and correction of logical errors). Good editing can be expensive but is indispensable to a polished, professional product.

Professional book cover design is critical to success. The book's title on the spine is the first thing seen on most bookstore shelves and must be legible from 10 feet away. Forget about not judging a book by its cover, because people do just that. Studies have shown that a well-designed cover lures browsers to pick up the book, after which they may spend 10-20 seconds looking at the cover. Only then might they actually open it. Good cover designers understand books and their covers, not just graphic design, and will provide a finished file ready for your book printer.

Few people appreciate good typesetting and interior layout for books, but they usually know when a book is poorly designed. They may find the reading experience annoying even if they cannot tell you why. The selection of page margins, font types and sizes, and the layout of tables, graphs, and images must all work together to support the book's subject matter and tone. A good design, which enhances the reading experience without drawing attention to its elements, requires special software and the ability to use it well. The final typeset interior, like the cover, will be complete and ready for the printer. Pete Masterson has written an excellent book on the subject, *Book Design and Production* (Aeonix, 2006), that every self-publisher should read.

Selecting a Printer

There are scores of book printers but only two basic printing technologies—offset and digital. Offset is the traditional method used for decades—think of movie scenes with huge paper rolls feeding through rollers and finished newspapers on the conveyor. Offset printing equipment may be sheetfed (using large sheets of paper) or web press (big paper rolls), and each has its preferred applications. Digital printing involves large-scale versions of your desktop laser printer, although faster with higher quality output. Trimming, collating, and binding machinery produces a finished book, either paperback or hardcover.

Offset usually produces sharper text and better graphics, although newer digital printers are closing the gap. Offset is cheaper for large print runs, with the cost breakpoint between 500–1,000 copies. Some digital printers offer true print-on-demand (POD) services and can economically produce from one to several hundred copies. The most successful POD printer is Lightning Source, Inc. (http://www.LightningSource.com/). As a subsidiary of the largest book wholesaler in the U.S. (Ingram Book Company), Lightning Source submits all books it prints to Ingram's huge database at no extra charge, and most bookstores order from Ingram.

Once you know the size and page count for your typeset book, you should request quotes from a dozen or more printers. Pete Masterson provides an excellent format for a request for quotation (RFQ) and an extensive list of offset and digital book printers at http://www.aeonix.com/bookprnt.htm.

Self-publishers either handle all order fulfillment themselves or contract those tasks to others. Wholesalers, who supply books to retailers and libraries, expect an average discount of 50 percent or more off list price. Distributors expect an even higher discount, since they employ sale representatives who contact bookstore buyers. The need for a wholesaler or distributor depends on your marketing plan.

Book marketing responsibility, regardless of publishing method, almost always falls on the author, unless that author is already a celebrity. For others, publishing success results from hard work, marketing savvy, and networking. You can, of course, hire expensive publicists to market your books. If you prefer to do it yourself, consider the following books:

1001 Ways to Market Your Books for Authors and Publishers
by John Kremer (Open Horizons, 2006)

Grassroots Marketing: Getting Noticed in a Noisy World by Shel Horowitz (Chelsea Green, 2000)

Guerrilla Marketing for Writers by Jay Conrad Levinson, Rick Frishman, Michael Larsen (Writer's Digest Books, 2001)

There are many books that can guide you through the self-publishing maze, but Dan Poynter's *Self-Publishing Manual: How to Write, Print and Sell Your Own Book* (Para Publishing, 2006) and Fern Reiss's *The Publishing Game: Publish a Book in 30 Days* (Peanut Butter and Jelly Press, 2003) are both excellent.

Potential Conflict Resolution Markets

Articles published in conflict resolution trade magazines average less than 1,500 words, with pay rates averaging four cents per word or $100 per article. Although not very lucrative, published articles in these trade magazines may increase your visibility and professional standing. There are two primary publishers for conflict resolution books and articles. The National Institute for Trial Advocacy publishes books on the subject, while Jossey-Bass (a publishing imprint of John Wiley and Sons, Inc.) publishes books and e-books as well as articles in several journals.

National Institute for Trial Advocacy
361 Centennial Pkwy, Ste 220
Louisville, CO 80027-1281
Website: http://www.nita.org/
Phone: 303-953-6800
Toll-Free: 800-225-6482
Fax: 720-890-7069

Jossey-Bass
989 Market Street
San Francisco, CA 94103-1741
Website: http://www.josseybass.com/
Phone: 415-433-1740
Fax: 415-433-0499

Conclusion

A single chapter can do little more than scratch the surface of writing and publishing, so take time to read the recommended books and, if you decide to self-publish a book, consider joining either the Small Publishers Association of North America (http://www.SPANnet.org/) or the Independent Book Publishers Association (http://www.PMA-online.org/). Also, consult John Culleton's list of books on writing and publishing at http://wexfordpress.com/tex/shortlist.pdf for more information.

Above all, read, study, learn... and write.

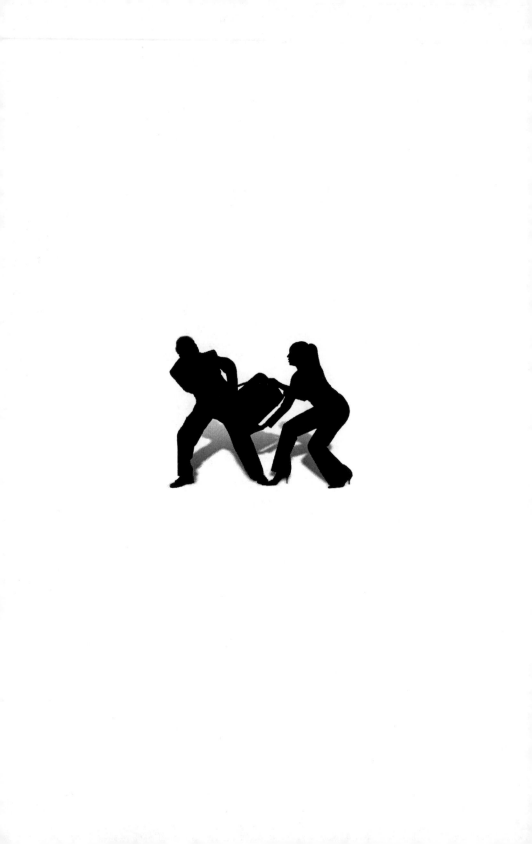

5

Want To Be a Conflict Resolution Trainer?

Objective
To provide information about becoming
a conflict resolution trainer/speaker.

What Is a Professional Trainer/Speaker

The career of a professional conflict resolution speaker/trainer looks attractive to many who enjoy working with audiences and feel proud of their potential to connect with strangers in an effective and convincing manner. There is a lot of value in learning to be a good public speaker or learning how to train a group of people to hone their professional skills. However, the career of a professional speaker or trainer is something more.

A professional speaker may speak in a variety of forums for a fee—keynote or banquet speeches or talks delivered at workshops, seminars, or conferences of local, regional, or international scale. A trainer is someone who professionally coaches a group of people. In corporate environments, a trainer will most often target a group of people committed to a certain area—for instance, the sales force. The task of the trainer is to develop a strategy that will bring out the utmost potential of the individuals and increase their expertise and skills in a given field.

How Much Do Professional Trainers/Speakers Earn?

According to data from the National Speakers Association, the "annual personal income of 26.3% of NSA members is between $75,000 and $150,000 with 10.5% in excess of $200,000" (NSA, 2004). The training industry is a 200-billion-dollar industry, according to Don Schrello, author of the book *How to Market Training and Information* (book available by calling 1-800-ENROLLX). This data only gives a general idea of how much a speaker can expect to earn in this profession. Income can vary widely depending on the number of speaking engagements a speaker has per annum. A survey of the speaking industry, prepared by Lilly Walters in 2002, demonstrates that the respondents of the survey earn 53% of their income from speaking arrangements. The opportunities for income growth for speakers will depend on growth or contraction in the market for speaking engagements, which depends directly on the number of meetings and fluctuations in the average spending on a meeting (NSA, 2004).

The price to charge for a speaking engagement is subject to many considerations. At present, the charge can vary from $25 for a speaking session to $100,000 if the person delivering the talk is a celebrity. Patricia Fripp—a famous keynote speaker, author, and trainer of speakers—believes that "you are not considered a professional speaker if you charge less than $2,500" (Fripp, 2005). However, some organizations may consider that $250 per speaking engagement is an excessive fee. How many speaking engagements a speaker can land is a matter of personal entrepreneurial spirit and ability to win audiences. NSA reports that its members average 30 engagements a year, with 10% going over 100 speeches (NSA, 2003).

The trainer's income can also depend on the number of engagements, especially if one is self-employed. Certified conflict-resolution trainers, for instance, may easily be able to obtain a $90,000 salary on average, but this requires a high degree of specialization. Salary.com gives the following information on the average salaries for trainers:

Median salary $79,292
Twenty-fifth percentile salary $66,886
Seventy-fifth percentile salary $96,341
(*Average Sales Training Manager Salary*)

Organizations which provide specialized certification training to prospective conflict-resolution trainers include the following:

Mediation Training Institute International

Dana Mediation Institute, Inc.
Mission Corporate Centre
5800 Foxridge Drive, Suite 412
Mission, KS 66202-2333

Phone:

Main:	913-432-2888
Registrar:	913-338-1113

Toll-free (USA and Canada):

Main:	888-222-3271
Registrar:	877-338-1113

Fax:	913-273-1919
E-mail:	info@mediationworks.com

Type of training offered: External training consultants and others who possess competencies in classroom instruction who wish to be certified to conduct the world's best conflict management training for their clients, to receive superb marketing support, and to qualify as a trainer subcontractor in MTI's corporate and government contracts.

American Center for Conflict Resolution Institute

5247 Wilson Mills Rd, #442
Richmond Heights, OH 44143

Phone: 216-255-6722
Email: support@accri.org

Type of training offered: A distance learning course will be offered beginning June 15, 2007. This train-the-trainer course's objective is to enable delegates to design, train, evaluate, and follow-up effective basic mediation, family mediation, and divorce mediation training programs. Successful graduates will also learn how to design training of any length for groups of varying sizes, learning styles, and experience. The session will also focus on delivery skills (effective body language and voice projection) and teach classic techniques for handling difficult trainees and maintaining control of a group.

The following textbook provides a design for basic mediation training. Mark D. Bennett and Scott H. Hughes have taken the performance-based training from the National Institute for Trial Advocacy (NITA) for trial lawyers and adapted it to training for mediators. The authors have used these materials extensively in their mediation training classes at law schools and in programs open to the public.

The Art of Mediation, Second Edition, sets the mediation process in context, provides basic definitions, contrasts mediation with other forms of dispute resolution, describes varieties of mediation, and lays out roles and functions of the mediators. The book also contains hypothetical situations for performance training. "Useful Teaching Notes" help plan, deliver, and evaluate mediation training. This text can be purchased by calling 1-800-225-6482 or through the NITA website at http://www.nita.org/.

What Is the Career Outlook for Professional Trainers/Speakers?

As the speaker/ trainer starts out on a career path, he will find that with time new opportunities for speaking open up, and there is a possibility to charge a higher fee. Thus, in Lilly Walters's survey of the speaking industry in 2002, she was able to locate 6,588 professional speakers, trainers, humorists, or seminar leaders who charge no less than $1,000 per engagement, delivering at least 40 presentations a year at this price level (Walters, 2002). She notes, too, that "the majority of those responding to the survey are in a much higher fee range, but these were the minimum requirements" (Walters, 2002).

Working for an agency—such as a speaker's bureau or seminar company—the speaker will be able to acquire more contracts as he wins recognition as a professional speaker or trainer and establishes a reputation. It makes sense to specialize. For instance, the speaker/trainer may prefer to devote his life to the career of a sales trainer or a speaker addressing financial or accounting conferences, especially if such an occupation resonates with his previous employment or education.

If he tires of speaking or training, he can start a seminar company or become a lecture agent, now moving to the other side of the table.

This occupation will allow him to select appropriate speakers for certain venues and is most suitable for someone with previous speaker/trainer experience. This can be a good way to expand revenue and increase entrepreneurial skills. Another transition can be to a job of a trainer for speakers or trainers. An experienced professional in the field can start working with novices in the subject area.

Where to Gain Skills

A person eager to begin a professional speaking or training career can develop expertise in a variety of ways. One way is to obtain the help of a professional speech coach able to give advice on improvement in this area. Another option is to join a course that will develop speaking or training abilities. For instance, former teachers or professors can go through a retraining course that will focus their skills and potential on areas specific to the trainer's profession.

Another way is to join a professional organization committed to helping novice speakers or trainers. One such example is Toastmasters International. The organization is a network of clubs that assist members in developing their public speaking skills and is committed to providing a friendly and stimulating learning environment to help every speaker bring out his full potential. Toastmasters provides training in such areas as prudent use of time and technology and dealing with various cultural and generational differences. You can enroll in a Toastmasters' club for a certain fee and attend the sessions of this club as long as you think there is a potential for learning new things there. The network of Toastmasters International clubs is continuously expanding.

Another opportunity to learn is to practice as much as possible. A novice speaker may find it difficult to come up with speaking engagements. This may prompt him to charge small fees or take up opportunities to speak free of charge. These chances can appear at small community organizations that are unable to pay the high speaking fees of prominent speakers but provide a platform for budding speakers willing to try out their skills. Success in volunteer engagements can lead to contracts that will generate fees.

Joining the National Speakers Association may be another option to contemplate. This organization unites professional speakers from all over the U.S. and is a real hub of experience and expertise and a valuable pool of knowledge providing a constant source of new resources for novices and well-established professional alike. The National Speakers Association, in existence since 1973, has provided resources and education to large numbers of people. Now, it unites experts in different fields who address meetings as trainers, educators, humorists, motivators, consultants, or authors.

The National Speakers Association issues a number of publications that may come in handy for a budding speaker, including: *Professional Speaker* magazine that discusses trends and prospects of the speaking industry, *Who's Who in Professional Speaking* that lists professional speakers with area of expertise, and *Voices of Experience Audio Magazine* that features interviews with renowned speakers. *Who's Who in Professional Speaking* can be instrumental in getting engagements since it is used by many meeting planners as a guide.

The NSA maintains an Academy for Professional Speaking, a one-year program that is a combination of face-to-face and distance learning. The end of the program is marked with a one-day session of the Cavett Institute. Another possibility to benefit from the expertise accumulated in the National Speakers Association is to join its workshops or other gatherings that provide excellent opportunities for networking.

Determine Your Options

First, you need to choose whether to become a full-time or a part-time speaker. To put your income in dependence on the number of engagements you can arrange in a self-employed position is a brave choice for the few people who are absolutely positive of their rapport with audiences and ability to market themselves to those who ultimately decide on meeting content. For this reason, many people prefer to balance between a permanent job and additional speaking/training contracts that supplement their income. The NSA 2003 survey showed that 64.5% of its members were full-time speakers or trainers,. while 19.9% regarded professional speaking as a part-time job that supplemented their other earnings. In the survey, 4.1% of respondents were part-time speakers who were contemplating a shift to full-time speaking in the next few years (NSA, 2003).

Next, you must define your areas of professional expertise. For instance, a speaker can specialize in talks delivered at workshops and seminars. A workshop is a course aimed at problem solving for a small group of people. The workshop presupposes intense exchange of ideas between participants, lively discussion, and practical orientation to teach participants how to apply their learned principles in the real world.

A seminar is usually "a presentation on a topic covering some facet of knowledge or skill delivered in a public or a private setting." A seminar is typically divided into modules and often includes a mix of lectures, visual aids, interaction with participants, and practical exercises, thus requiring a great deal of versatility from the person delivering the seminar. The objective of this venue is to share the speaker's knowledge with the audience through a combination of teaching methods.

A speaker choosing to specialize in keynote addresses will have to address larger audiences. A keynote address is "the main speech at a meeting or for that day of the meeting" (Women's Calendar). A typical keynote setting is a breakfast, lunch, or dinner at a large conference of professionals in a particular field. Keynote speeches tend to be rather long and can take between a half hour and an hour and a half. These speeches most typically cover broad topics that all listeners may find of interest. It is usual to pay a large fee to a keynote speaker, and this speaker is often a celebrity or a renowned professional in the field. For instance, "at an advertising association meeting, science fiction writer Ray Bradbury gave a keynote on creativity."

There are several ways to sell your services. The most straightforward is to enter into a contract with a seminar company that will hire you and then put you in contact with meeting organizers willing to obtain your services. The company will surely charge a commission for their services but, on the bright side, the speaker gains access to a well-researched market and can utilize the company's long-lasting partnerships. There are a number of speaker's bureaus that will hire speakers to talk at various occasions and, with application of some effort, a person can strike a contract with one of those—first for a small engagement, followed by a larger contract.

Alternatively, one can choose to be self-employed, chasing customers single-handedly. The bright side of this approach is that the self-employed speaker will not need to pay a commission to the bureau for the engagement. However, this means investing more funds, energy, and time into the challenging job of finding clients. Without enough experience, this may prove a daunting undertaking. Even so, this may allow the speaker/trainer to upgrade his promotional material and gain an opportunity to start his own seminar company.

Finally, the speaker or trainer needs to decide whether to operate on a regional, national, or international level. For most speakers, the regional events are a good place to start a career due to the ease of finding contracts and an extensive network of local acquaintances. After establishing a reputation in a local setting, the speaker may find it easier to proceed to the next level, receiving contracts for national-level engagements.

The next logical step is going international. One should not forget, however, that advancing to the international level is not a matter of transferring his skills to the next level. Other issues come into play, such as legal and organizational challenges, logistics, and—above all—cross-cultural differences. In public speaking, the chance of cross-cultural blunders is very high, and these mistakes are not as easy to correct as in personal communication. One area in which a speaker surely has to take the greatest precaution is humor, since jokes that appeal to audiences in one nation may not produce the same effect in other nations. Speaking through an interpreter can be tricky as well, since translation can often distort meaning to some degree. For this reason, a move to international speaking will require a great concentration of abilities and struggling with many new issues and details.

How to Develop Your Content

A serious issue to ponder is the content of the speeches the speaker/trainer plans to deliver. Clearly, someone with a Bachelor of Arts degree will not want to deliver a lecture on the prospects of the air and space industry. That is why the first step is to evaluate expertise and to search for appropriate fields, topics, and content. Ideally, the content should be somehow connected with the speaker's previous occupation, education, or other background. A speaker/trainer with a professional history in an investment firm will be perceived better by an audience of financiers than someone lacking such a background. Even if you have an amateur background, this is better than nothing—such as volunteering at a medical center or acting in an amateur club.

Expertise is important, but expertise alone will not make a brilliant speech. The speaker should have a passion for the topic. There are numerous devices to let the audience see a trace of the speaker's enthusiasm. Although some highly qualified professionals may fake their interest in the subject, this is not recommended. In order to avoid fooling the audience or delivering a lukewarm presentation, therefore, the speaker should either tackle only subjects he has long been interested in or learn more about the subject.

Preparing for delivering a speech, a trainer/speaker can surely purchase canned material to present. Alternatively, a speaker can develop materials to support his presentation that will probably be best-suited to the occasion. This is the problem with canned material—the speaker often has to rework it to make it suitable for a particular lecture or workshop. There is always the danger that there will be no materials available suitable for such purposes. Besides, there is a chance that some of the listeners are already familiar with the materials, which will reduce the novelty of the talk to them and create a worse impression than custom-made materials.

A speaker should always be careful to develop a resource base. This is easy to do with a specialty in a particular field. Therefore, it makes sense to keep up with all developments in the given field. On the contrary, a speaker may find it necessary to work with different topics, undertaking in-depth research on each one. Library resources, credible online content, and government publications all are good resources for incorporation in speeches. Another good resource base is interactions with professionals who may provide insight on specific topics to be incorporated in speech content..

Marketing and Selling Your Services

There is plenty of information on how to market one's services to lecture agents and seminar companies, as well as directly to meeting organizers. In the first place, the speaker's individual marketing campaign has to focus on attaining the objectives present in any marketing campaign. Thus, the campaign has to present to the prospective buyers the advantages and benefits of hiring a particular speaker. Although there may be several benefits, it is wise to choose a particular focus on which to concentrate. The speaker can emphasize his own expertise in the field, confirmed by a record of engagements dealing with similar topics and previous professional experience in the given area. Another possible focus is the enthusiasm of the audience and enthusiastic evaluations from listeners and meeting organizers. Finally, the speaker can choose to highlight the quality of the speech itself, providing audio or video clips of the most successful moments in marketing materials.

The next step is to create a business plan for selling services. A business plan will most typically contain steps to be undertaken in order to increase bookings, along with expected results. This document can include, among other things, plans for agency search and for marketing services. As a way to boost the number of bookings, the speaker can engage in an online search and make a point of contacting a set number of agencies per week with e-mails or deliveries of promotional materials.

The plan can also include elements of the marketing campaign, such as purchase of speaker bureaus' lists or creation of promo materials. Thus, the speaker may want to use the services of Emailing Speakers Bureau Blast that charges $199 for putting him in contact with agencies. Walters Speaker Services will give access to the International Directory of Lecture Agencies and Speakers Bureaus, which contains about 430 agents and bureaus from all over the globe to subscribers to their magazine who pay $95 a year. Free databases are available from the websites of the National Speakers Association and the International Association of Speakers Bureaus (Walters, 2002).

The creation of promo materials can cost as much as one wants. In the initial stages of a speaking/training career, however, it makes sense to limit the expenses by, for instance, ordering two-color brochures instead of four-color ones. While a video featuring one's most successful speeches is recommended, an audio demo tape will do for budding speakers. The speaker may want to order promotional materials in small quantities of 30 to 50 packages at a time to allow for later modification to provide more individualized messages.

The resumé is one of the most effective tools for personal promotion in the speaking industry, much as in any other field. A speaker has to rethink the scope of the resumé, discarding items that have little bearing on speaking skills and updating information that can be instrumental in demonstrating speaking abilities. If a speaker targets several fields, it makes sense to have a few variations of the resumé ready so that a person can have different focal points receiving more extensive coverage in each version.

As the discussion of speakers' fees suggests, there is a wide range of salaries and fees in this area. A beginning speaker can consider setting fees that are one step below the range exhibited by more experienced speakers. The data of various surveys available from the website of the National Speakers Association and other similar organizations can allow one to gather reliable information about average rates and adjust requirements accordingly. Most speakers in the National Speakers Association's 2003 survey indicate that the range of fees is continuing to rise.

How to Find Venues for Speaking

The most obvious way to find venues for speaking is to connect with a seminar company that can put the speaker in contact with potential employers. However, a budding speaker will find it difficult to assure the seminar company that his services are the high-quality the company needs and, thus, it may be more sensible to build a track record before selling services to one of the companies or lecture agents.

There are multiple venues for speaking, including adult education classes, college events, schools, and government agencies. Some recruiters at non-profit organizations, for instance, may be interested in beginners willing to talk for a small fee or even free of charge. A speaker may also get an engagement by contacting large companies that "realize the tremendous marketing and good will benefits available to them by sending presenters into the public to teach them about their product and industry" (Walters, 2002). Even if the fees are at first small, the speaker can use speeches as opportunities for networking that, in the future, will bring more paid engagements. Those with professional expertise in some field may find that talking to school audiences or addressing college events is a viable option. Speakers with strong academic backgrounds and research interests or records can find it appealing to address conferences, professional seminars, or conventions. Corporate training programs, cruise ships, government agencies, and trade shows can be potential venues for public speaking.

Here are three national seminar companies which actively recruit speakers:

> Attn: Screening Committee
> National Seminars Group/Padgett-Thompson
> 6901 W 63rd Street, 3rd floor
> Overland Park, KS 66202-4007
> E-mail: screeningcommittee@natsem.com

> Attn: Faculty Recruiter
> SkillPath Seminars
> P.O. Box 2768
> Mission, KS 66201
> E-mail: recruit@skillpath.net

> Trainer Review Committee
> Fred Pryor Seminars and CareerTrack
> 9757 Metcalf Ave.
> Overland Park, KS 66212
> Email: speakerapp@pryor.com

Sample Forms

Sample Speaking Contract

Contract for Speaking Appearance of Jack Johnson
Contact Jane Dimensa to confirm an engagement.

Title of Program: _____

Scheduled to appear on August 12, 2005, for fee of $1,000 plus expenditures enumerated below.

1. Expenses payable by the host of the program involve first-class airfare to and from JFK Airport, NYC; hotel charge of approximately $300; transportation from the airport to the hotel; rent of the vehicle for three days. The accommodation site has to be negotiated by the host group and the speaker and has to be a four- or five-star hotel. The host group is expected to pay for the hotel room with a credit card to secure accommodation prior to the speaker's arrival. The other expenses will be sent to the host group as an invoice.

2. The speaker's fee is payable on the day of the engagement and should be paid to Jack Johnson.

3. If the host group is forced to cancel the presentation within 30 days of the scheduled date, the penalty of 30% of the approved speaker's fee is payable to the speaker. The penalty does not apply to special cases such as natural calamities. If the speaker cannot arrive at the site of the presentation for a valid reason, he undertakes to refund the expenses pre-paid by the host group.

4. The host group will provide the necessary equipment that will be previously agreed upon. If the audience exceeds 60 people, the speaker has to be supplied with a podium and either a lavalier or a free-standing microphone.

5. Videotaping is allowed, but additional fees for that service are to be negotiated.

6. If you are willing to purchase the samples of hand-outs that will be distributed at the meeting, you have to contact the speaker at least 7 days before the venue so that sufficient number of materials can be prepared.

Signature: _____

Signature of the host group representative: _____

Sample Forms, Cont.

Sample Program Evaluation Form

Presentation Evaluation Form
(to be completed by participants of the program)

I appreciate your contribution in helping me further develop the content and style of my presentation. Please take time to complete this evaluation form and return it to:

> Name of Speaker
> Date of Program
> Title of Program

1. Did the presentation meet your expectations?
   Yes   No

2. Do you believe the topic was appropriate?
   Yes   No

3. Are you satisfied with the level of the speech?
   Yes   Too simple   Too complicated

4. How would you rate the speaker's familiarity with the topic?
   Poor   Adequate   Good   Excellent

5. Did you find the supporting materials helpful in understanding the topic of the presentation?
   Very helpful   Rather helpful   Useless

6. Did the presentation in general help your understanding of the subject?
   Yes, very much   Yes   Not really   No

7. Would you like to listen to another lecture from this speaker?
   Yes   No

8. Your overall impression of the speech:

9. Do you have any suggestions for improving the speaker's techniques and style?

10. Do you have any suggestions concerning topics for discussion for the following presentations?

Sample Forms, Cont.

Sample Promotional Package

Add a cutting edge to your business by inviting a talented speaker to talk to your employees!

Electrifying lectures from Jack Johnson—an experienced speaker with tremendous potential!

Invite a speaker who has:

- A proven record of speeches at top companies including Citigroup, PriceWaterHouse Coopers, Ernst & Young, and others
- A close knowledge of the local market developed over a decade of employment in the Jensen truck factory, the leading employer in the area
- Over 20 years of experience in the speaking industries
- Averaged 50 speaking engagements per year
- Satisfied and enthused over 95% of his listeners

See my demo video to get a glimpse of how I deliver speeches that will make a memorable impression on your audience.

Take a chance to live an exciting moment by attending Jack Johnson's lecture!

Sample Rate Sheet

Typical Rates for Jack Johnson

A 20-minute presentation $1,000
A keynote address .... $3,000–$5,000
In case the address
exceeds 60 minutes .... $5,000–$8,000

Note: the rate will vary depending on the complexity of the topic, the knowledge level of the audience, and the location of the venue. In any case, the exact fee is subject to negotiation.

Sample Forms, Cont.

Sample Testimonial Letter

Our company, Trend Issues Inc., has a long record of working with Jack Johnson, and we have been invariably satisfied with our partnership. We invited Jack to talk to our sales personnel for the first time six years ago, and the enthusiastic response of our staff to his lectures convinced us that we must invite Jack again. Since that time we have been so happy with our cooperation that we never contemplated inviting a different speaker to address our employees.

One of the reasons we did not try to change the speaker for several years was the obvious effect of Jack's lectures and the superior results delivered by his presentations. As a result of Jack's work, sales in our unit picked up 20% a year on average. We connect this progress not only with the economic trends in our area, but also with the positive effect of Jack's training sessions. Besides, we noted that his sessions are accompanied with a surge in sales volume, as sales staff return to their work invigorated and full of new ideas. Evaluation forms filled out by our employees after the talks confirm our view that Jack's influence on the performance of our sales staff is significant.

I would like to note that Jack does not restrict his area of expertise only to the sales department. Over the years, we have asked him to talk to our customer service representatives, designers, and administrative staff. Each time, we obtained positive feedback that convinced us to continue our cooperation.

We are determined to invite Jack Johnson for most or all of the speaking events in our company, if he has the time and desire to participate. We found that his speeches were an excellent investment and are highly pleased with our cooperation.

Sincerely,

Linda Johnson
Human Resource Manager
Trend Issues Inc.

Conclusion

Professional speaking/training is an attractive occupation that allows a person with a talent for influencing audiences to realize his full potential and bring out both intellectual abilities and emotional maturity. Although this profession calls for constant improvement, painstaking perfection of speaking skills, and overcoming of barriers such as stage fright, it is also associated with an attractive compensation and a great degree of flexibility. A speaker/trainer can choose this career as a part-time occupation to supplement income or opt for full-time employment to make professional speaking the most important source of income. Regardless of the degree of involvement, the profession of a conflict-resolution speaker/trainer can deliver exciting opportunities and great job satisfaction.

6

Becoming a Mediator

Objective
To identify ways to become a private practice mediator and/or a court-connected mediator.

Introduction

In recent years, the profession of a mediator has become more and more popular. It is not simply a trend of the contemporary times but rather an subjective necessity that stimulates people to focus their attention on mediation when choosing a profession. It is also noteworthy that mediation may also be very helpful for those who have made the decision to change careers and start a new mediation practice. It is never too late to become a mediator, and varied experiences working with others among different fields will help those wishing to become mediators.

On the other hand, it is also necessary to take into consideration the position and interests of those who use the services offered by mediators. Traditionally, mediators to a certain extent have replaced courts, which were always referred to when different conflicts could not be resolved by their participants. In a court setting there is usually a winner and a loser. In such situations, it is quite natural that the opposing parties in conflicts would more readily refer to mediators to resolve their problem efficiently, and profitably for all participants, than turn their views to courts with their bureaucracy and often quite a low efficiency. Anyway, I believe that often both parties appealing to a court remain unsatisfied with the outcome of the trial, while mediators can lead them to a mutually satisfactory solution.

The current world simply cannot exist without the role a of peacemakers especially in the growing role of mediators, since conflicts are occurring more often and are becoming more complicated. As a result, it is very important to clearly realize how one can become a mediator—what education, training, skills, and abilities he must have and, what is more, how he can work efficiently so that it is profitable both for clients and the mediator.

Licensing or Certification Of Mediators

Currently in the United States, although many states recommend qualifications for mediators, no state has requirements for the private practice of mediation. In any state, a mediator can practice in private settings without being licensed, certified, or listed. States have implemented requirements for mediators only for those who desire to receive court case referrals or work within a court-connected program; all other mediators are exempt from such requirements. Therefore, any person, with no training or experience, could simply hang out a shingle calling themselves a professional mediator; although, this is not advisable due to the unique set of skills required to become a professional, successful mediator.

Obviously, it is possible to start without any serious professional experience, but it is practically impossible to obtain and retain clients without completing an appropriate training course. This is why training and education are becoming the hallmarks of a mediator's professionalism. The training courses or special education a mediator receives from an educational establishment—including universities—is very important, primarily to maintain his good reputation and his customers' respect.

At the present time, educational establishments and companies operating in the field of education offer a variety of courses to provide necessary training for the professional mediator. In general, for one to become a proficient mediator, one should complete, as a minimum, both a basic mediation course and an advanced family/divorce mediation course with a reputable training organization.

It is also worthy to note that, in recent years, the offers of distance learning for, and training of, mediators via the Internet have progressed dramatically, and in all probability, their popularity soon will be extremely high. The American Center for Conflict Resolution Institute offers a distance education Professional Mediation Certification program, which can be completed online or through correspondence and can be found at http://www.accri.org/. Such distance learning alternatives to conventional "brick and mortar" education and training of mediators are very pervasive, since often mediators enter this profession on a part-time basis while keeping their current position while building a profitable practice.

The following pages list organizations that provide mediation training.

Program: Participated in several workshops on conflict resolution in Africa. Location: Nigeria and Ghana Description: I was chairman of a committee of the 7-day seminar on the Enhancement Of African Peace Keeping Capability held at the Koffi Anan Institute For Conflict Resolution in Ghana in 2005.	Contact: Dr. Ozichi Joel Alimole PhD Work Phone: 673-217-41 Home Phone: 673-291-45 Mobile Phone: 915-042-34 Fax: 673-217-42 Work: ozichialimole@msn.com 72 Anson Road #08-02 Anson House Singapore 079911 Singapore
Program: American Center for Conflict Resolution Institute Location: Cleveland, Ohio Description: Offer classroom attended basic, business, family, divorce trainings. Also, online and correspondence professional mediation certification training.	Contact: Tanya Dominick Work Phone: 800-517-0857 Work Phone: 216-255-6722 Fax: 216-373-6710 Work: suport@accri.org 5247 Wilson Mills Road, #442 Richmond Heights, OH 44143 United States

Program: Coast to Coast Mediation Center Location: Encintas CA	Contact: Elizabeth Allen Work Phone: 800-748-6462 Work Phone: 760-436-8414 Fax: 760-634-2628 Work: staff@ctcmediation.com PO Box 230637 Encinitas, CA 92023 United States
Program: Paralegal Certificate Location: Columbus State Community College	Contact: Thomas L. Bailey Jr. Work Phone: 614-890-7014 Fax: 614-890-1118 Work: thomasbailey@pobox.com 373 Scottsdale Court Westerville, OH 43082 United States
Program: Current Student - Mediation Certificate Program Location: Capital University Law School, Columbus OH	Contact: Thomas L. Bailey Jr. Work Phone: 614-890-7014 Fax: 614-890-1118 Work: thomasbailey@pobox.com 373 Scottsdale Court Westerville, OH 43082 United States

Program: Mediation and Conflict Management Services Location: Portland OR	Contact: Robert D. Benjamin MSW, JD Work Phone: 503-417-2655 Work: rbenjamin@mediate.com 3246 SW Cascade Ter Portland, OR 97205 United States Website: www.rbenjamin.com
Program: Decision Management Associates, Inc. Location: Macon GA	Contact: Robert A. Berlin Work Phone: 478-477-3317 Fax: 478-477-1115 Work: dma-adr@mindspring.com 1100 Hill Place Macon, GA 31210-3337 United States Website: www.dma-adr.com

Program: Law & Mediation Offices Location: Teaneck NJ; New York NY	Contact: Adam J. Berner JD, MA Work Phone: 201-836-0666 Work Phone: 212-721-7555 Fax: 201-336-9130 Work: Adam@MediationOffices.com 179 Cedar Lane Teanack, NJ 07666 United States 450 Seventh Avenue, Suite 1400 New York, NY 10123 United States Website: www.MediationOffices.com
Program: Mediation Consultants, Inc. Location: Pawtucket RI	Contact: Bryna B. Bettigole LICSW, BCD Work Phone: 401-723-0353 Fax: 401-722-1382 Work: bbbettigole@cox.net 29 Wilcox Ave Pawtucket, RI 02860 United States

Program: Key Bridge Therapy and Mediation Center Location: Arlington VA	Contact: Emily M. Brown LCSW Work Phone: 703-528-3900 Fax: 703-524-7525 Work: keybridgectr@aol.com 1600 Wilson Blvd Suite 702 Arlington, VA 22209 United States
Program: Worklife Institute Center for Mediation and Conflict Resolution Location: Houston, TX Description: Basic 4-Hour, Family and Divorce, Work- place Conflict Resolution, Transformative, Ad- vanced Transformative	Contact: Elizabeth F. Burleigh Work Phone: 713-334-0499 Fax: 713-266-0845 Home: EFBurleigh@aol.com 1900 St. James Place, Suite 880 Houston, TX 77056 United States Website: www.worklifeinstitute.com

Program / Location / Description	Contact
Program: Cramer & Associates Dispute Resolution Services Location: Gilbert, AZ Description: Basic 30 hour Family Mediation Training, specializing in child custody and parenting time mediation. Also specializing in establishing court mediation programs. Basic 40 hour mediation training focusing on the dynamics of family and divorce conflict resolution. Advanced mediation workshops.	Contact: Clarence Cramer MA, LPC Home Phone: 480-545-9048 Work Phone: 520-723-3077 Fax: 520-866-7354 Work: Clarence.Cramer@co.pinal.az.us 561 W. Spur Ave. Gilbert, AZ 85233 United States
Program: Foreign Exchanges Location: Los Angeles, CA Description: Foreign Exchanges, a consortium of artists, designers, mediators, and cultural workers directed by Aya Dorit Cypis, develops new tools of engagement exploring the social, physical and psychological aspects of identity, representation and social relations. Drawing on aesthetics, ethics, conflict studies, and body healing arts, Foreign Exchanges develops public programs and offers training and consultation to leaders in culture, education, business and philanthropy to expand understanding of who we are to ourselves and to each other, encouraging new paradigms of social activisms.	Contact: Ms. Dorit Aya Cypis Work Phone: 323-653-5988 Fax: 323-651-4590 Work: mediate@doritcypis.com 8417 Waring Avenue Los Angeles, CA 90069 United States Website: www.doritcypis.com

Program	Contact
Program: Conflict Management Skills Location: St. Louis, MO Description: 40-hour Mediation workshop	Contact: Suzanna G. Davis Work Phone: 770-200-8775 Fax: 770-989-3619 Work: suzdavis@na.cokecce.com 2500 Windy Ridge Parkway Atlanta, GA 30339 United States
Program: Dorothy J. Della Noce Mediation Location: Penn Land VA	Contact: Dorothy J. Della Noce JD, PhD Work Phone: 540-421-9226 Work: deallndj@jmu.edu 3910 Dixie Ridge Run Rd Penn Laird, VA 22846 United States
Program: Basic Mediation Training Location: North Shore Community College Danvers, MA 01923 Description: 40 hour - 13 week, three credit full semester course in the skills and techniques of mediation. Complies with the Massachusetts Trial Courts standards of mediation training with opportunities for practice and apprenticeship with a court approved community mediation program.	Contact: Ms. Jean M. Deschene Work Phone: 978-744-3420 School/University Phone: 978-762-4084 Fax: 978-744-3420 Home: myfelina@msn.com School: JDESCHEN01@nscc.mass.edu Work: JeanDeschene@msn.com 10 Greenway Rd Salem, MA 01970 United States

Program: Erickson Mediation Institute Location: 3800 W 80th St Suite 530, Minneapolis, MN 55431	Contact: Stephen K. Erickson JD Work Phone: 952-835-3688 Fax: 952-835-3689 Work: steve@ericksonmediation.com 3600 American Blvd. W Ste 530 Minneapolis, MN 55431 United States Website: www.ericksonmediation.com
Program: Gregory Firestone Location: Tampa FL	Contact: Gregory Firestone PhD Work Phone: 813-494-7655 Fax: 813-974-7655 Work: firestoneg@aol.com 12901 Bruce B Downs Blvd, MDC46 Tampa, FL 33612 United States
Program: Divorce Mediation Training Associates Location: Cambridge, MA	Contact: John Fiske Work Phone: 617-354-7133 Fax: 617-354-5830 Work: info@dmtatraining.com 189 Cambridge St Cambridge, MA 02141 United States Website: http://www.dmtatraining.com

Program: Dr. Larry S. Fong & Associates Ltd. Location: 115-1st St. SW; Calgary, AB; CAN T2P0B3 Description: One of Canada's longest running inter-est based training programs, the techniques of the program has been used in training mediators worldwide in at least 25 different countries.	Contact: Dr. Larry Sun Fong Work Phone: 403-233-7533 Fax: 403-266-4998 Work: lsfong@web.net 115 - 1st Street SW Calgary, AB T2P 0B3 Canada Website: www.fongmediate.com
Program: Northern California Mediation Center Location: Greenbrae CA	Contact: Ms. Nancy J. Foster JD Work Phone: 415-461-6392 Fax: 415-461-7492 Work: njfoster@ncmc-mediate.org 175 North Redwood Drive Suite 295 San Rafael, CA 94903 United States

Program: DePaul University - Center for Dispute Resolution Location: Chicago, Illinois IL Description: 1 East Jackson Blvd. Chicago, IL 60604 312-362-6300 dcolliso@depaul.edu	Contact: Lynn A. Gaffigan J.D. Work Phone: 847-615-7220 Fax: 847-615-7279 Work: gaffigan@msn.com 736 N Western Ave, #122 Lake Forest, IL 60045 United States Website: https://learning.depaul.edu/about/bios/lynn_gaffigan.asp

Program: Mediation through Education
Location: Miami Florida
Description: American Academy of Family Mediators,
  orginal member.
Association of Family and Conciliation Courts training
  1990
	Contact: Carla A. Goodwin PhD
	Work Phone: 508-238-3722
	Fax: 508-238-5964
	Work: ForumForNewDirections@comcast.net
	855 Washington St
	South Easton, MA 02375
	United States

Program: Northwestern University School of Continu- ing Studies Location: Chicago, Illinois IL Description: Northwestern University School of Continuing Studies 339 E. Chicago Ave 6th Floor Chicago, IL 60611 (312) 503-3917 (312) 503-4942 (fax) jclegg@northwestern.edu	Contact: Ms. Ericka B. Gray Work Phone: 781-643-3577 Fax: 781-648-1234 Work: ebgray@disputed.com 26 Berkeley St Arlington, MA 02474 United States Website: www.disputed.com
Program: Penninsula Mediation Center Location: Hampton VA	Contact: Merri L. Hanson Work Phone: 757-722-1228 Fax: 757-728-1312 Work: merrihe@aol.com 1 W Queens Way Hampton, VA 23669 United States

Program: Family & Divorce Mediation Location: Tulsa, Oklahoma Description: The Mediation Institute- 40 hr. Comprehensive Mediation Program focusing on the dynamics of family and divorce conflict resolution. Approved couse by the Oklahoma Bar Association	Contact: Mrs. Shelly D Harvill-Kamm Work Phone: 918-877-1447 Fax: 918-376-2266 Work: shkamm@tulsamediation.com 1408 S. Denver Avenue Tulsa, OK 74119 United States Website: www.TulsaMediation.com
Program: Civil, Commercial, Employment Mediaiton Program Location: Tulsa, Oklahoma Description: The Mediation Institute- 24 hr. Comprehensive Mediation Program focusing on the dynamics of civil and commercial and employment conflict resolution. Approved couse by the Oklahoma Bar Association	Contact: Mrs. Shelly D Harvill-Kamm Work Phone: 918-877-1447 Fax: 918-376-2266 Work: shkamm@tulsamediation.com 1408 S. Denver Avenue Tulsa, OK 74119 United States Website: www.TulsaMediation.com
Program: Mediation Center of Rochester Location: Rochester NY	Contact: John W. Heister PhD Work Phone: 716-272-1990 Fax: 716-272-1978 Work: heister@mediationctr.com 2024 W Henrietta Rd Ste 5g Rochester, NY 14623 United States

Program: Syracuse University College of Law Location: Syracuse NY	Contact: Christine Hickey Esq. Work Phone: 315-422-9756 Fax: 315-479-5651 Work: mchickey@a-znet.com 120 E Washington St Ste 711 Syracuse, NY 13202 United States Website: www.christine-hickey.com
Program: Beech Acres Mediation Center Location: Cincinnati OH	Contact: Marie Hill LPCC Work Phone: 513-351-2231 Mobile Phone: 513-378-8548 Home: mmhill@fuse.net 3726 Isabella Avenue Cincinnati, OH 45209 United States
Program: ACR Staff Location: Washington Description: Staff	Contact: Emma Johnson Work Phone: 202-464-9700 Fax: 202-464-9720 Work: emma@ACRnet.org 1015 18th Street NW Suite 1150 Washington, DC 20036 United States

Program: S.A.F.E. Crisis Intervention Model Location: Fairfax County Criminal Justice Academy Description: Advanced course in crisis intervention and hostage negotiation techniques using actual equipment and HRT scenarios. Certifies participants to work with law enforcment.	Contact: Lynne Kinnucan Home Phone: 631-424-1889 HomeFax Phone: 631-549-7241 Home: kinnucan@patriot.net 10 Ardsley Place Huntington Station, NY 11746 United States
Program: Mediation Services of Annapolis Location: Annapolis MD	Contact: Martin Alan Kranitz MA Work Phone: 410-974-8888 Fax: 410-295-9190 Work: makranitz@aol.com 1160 Spa Rd, 1B Annapolis, MD 21403 United States
Program: Cooperative Solutions Location: Toronto ON, Canada	Contact: Barbara Landau Ph.D., LL.B., LL.M. Work Phone: 416-391-3110 Fax: 416-391-2347 Work: barb@coop-solutions.ca 76 Truman Road Toronto, ON M2L 2L6 Canada Website: www.coop-solutions.com.ca

Program	Contact
Program: The Art and Soul of Peacemaking Location: Tucson, AZ Description: One-day workshop with John Paul Lederach focusing on the role of storytelling in peacemaking	Contact: Ms. Christie Lapitan Home Phone: 520-296-6629 Work: clapitan@yahoo.com Tucson, AZ 85748 United States
Program: Mediation Skills for Resolving Conflicts Location: Tucson, AZ Description: 40-hour mediation training course conducted by ACCORD Mediation Services and Ann Yellott	Contact: Ms. Christie Lapitan Home Phone: 520-296-6629 Work: clapitan@yahoo.com Tucson, AZ 85748 United States
Program: Community Mediation Training Program Location: Tucson, AZ Description: 40-hour mediation training conducted by Our Family (service agency)	Contact: Ms. Christie Lapitan Home Phone: 520-296-6629 Work: clapitan@yahoo.com Tucson, AZ 85748 United States
Program: ADR, Inc. Location: Metairie LA	Contact: Ms. Nell I. Lipscomb Work Phone: 504-733-1360 Fax: 504-838-9555 Work: Helenell@cox.net 317 Jefferson Heights Ave Jefferson, LA 70121 United States

Program: Montana Mediators Location: Missoula MT	Contact: Arthur W. Lusse Work Phone: 406-543-1113 Work: artlusse@montana.com 300 Brooks St. Missoula, MT 59801 United States	
Program: Lynn E. MacBeth Location: Pittsburgh PA	Contact: Lynn E. MacBeth JD Work Phone: 412-391-7659 Fax: 412-391-7606 Work: macbethlynn@aol.com 1301 Grant Building, #310 Pittsburgh, PA 15219 United States	
Program: Atlanta Divorce Mediators Location: Atlanta GA	Contact: E. Elizabeth Manley M.Ed., J.D., LMFT Work Phone: 404-378-3238, Fax: 404-577-6505 Work: EManley532@aol.com 1149 Austin Ave NE Atlanta, GA 30307 United States Website: www.mediationtraining.net	

Program: Multnomah County Small Claims Court Mediation Program Location: Portland, OR Description: Small Claims Court mediation program, volunteer-based. Includes all civil cases, with an amount in dispute less than $5000.	Contact: Dena Marshall Work Phone: 503-234-1191 Work: dena@marshallmediation.net Work: dmarshall29@yahoo.com 3587 SE Sherman St. Portland, OR 97214 United States Website: www.marshallmediation.net
Program: Resolutions Northwest Basic Mediation Training Location: Portland, OR Description: Basic 40-hour mediation training, taught by Chris Sheesley, In-Accord, Inc.	Contact: Dena Marshall Work Phone: 503-234-1191 Work: dena@marshallmediation.net Work: dmarshall29@yahoo.com 3587 SE Sherman St. Portland, OR 97214 United States Website: www.marshallmediation.net
Program: Virginia Commonwealth Mediation Group Location: Sandston VA	Contact: Ervin J. Mast LCSW Work Phone: 804-737-3747 Work: emmast@earthlink.net 5448 White Oak Cir. Sandston, VA 23150 United States Website: www.cmgmediates.com

Program: Mediating the Litigated	Contact: Mr. Thomas Matychowiak Work Phone: 559-347-7807 Work: tom@reasonablelaw.com 2067 W. Barstow Avenue Fresno, CA 93711 United States Website: http://www.reasonablelaw.com
Program: Mediating the Litigated Case Location: Pepperdine University Description: 42-hour course at Straus Institute, Pepperdine Unviersity, Malibu, California	Contact: Mr. Thomas Matychowiak Work Phone: 559-347-7807 Work: tom@reasonablelaw.com 2067 W. Barstow Avenue Fresno, CA 93711 United States Website: http://www.reasonablelaw.com
Program: CDR Associates Location: Boulder CO	Contact: Bernie Mayer Work Phone: 303-442-7367 Work Phone: 519-733-4849 Fax: 303-442-7442 Work: bmayer@mediate.org 100 Arapahoe Ave Ste 12 Boulder, CO 80302 United States

Program: Danuta McDaniel Location: Wheaton, Illinois IL Description: 40-hour Divorce and Family Mediation trainings, led by Danuta McDaniel, in College of Dupage, Illinois (IL). For more information, contact danutamcd@aol.com, or 630-668-4184.	Contact: Ms. Danuta Maria McDaniel MA, LCPC, CADC, MISAII Work Phone: 630-668-4184 Fax: 630-668-4192 Work: danutamcd@aol.com 1039 College Ave. Suite F Wheaton, IL 60187 United States Website: http://www.mediate.com/Danuta
Program: Divorce Mediation Training Location: Minneapolis, MN Description: Forty hour divorce mediation training for beginners. 100 hour internship in divorce mediation training. One day advanced mediation training.	Contact: Marilyn McKnight MA Work Phone: 952-835-3688 Fax: 952-835-3689 Work: marilyn@ericksonmediation.com 3600 American Blvd W Suite 530 Minneapolis, MN 55431 United States Website: www.ericksonmediation.com

Program: Forty-four hour Family Law Mediation Course Location: William Mitchell College of Law Description: Adjunct Professor co-teaching with Stephen K. Erickson Beginning course in divorce mediation for law students including training in mediating divorces in which there is domestic violence.	Contact: Marilyn McKnight MA Work Phone: 952-835-3688 Fax: 952-835-3689 Work: marilyn@ericksonmediation.com 3600 American Blvd W Suite 530 Minneapolis, MN 55431 United States Website: www.ericksonmediation.com
Program: Mediation Center for Family Law Location: Ventura CA	Contact: Nina R. Meierding MS, JD Work Phone: 805-643-3543 Fax: 805-653-6107 Work: Meierding@sbcglobal.net 857 E Main St Ventura, CA 93001 United States Website: www.mediate.com/ninameierding

Program	Contact
Program: The Mediation Center Location: Eugene OR	Contact: Mr. James C. Melamed Work Phone: 541-345-1456 Fax: 801-382-3031 Work: jmelamed@mediate.com PO Box 51119 Eugene, OR 97405 United States Website: www.smartmediator.com
Program: Supervisory Training 1 and 2 Location: Brookings, SD Description: Intense management training concentrating on interpersonal relationships and how to encourage cooperation and goal accomplishment. Also focused on the importance of diversity and communication.	Contact: Pamela Mertens-Dronski Work Phone: 386-447-8488 Work: p.dronski@counterpointmediations.com 10 Florida Park Drive Suite D-2 Palm Coast, FL 32137 United States Website: www.counterpointmediations.com
Program: Videoteleconferencing Location: USMC Quantico, VA Description: AT&T Operation and troubleshooting techniques and skills required to operate and maintain reliable VTC eqipment for USMC official use.	Contact: Pamela Mertens-Dronski Work Phone: 386-447-8488 Work: p.dronski@counterpointmediations.com 10 Florida Park Drive Suite D-2 Palm Coast, FL 32137 United States Website: www.counterpointmediations.com

Program: George Mason University Location: Faifax, Virginia Description: Various mediation courses	Contact: Frederick Michaud Work Phone: 202-251-2975 Fax: 202-585-1039 Work: fred.michaud@bakerbotts.com 1299 Pennsylvania Ave NW Washington, DC 20004 United States Website: www.bakerbotts.com
Program: Multi-Door Family Mediation Program Location: Washington, DC Description: Family mediation training program leading to mediation of custody and support disputes for the Superior Court of the District of Columbia	Contact: Frederick Michaud Work Phone: 202-251-2975 Fax: 202-585-1039 Work: fred.michaud@bakerbotts.com 1299 Pennsylvania Ave NW Washington, DC 20004 United States Website: www.bakerbotts.com
Program: Mosten Mediation Training Location: Los Angeles CA	Contact: Forrest S. Mosten Work Phone: 310-473-7611 Fax: 310-473-7422 Work: mosten@mediate.com 11661 San Vicente Blvd Ste 414 Los Angeles, CA 90049 United States Website: www.MostenMediation.com

Program: Center for Family & Divorce Mediation Location: New York NY	Contact: Kenneth Neumann Work Phone: 212-799-4302 Fax: 212-721-1012 Work: kenneumann@juno.com 111 W 90th St., Townhouse B New York, NY 10024 United States Website: www.divorcemediation.com
Program: Mediation Center for Dispute Resolution Location: Saint Paul MN	Contact: Dr. Katherine J. Nevins Work Phone: 651-638-6292 Fax: 651-638-6001 Work: k-nevins@bethel.edu 3900 Bethel Dr. Saint Paul, MN 55112 United States
Program: Eagles Mediation and Counseling Centre Location: Eagles Center Singapore Singapore	Contact: Dr. John Sk Ng Work Phone: 67888220 Fax: 67888218 Work: emcc@eagles.org.sg 31 Boon Tat Street #02-01, Eagles Center Singapore, 69625 Singapore

Program Information	Contact
Program: Mediation Inc. Location: Brevard NC	Contact: Celia O'Briant MEd, NCC Work Phone: 828-674-3010 Fax: 828-877-5001 Work: celia@celiaobriant.com PO Box 2256 Brevard, NC 28712 United States
Program: Certified Knowledge Manager Location: Washington, DC Description: International Knowledge Management Institute Certified Knowledge Manager	Contact: Manny Ovalle Home Phone: 703-550-0322 Work: movalle@usa.com 6538 Old Carriage Drive Alexandria, VA 22315 United States
Program: Organizational Mediation Location: Front Royal, VA Description: Conflict Management Consortium	Contact: Manny Ovalle Home Phone: 703-550-0322 Work: movalle@usa.com 6538 Old Carriage Drive Alexandria, VA 22315 United States

Program: Private Investigator Location: Falls Church, VA Description: American Security Programs	Contact: Manny Ovalle Home Phone: 703-550-0322 Work: movalle@usa.com 6538 Old Carriage Drive Alexandria, VA 22315 United States	
Program: Ombudsman Location: Boston, MA Description: The Ombudsman Association	Contact: Manny Ovalle Home Phone: 703-550-0322 Work: movalle@usa.com 6538 Old Carriage Drive Alexandria, VA 22315 United States	
Program: School for Dispute Resolution Location: Decatur GA	Contact: Lemoine D. Pierce MEd, JD Work Phone: 404-373-4457 Fax: 404-377-4244 Work: LEMOINEPIERCE@aol.com PO Box 2372 Decatur, GA 30031 United States	

Program: Institute for the Study of Conflict Transformation, Hofstra University Location: Hempstead NY	Contact: Ms. Sally Ganong Pope Work Phone: 212-721-0770 Fax: 212-721-0773 Work: spnyc@earthlink.net PO Box 225 Remsenburg, NY 11960 United States
Program: Northwestern University School of Continuing Studies Location: Chicago, Illinois Description: Northwestern University School of Continuing Studies 339 E. Chicago Ave 6th Floor Chicago, Illinois 60611 (312) 503-3917 (312) 503-4942 jclegg@northwestern.edu	Contact: Margaret S. Powers Work Phone: 847-398-1969 Fax: 847-670-0036 Work: mspowers09@aol.com 120 W Eastman St Ste 106 Arlington Heights, IL 60004 United States Website: www.margaretspowers.com

Program: M. S. Powers and Associates Location: Arlington Heights, Illinois Description: M.S. Powers and Associates, Inc. 120 W Eastman St Ste 106 Arlington Heights, IL 60004 847-398-1969 847-670-0036 (fax) mspowers09@aol.com	Contact: Margaret S. Powers Work Phone: 847-398-1969 Fax: 847-670-0036 Work: mspowers09@aol.com 120 W Eastman St Ste 106 Arlington Heights, IL 60004 United States Website: www.margaretspowers.com
Program: ACRI 40 Hour Basic Mediation Location: Decatur, GA Description: This 40 hour Basic Mediation class meets the requirements of the Georgia Office of Dispute Resolution for registration as a neutral. The class agenda includes the 28 hour General/Civil mediation training and the 12 hour Mediation Practicum.	Contact: Thomas G. Prince Th.D. Home Phone: 404-431-4514 Fax: 770-498-8280 Work: thomas.prince@atlantacenter4reconciliation.com 5295 Stone Mountain Highway Suite D-300 Stone Mountain, GA 30087 United States Website: www.atlantacenter4reconciliation.com

Program: 40-Hour Domestic Relations Mediation Training Location: 3778 Hardee Drive NW, Kennesaw GA 30152 Description: This training meets the requirements for registration as a domestic relations mediator in the State of Georgia. Taught by Professor and mediator, Susan Raines, this course pays particular attention to the types of divorce, custody, and property issues commonly encountered in the court-connected setting, including issues of domestic violence and recent changes to the child support guidelines. For more information call:1-770-423-6081	Contact: Susan Summers Raines Work Phone: 770-423-6081 Fax: 770-423-6312 Work: sraines@kennesaw.edu 1000 Chastain Road, Mb #2302 Kennesaw, GA 30152 United States
Program: Resolution Resources Corporation Location: Fayetteville, Georgia Description: Georgia, GA	Contact: Raytheon M. Rawls Work Phone: 706-542-1108 Fax: 706-542-7007 Work: rrawls@fanning.uga.edu 1240 S Lumpkin St Athens, GA 30602 United States

Program: North Carolina Central University School of Law Dispute Resolution Institute Location: North Carolina Central University Description: This was a 40 hour training course in Superior Court Mediation conducted by the Carolina Dispute Settlement Service and the Dispute Resolution Institute at the School of Law North Carolina Central University.	Contact: Dr. Isaac A. Robinson Home Phone: 919-530-6287 Fax: 919-530-6287 Home: irobinson2@verizon.net Home: irobinson@nccu.edu 4013 Trotter Ridge Road Durham, NC 27707 United States
Program: Divorce Mediation Location: Kennesaw State University, Kennesaw, GA Description: 40 Hour Divorce Mediation Training provided by Atlanta Divorce Mediators, Inc.	Contact: Alys Anne Roux Home Phone: 239-263-7722 Work: vgirlalys@aol.com 499 Forest Lakes Blvd, Apt #205 Naples, FL 34105 United States

Program: Mediation Skills Training Institute
Location: Lombard Mennonite Peace Center
Description: Basic mediation training (28 hours). Richard Blackburn, primary instructor.

Contact: Mr. Mark A. Roy
Work Phone: 559-256-6325
Work Phone: 800-675-8118
Mobile Phone: 559-708-8799
Fax: 559-228-6518
Work: mark@valleymediation.net
Home: medi8r@comcast.net
BBB Mediation Center of Fresno County
4201 W. Shaw Ave., Ste. 107
Fresno, CA 93722
United States

BBB Mediation Center of Kern County
1601 H St., Ste. 101
Bakersfield, CA 93301
United States

1919 W. Dakota Ave., Apt. 133-J
Fresno, CA 93705
United States
Website: www.valleymediation.net

Program: VORP Mediator Training
Location: Mediation Services of Tippecanoe County
Description: Victim-offender mediation training (15
    hours). Paul Landskroener, primary trainer.

Contact: Mr. Mark A. Roy
Work Phone: 559-256-6325
Work Phone: 800-675-8118
Mobile Phone: 559-708-8799
Fax: 559-228-6518
Work: mark@valleymediation.net
Home: medi8r@comcast.net
BBB Mediation Center of Fresno County
4201 W. Shaw Ave., Ste. 107
Fresno, CA 93722
United States

BBB Mediation Center of Kern County
1601 H St., Ste. 101
Bakersfield, CA 93301
United States

1919 W. Dakota Ave., Apt. 133-J
Fresno, CA 93705
United States
Website: www.valleymediation.net

Program: Basic Institute in Conflict Management and Mediation
Location: Center for Peacemaking and Conflict Studies, Fresno Pacific University
Description: Mediation and conflict management training (30 hours). Dalton Reimer and Ron Claassen, primary trainers.

Contact: Mr. Mark A. Roy
Work Phone: 559-256-6325
Work Phone: 800-675-8118
Mobile Phone: 559-708-8799
Fax: 559-228-6518
Work: mark@valleymediation.net
Home: medi8r@comcast.net

BBB Mediation Center of Fresno County
4201 W. Shaw Ave., Ste. 107
Fresno, CA 93722
United States

BBB Mediation Center of Kern County
1601 H St., Ste. 101
Bakersfield, CA 93301
United States

1919 W. Dakota Ave., Apt. 133-J
Fresno, CA 93705
United States
Website: www.valleymediation.net

Program: How to Start a Church-Based VORP
Location: Fresno Pacific University
Description: Organizing and operating a church-based victim-offender reconciliation program. Ron Claassen and Elaine Enns, primary trainers.

Contact: Mr. Mark A. Roy
Work Phone: 559-256-6325
Work Phone: 800-675-8118
Mobile Phone: 559-708-8799
Fax: 559-228-6518
Work: mark@valleymediation.net
Home: medi8r@comcast.net

BBB Mediation Center of Fresno County
4201 W. Shaw Ave., Ste. 107
Fresno, CA 93722
United States

BBB Mediation Center of Kern County
1601 H St., Ste. 101
Bakersfield, CA 93301
United States

1919 W. Dakota Ave., Apt. 133-J
Fresno, CA 93705
United States
Website: www.valleymediation.net

Program: Divorce Mediation Institute
Location: Lancaster Mediation Center
Description: Divorce mediation training (40 hours).
Zena Zumeta and Carl Schneider, primary trainers.

Contact: Mr. Mark A. Roy
Work Phone: 559-256-6325
Work Phone: 800-675-8118
Mobile Phone: 559-708-8799
Fax: 559-228-6518
Work: mark@valleymediation.net
Home: medi8r@comcast.net

BBB Mediation Center of Fresno County
4201 W. Shaw Ave., Ste. 107
Fresno, CA 93722
United States

BBB Mediation Center of Kern County
1601 H St., Ste. 101
Bakersfield, CA 93301
United States

1919 W. Dakota Ave., Apt. 133-J
Fresno, CA 93705
United States
Website: www.valleymediation.net

Program: Family Mediation
Location: San Joaquin College of Law
Description: Family law and divorce mediation training (16 hours). Richard Cartier, primary trainer.

Contact: Mr. Mark A. Roy
Work Phone: 559-256-6325
Work Phone: 800-675-8118
Mobile Phone: 559-708-8799
Fax: 559-228-6518
Work: mark@valleymediation.net
Home: medi8r@comcast.net

BBB Mediation Center of Fresno County
4201 W. Shaw Ave., Ste. 107
Fresno, CA 93722
United States

BBB Mediation Center of Kern County
1601 H St., Ste. 101
Bakersfield, CA 93301
United States

1919 W. Dakota Ave., Apt. 133-J
Fresno, CA 93705
United States
Website: www.valleymediation.net

Program: Mediation Skills Training for Professionals
Location: BBB Mediation Center of Fresno County
Description: Basic mediation training (25 hours).
Doug Noll, Richard Cartier, Daniel DeSantis, Mari
Henson, primary trainers.

Contact: Mr. Mark A. Roy
Work Phone: 559-256-6325
Work Phone: 800-675-8118
Mobile Phone: 559-708-8799
Fax: 559-228-6518
Work: mark@valleymediation.net
Home: medi8r@comcast.net

BBB Mediation Center of Fresno County
4201 W. Shaw Ave., Ste. 107
Fresno, CA 93722
United States

BBB Mediation Center of Kern County
1601 H St., Ste. 101
Bakersfield, CA 93301
United States

1919 W. Dakota Ave., Apt. 133-J
Fresno, CA 93705
United States
Website: www.valleymediation.net

Program: Alternative: A Center for Mediation & Training in New England Location: Keene NH	Contact: Olivia A. Ruel PhD Work Phone: 603-355-8066 Work: mediation@ne.rr.com 4 Felt Rd PO Box 1085 Keene, NH 03431 United States
Program: Credentialed Mediator Location: National Conflict Resolution Center (NCRC), San Diego CA Description: Completed full training plus specialized program for credential, appointed to Superior Court Mediation Panel, volunteer mediator court-referred disputes	Contact: Anita Rufus J.D. Work Phone: 619-523-0971 Work: AnitaRufus@TheLivingEndBook.com 3098 Rue D'Orleans #324 San Diego, CA 92110 United States Website: www.TheLivingEndBook.com
Program: Advanced Mediation Training Location: Straus Institute, Pepperdine (CA) Description: Completed intensive Advanced Mediation Training	Contact: Anita Rufus J.D. Work Phone: 619-523-0971 Work: AnitaRufus@TheLivingEndBook.com 3098 Rue D'Orleans #324 San Diego, CA 92110 United States Website: www.TheLivingEndBook.com

Program: JAMS Location: San Diego CA Description: Internship, Mediation and Arbitration	Contact: Anita Rufus J.D. Work Phone: 619-523-0971 Work: AnitaRufus@TheLivingEndBook.com 3098 Rue D'Orleans #324 San Diego, CA 92110 United States Website: www.TheLivingEndBook.com
Program: ADR - Mediation Location: Cal Western School of Law Description: Seminar courses, law school, received Academic Achievement Awards (highest class grade) for scholarly writing	Contact: Anita Rufus J.D. Work Phone: 619-523-0971 Work: AnitaRufusf@TheLivingEndBook.com 3098 Rue D'Orleans #324 San Diego, CA 92110 United States Website: www.TheLivingEndBook.com
Program: Association of Family and Conciliation Courts Location: Madison WI	Contact: Peter Salem Work Phone: 608-664-3750 Fax: 608-664-3751 Work: psalem@afccnet.org 6525 Grand Teton Plaza Madison, WI 53719 United States Website: www.afccnet.org

Program	Contact Info
Program: Clackamas County Family Court Services Location: Oregon City, Oregon Description: One-year internship as a family court service mediator. Included reading and classwork as well as casework. 1989-90	Contact: Linda R. Scher Work Phone: 503-232-8550 Fax: 503-232-8494 Work: linda@schermediate.com 3282 SE Hawthorne Blvd Portland, OR 97214 United States Website: www.schermediate.com
Program: Pacific Family Mediation Institute Location: Bellevue, Washington Description: Basic Family Mediation Training, 1987	Contact: Linda R. Scher Work Phone: 503-232-8550 Fax: 503-232-8494 Work: linda@schermediate.com 3282 SE Hawthorne Blvd Portland, OR 97214 United States Website: www.schermediate.com
Program: Mulntomah County Court Location: Portland, Oregon Description: Training to be a mediation trainer.	Contact: Linda R. Scher Work Phone: 503-232-8550 Fax: 503-232-8494 Work: linda@schermediate.com 3282 SE Hawthorne Blvd Portland, OR 97214 United States Website: www.schermediate.com

Program: Mediation Matters Location: Bethesda MD	Contact: Carl D. Schneider PhD Work Phone: 301-581-0330 Fax: 301-581-0346 Work: cdschneider@igc.org 9816 Parkwood Drive Bethesda, MD 20814 United States Website: www.mediationmatters.com
Program: Mediation Skills Training Location: Northwestern School of Continuing Studies-Chicago, IL Description: 40 Hour skills course	Contact: Mr. Scott P. Seagren Work Phone: 847-382-4167 Work: scott.seagren@sbcglobal.net 711 Prairie Avenue Barrington, IL 60010 United States
Program: Mediation Skills Training Location: Center for Conflict Resolution-Chicago, IL Description: Performance based skills training. Includes certification as CCR volunteer August 30,2006	Contact: Mr. Scott P. Seagren Work Phone: 847-382-4167 Work: scott.seagren@sbcglobal.net 711 Prairie Avenue Barrington, IL 60010 United States

Program: Sovern Mediation Training Location: Cedar Rapids, IA; MN; WI, IL; MO; NE; SD Description: Basic 40 Hour Divorce and Custody Mediation Training	Contact: Steve Sovern JD Work Phone: 319-841-5151 Fax: 319-841-5152 Work: sovern@mediate.com Resolution Center 8710 Earhart Lane S.W. Cedar Rapids, IA 52404 United States Website: www.mediate.com/stevesovern
Program: Mediation Institute Location: Nashville, TN Description: Certificate of Completion in Alternative Dispute Resolution (40 units) by the Mediation Institute in Nashville, TN, Approved by the Tennessee Supreme Court	Contact: Mr. Raymond L. Stevenson Work Phone: 731-571-4408 Home Phone: 731-587-9819 Fax: 731-587-9796 Work: ray_stevenson@charter.net 159 Strawberry Lane Martin, TN 38237-1633 United States Website: tennmediators.org/raymondstevenson

Program: Littler Mendelson and Epstein Becker & Green, P.C Location: Nashville, TN Description: Certificate of Completion by Littler Mendelson and Epstein Becker & Green, P.C., Advanced Topics In The Family And Medical Leave Act, 6.0 recertification credit hours toward PHR and SPHR recertification through the Human Resource Certification Institute (HRCI).	Contact: Mr. Raymond L. Stevenson Work Phone: 731-571-4408 Home Phone: 731-587-9819 Fax: 731-587-9796 Work: ray_stevenson@charter.net 159 Strawberry Lane Martin, TN 38237-1633 United States Website: tennmediators.org/raymondstevenson
Program: Leadership Location: Memphis, TN Description: Leadership: A Modern Guide To Communication with employees. Human resource professionals; Courtney Elizabeth Anderson, J.D., M.B.A., Courtney Anderson and Associates, LLC	Contact: Mr. Raymond L. Stevenson Work Phone: 731-571-4408 Home Phone: 731-587-9819 Fax: 731-587-9796 Work: ray_stevenson@charter.net 159 Strawberry Lane Martin, TN 38237-1633 United States Website: tennmediators.org/raymondstevenson

| Program: Human Resource Professional Development
Location: Washington, DC
Description: Human Resource Professional Development; HRPD Certification, George Washington University School of Business, Washington DC | Contact: Mr. Raymond L. Stevenson
Work Phone: 731-571-4408
Home Phone: 731-587-9819
Fax: 731-587-9796
Work: ray_stevenson@charter.net
159 Strawberry Lane
Martin, TN 38237-1633
United States
Website: tennmediators.org/raymondstevenson |
| Program: Employee Relations L
Location: Newport Beach, CA
Description: Certification in Employee Relations Law - Institute for Applied Management & Law, Newport Beach, CA | Contact: Mr. Raymond L. Stevenson
Work Phone: 731-571-4408
Home Phone: 731-587-9819
Fax: 731-587-9796
Work: ray_stevenson@charter.net
159 Strawberry Lane
Martin, TN 38237-1633
United States
Website: tennmediators.org/raymondstevenson |

Program: Alternative Dispute Resolution Location: Nashville, TN Description: Approved by the Tennessee Supreme Court Approved by the Kentucky Supreme Court Approved by the George Supreme Court	Contact: Mr. Raymond L. Stevenson Work Phone: 731-571-4408 Home Phone: 731-587-9819 Fax: 731-587-9796 Work: ray_stevenson@charter.net 159 Strawberry Lane Martin, TN 38237-1633 United States Website: tennmediators.org/raymondstevenson
Program: Academy of Family Mediators Location: Seattle Description: 40 hour training program in mediating family disputes	Contact: Darcia C. Tudor JD, MA Work Phone: 206-547-3166 Fax: 425-883-4751 Work: darciatudor@aol.com 2018 156 Avenue NE #100 Bellevue, WA 98007 United States Website: www.darciatudor.com

Program: Advanced Training For Family Mediators Location: University of Washington	Contact: Darcia C. Tudor JD, MA Work Phone: 206-547-3166 Fax: 425-883-4751 Work: darciatudor@aol.com 2018 156 Avenue NE #100 Bellevue, WA 98007 United States Website: www.darciatudor.com
Program: Dispute Resolution Location: Seattle, Washington Description: 40 hour training program in community dispute mediation	Contact: Darcia C. Tudor JD, MA Work Phone: 206-547-3166 Fax: 425-883-4751 Work: darciatudor@aol.com 2018 156 Avenue NE #100 Bellevue, WA 98007 United States Website: www.darciatudor.com

Program: Parenting Evaluation Training Program Location: University of Washington Description: Training for Graduate Level Therapists in court ordered evaluation of parenting capacity in custody disputes.	Contact: Darcia C. Tudor JD, MA Work Phone: 206-547-3166 Fax: 425-883-4751 Work: darciatudor@aol.com 2018 156 Avenue NE #100 Bellevue, WA 98007 United States Website: www.darciatudor.com
Program: Center for Alternative Dispute Resolution Location: Prince Georges County Maryland Description: 40 hour Skill Based Mediation	Contact: Mrs. Mae R. Whitehead Work Phone: 301-572-7464 Fax: 301-937-6933 Work: maewhitehead@adrready.com 11421 Cedar Ln Beltsville, MD 20705 United States Website: www.adrready.com
Program: Michael Williams Location: Dublin Ireland	Contact: Michael Williams Work Phone: 01135314978402 Fax: 01135314978402 Work: miwil@indigo.ie 65 Grosvenor Square Rathmines Dublin, 6 Ireland

Program: Mediation Training & Consultation Institute
Location: Ann Arbor MI and National
Description: Trainings held in Michigan, Illinois, Pennsylvania, Arkansas, Ohio, Minnesota. See schedule http://learn2mediate.com/calendar.php

Contact: Zena D. Zumeta JD
Work Phone: 734-663-1155
School/University Phone: 800-535-1155
Fax: 734-663-0524
Work: zzumeta@igc.org
330 E Liberty St Suite 3A
Ann Arbor, MI 48104
United States
Website: http://www.learn2mediate.com

It is also possible to receive a certificate through training in a University, for instance, it is possible to get a certain degree. However obtaining a certificate by a reputable training organization, as mentioned above, is the most sought method of obtaining entrance into the mediation profession. In fact, such a certificate should be considered an essential condition for an individual to work successfully as a professional mediator. Although it is possible to remain uncertified and attempt to work in the field of mediation, most respectable companies, organizations, or disputing parties would not appeal to such a mediator for assistance. It is also necessary to pay attention to the fact that the receipt of a certificate contributes to the professional growth of a mediator because he has to pass through a course of training and, consequently, is educated and in such a situation which provides a reward for his efforts to gain more success and improve his professionalism.

Success in any field comes after instruction. You may hear many people say that someone has achieved success as a result of good luck. I agree with Oprah Winfrey's statement that there is only one kind of LUCK—an acronym for Learning Under Correct Knowledge. Successful mediators constantly participate in ongoing training to develop their knowledge, since the field is ever developing and changing. In light of this, included below are some of the most respected mediation training degree programs in the country.

Academic Training Programs

Dispute Resolution Institute
Hamline University School of Law
1536 Hewitt Avenue
St. Paul, MN 55104
Contact: Kitty Atkins, Associate Director
Phone: 651-523-2897
Fax: 651-523-2435
E-mail: katkins@gw.hamline.edu

Antioch University
The McGregor School Program in Conflict Resolution
800 Livermore Street
Yellow Springs, OH 45387
Phone: 937-767-6321
Email: admiss@mcgregor.edu
Website: http://www.mcgregor.edu/imacr.html

Royal Roads University
Master of Arts in Conflict Analysis and Management
Royal Roads University
2005 Sooke Road
Victoria, BC, Canada V9B5Y2
Phone: 800-788-8028
Email: jim.bayer@royalroads.ca
Website: http://www.royalroads.ca/

A Behavioral Science: Negotiation and Conflict Management (online)
California State University, Dominguez Hills
Division of Extended Education
1000 E. Victoria St.
Carson, CA 90747
Contact: Penny Putz, Program Coordinator
Phone: 310-243-2162
Fax: 310-516-3753
Email: negotiation@csudh.edu

University of Missouri-Columbia School of Law
Master of Laws in Dispute Resolution Degree Program
Center for the Study of Dispute Resolution
206 Hulston Hall
Columbia MO 65211
Website: http://www.law.missouri.edu/

City University of New York
Dispute Resolution Consortium (CUNY DRC)
at John Jay College of Criminal Justice
445 West 59th Street, Rm. 2111
NY, NY 10019

Nova Southeastern University
3301 College Avenue
Fort Lauderdale, FL 33314

Woodbury College
660 Elm Street
Montpelier, VT 05602

Nonetheless, although it is not obligatory to have special training or education to become a mediator, it is necessary to remember that a mediator may have great difficulty retaining clients without it. Naturally, such a mediator practice may be sufficient for an individual's survival but is absolutely insufficient if an individual really wants to become a professional mediator having the benefit of being a well-paid mediator.

The Level of Earnings of Professional Mediators

The question of earnings is probably the first question an individual willing to enter a new profession asks, but the answer is not as simple as it may seem to be. It is necessary to take into consideration a variety of factors that influence the level of earnings of each individual mediator. This is why it is hardly possible to name a definite sum of money as a norm of earnings for a mediator.

In fact, there is practically no maximum for a mediator's earnings. To properly assess the earnings of a mediator, you must pay attention to several factors. It is no surprise that an experienced mediator earns more, significantly more, than an inexperienced one. Experience means not only years spent in the business but also the number and quality of cases. A mediator may deal with many conflicts that are quite simple to resolve or a few very complicated ones.

Education also contributes to increasing a mediator's earnings, although education alone is useless if the mediator lacks natural skills and abilities.

Finally, it is also important to pay attention to the area where a mediator works. It means that a mediator may work with respectable companies or individuals and this contributes to his professional level and public image. As a result, he earns more than a mediator working with smaller companies which are not widely known even among professionals. Nonetheless, it does not necessarily mean that the latter will not earn a lot since it is his experience and the workability that defines the level of his earnings. A mediator's earnings may vary from as little as $700 per day to as much as several thousands of dollars per day. Most mediators report an hourly rate of $150–$500 per hour for services rendered. According to the U.S. Department of Labor, mediators average $54,760 per year For instance, mediators in the USA earn in excess of this sum per year only working for a few days per week (Schmitt, 2001) and six figure incomes are also possible on the condition of hard, professional and reliable work of a mediator. Basically, it is necessary to remember that, above all, the fee of a mediator is based on number of parties and length of mediation.

The Importance of Having A Law Degree

Many people mistakenly believe that it is obligatory to be a lawyer or at least have a law degree to become a mediator. My ten years of experience in this emerging field has shown me that accountants, realtors, counselors, clergy, and business people—among others—are becoming mediators and often become very successful and skilled mediators. It is extremely helpful for a mediator to have experience in a variety of fields, and an individual with other than legal experience can find a niche in the mediation market.

Sometimes, in very few settings, a law degree may be required even when it is not essential in the resolution of a particular dispute. Basically, these are the few cases in mediation when a profound knowledge of law and legislative system and principles are required.

However, in general, mediation is focused on an individual's qualities, abilities, skills, and experience rather than on a law degree.

Gaining Mediation Ability and Skills

Although education and experience are extremely important for mediation, a mediator can gain the necessary abilities and skills from three basic sources.

First, are the natural abilities and skills which an individual possesses. In such a situation, it is possible to speak about innate predisposition of an individual to such a job as a mediator. Those traits are as follows:

Trustworthiness
Honesty
Integrity
Ethical standards
Ability to maintain and demonstrate neutrality toward all parties
Ability to control own biases, prejudices and emotions
Credibility—Knowledge of the mediation process—Commitment
   to the mediation process (advocate for resolution).
Sincerity
Tactfulness
Patience

Ability to maintain control of disputing parties
Flexibility
Understanding
Empathetic—Sensitivity to strongly held values of other
Awareness of cultural, economic, social and gender differences
Respect for others and opposing views
Open-minded
Good listening skills
Good oral communications skills, in clear and neutral tone
Good questioning skills and techniques
Nonjudgmental
Positive/Optimistic
Persistent but not overpowering
Ability to facilitate firm conclusions regarding settlement value
A good listener
A good communicator
Able to identify the fundamental issues
Able to focus on the matter in hand and push aside the roadblocks created by assumptions and emotions
Someone who commands the respect of all parties involved
Creative in envisioning solutions
Patient and determined

It is not a secret that many people possess such traits naturally and they are essential for the professional mediator to the extent that people naturally choose them when resolving conflicts. However these skills can also be developed through continued work as a mediator.

Second is an individual's professional experience. It has been already mentioned that mediators enter the mediation profession from a variety of fields, where they often have to solve conflicts and problems and, willingly or not, served as mediators. In such former roles the development of the abilities and skills provide the perfect entrance to that of a professional mediator. At the same time, professional mediators never stop developing their skills and abilities once entering the profession.

Finally, probably the most accessible and widespread way of gaining a mediator's abilities and skills are through special education and training. Obviously, education and training may enhance natural abilities and skills of an individual as a mediator such abilities and skills among individuals who are not naturally predisposed for such a job.

Getting a Job and Getting Paid

Naturally, there is no use of skills and abilities of a mediator if they are not beneficial for a mediator himself. This is why it is very important to find a niche and get paid for this niche, especially for a beginning mediator. On analyzing the perspectives of getting a well paid position as a mediator, it is necessary to point out that it is very difficult to find such a position if a mediator is unsure where to begin even with the appropriate training and skills. It may be beneficial for an individual to seek to find a job in a company dealing with mediation and acquire essential experience while working for such a company. At the same time, it is obvious that a mediator may be well paid from the beginning Such companies such as http://www.ADRpracticebuilder .com/ provides resources, mentoring and coaching to facilitate mediators to reach the next level in their practice.

The state dispute resolution programs in the list below are funded, fully or in part, by state government or are nonprofit partnerships with state government. Contacting agencies within your state may be a great place to start, if you are more interested in employment than in working in your own private practice as a mediator.

Alabama

Alabama Center for Dispute Resolution
Judy Keegan, Executive Director
415 Dexter Avenue
P.O. Box 671
Montgomery, AL 36101
334-269-1515
fax 334-261-6310
judy.keegan@alabar.org
Website: http://www.alabamaadr.org/
>   *The Center is the administrative arm of the Alabama Supreme Court Commission on Dispute Resolution and provides broad services to all branches of state government.*

Alabama Office of the Attorney General
Office of Administrative Hearings
Tori L. Adams-Burks, Administrative Law Judge
11 South Union Street, Room 224
Montgomery, AL 36130
334-242-7395

fax 334-353-9050

taburks@ago.state.al.us

> *The task force created by an Executive Order of the Governor of Alabama, which is transitioning in the support group, has: educated, trained, and assisted state agency department heads, managers, legal representatives, and labor representatives on the processes and benefits of ADR; trained agency in-house mediator coordinators who are available to serve as mediators in agency related disputes; and started a pilot employment mediation program for nine mostly large agencies to assist in the ultimate integration of the use of mediation in all state entities.*

Alabama State Agency ADR Support Group

John Wible, Esq., Co-Chair

P.O. Box 303017

Suite 1540, The RSA Tower, 201 Monroe Street

Montgomery, AL 36130-3017

334-206-5209

fax 334-206-5874

jwible@adph.state.al.us

http://alabamaadr.org/flashSite/stateAgencyAdr/stateAgency.cfm

> *Established in 2002 to promote state wide efforts involving the use of collaborative processes in government.*

State Agency Workplace Mediation Program

Alabama Department of Personnel

Douglas Lunsford

Suite 363

64 North Union Street

Montgomery, AL 36130-4100

334-242-3410

fax 334-353-3935

dlunsford@personnel.state.al.us

> *Responsible for development and implementation of employee DR programs in agencies.*

Alaska

Alaska Court System

Karen Largent, Dispute Resolution Coordinator

820 W. 4th Ave., Room 223

Anchorage, AK 99501

907-264-8236

fax 907-264-8291
klargent@courts.state.ak.us
http://www.state.ak.us/courts/mediat.htm

Offers two programs: The child-in-need-of-aid mediation program offers free mediation of child protection cases. The access and visitation mediation program offers parents free mediation of child custody and access issues. Both programs use contract mediators and are funded by federal grants.

Alaska State Commission for Human Rights
Paula Haley, Executive Director
800 A Street, Suite 204
Anchorage, AK 99501-3669
907-276-3177
fax 907-278-8588
http://gov.state.ak.us/aschr/

The Commission investigates discrimination complaints involving employment, housing, finances, public accommodations and practices by the state and its political subdivisions. The Commission also offers free, voluntary mediation to parties involved in these complaints as an alternative to investigation. In addition, telephone mediation is available if the parties are willing to pay the cost of the telephone call.

University of Alaska
Environment and Natural Resources Institute
Margaret King
University of Alaska
707 A Street
Anchorage, AK 99501
907-257-2716
fax 907-257-2754
anmjk@uaa.alaska.edu
http://enri.uaa.alaska.edu/

Provides broad services primarily focusing on natural resource and environmental issues.

Arizona

Arizona Supreme Court ADR Program
Patrick Scott, Manager
1501 W. Washington, Suite 411
Phoenix, AZ 85007

602-542-9255
fax 602-542-9659
pscott@supreme.sp.state.az.us
> *The program administers an Alternative Dispute Resolution Fund which grants monies to establish, maintain, improve or enhance local, regional, or statewide ADR programs in the courts.*

Department of Transportation Partnering Section
Ginger Murdough
206 S 17th Ave., Rm. 192
Maildrop 175-A
Phoenix, AZ 85007
602-712-7120
Gmurdough@dot.state.az.us
> *The Partnering Office provides resources for workshop facilitation, facilitated problem solving, and mediation through contracted services. Project team feedback is provided through software titled "Partnering Evaluation Program (PEP)."*

Office of the Attorney General
Civil Rights Division
Ann E. Woodley, Chief Counsel
Litigation and Community Services
S 1275 W. Washington St.
Phoenix, AZ 85007
602-542-8608
fax 602-542-8899
ann.woodley@azag.gov
> *The Civil Rights Division includes the Litigation and Community Services Section (which has a Conflict Resolution Unit), and the Compliance Section. The division also works with the Arizona Civil Rights Advisory Board ("ACRAB") to provide policy guidance and assistance through public hearings and forums addressing civil rights issues.*

Arkansas

Arkansas Access and Visitation Mediation Program
Shannon Hall, Director
625 Marshall St.
Justice Building
Little Rock, AR 72201

501-682-9400
fax 501-682-9410
shannon.hall@mail.state.ar.us

A Statewide Federal Program to support and facilitate non-custodial parents' access to and visitation with their children. Mediation is provided for divorcing or never married couples working through the issues of access, custody, and visitation.

Arkansas ADR Commission
Jennifer Jones Taylor, Director
625 Marshall Street
Justice Building
Little Rock, AR 72201-1020
501-682-9400
fax 501-682-9410
jennifer.taylor@mail.state.ar.us

Serves the state judiciary, working most closely with courts. Sets standards for certification, professional conduct, discipline and training of ADR neutrals in and for state and local courts. Also provides expertise on mediation systems to all branches of government. Provides no direct mediation services.

Center for Conflict Management
University of Arkansas--Little Rock
Ruth Craw, Director
2801 S. University Avenue
Little Rock, AR 72204
501-569-8562
fax 501-569-8514
rxcraw@ualr.edu

Department of Finance and Administration
Arkansas Inter-Agency Mediation Pilot Program
Don Lukas, Personnel Management
P.O. Box 3278
Little Rock, AR 72203
501-682-2252
fax 501-682-5335
don.lukas@dfa.state.ar.us

Provides option to mediate to state employees filing an employment grievance. At present at least eight state agencies participate in the pilot program. If the governor signs an executive order, the program will become a permanent part of the grievance process for state employees.

Office of the Attorney General
Darrin Williams, Chief Deputy Attorney General
200 Tower Building
323 Center St., Suite 200
Little Rock, AR 72201-2610
501-682-2081
fax 501-682-8084
darrinw@ag.state.ar.us

California

Administrative Office of the Courts
Judicial Council of California
Heather Anderson, Senior Attorney
455 Golden Gate Avenue
San Francisco, CA 94102-3660
415-865-7691
fax 415-865-7664
heather.anderson@jud.ca.gov
> *Supports the appropriate development, maintenance, and expansion of court-connected alternative dispute resolution programs by developing statewide court rules and ethics standards, conducting research, and providing education and training.*

Attorney General's Office
Rick Frank, Deputy Attorney General
1300 "I" St.
Sacramento, CA 95814
916-445-8178
fax 916-324-4293
rick.frank@doj.ca.gov

CA Dispute Resolution Council
Robert Barrett, Executive Director
760 Market St., Suite 516
San Francisco, CA 94102-2406
866-285-6500
fax 866-285-6600

rbarrett@igc.org

http://www.cdrc.net

> *Services the DR field in Sacramento and other policy-making arenas.*
> *Provides informed opinions on proposed legislation and develops principles*
> *and standards that shape DR policy in the state of*

California Center for Collaborative Policy

Susan Sherry, Director

1303 J Street, Suite 250

Sacramento, CA 95814

916-445-2079

fax 916-445-2087

ssherry@ccp.csus.edu

http://www.csus.edu/ccp

> *A joint program of CSU-Sacramento and McGeorge School of Law, the*
> *Center provides a variety of dispute resolution services to state agencies*
> *and the legislative branch.*

California Department of Consumer Affairs

Albert Balingit, Coordinator and Staff Attorney

400 R St., Suite 3090

Sacramento, CA 95818-1368

916-322-5254

fax 916-324-1368

albert_balingit@dca.ca.gov

http://www.dca.ca.gov./complainthelp/

> *Oversees the State Dispute Resolution Programs Act.*

Common Ground: Center for Cooperative Solutions

Beth Greenwood and Carolyn Penny, Co-Directors

1333 Research Park Drive

Davis, CA 95616-4852

530-754-7060

fax 530-754-5105

commonground@unexmail.ucdavis.edu

http://www.extension.ucdavis.edu/commonground/

> *Common Ground helps government entities, agencies, private sector*
> *organizations, nonprofits, and communities come together and work out*
> *solutions to public policy issues including land use, water quality, health,*
> *education, and transportation. In order to accomplish this work, Common*
> *Ground provides facilitation and mediation services, educates communities*

and organizations in order to build capacity in collaboration, and conducts and conveys research on what helps and hinders cooperative process and solutions.

Colorado

Colorado Bar Association
ADR Section, ADR Government Subcommittee
Marshall Snider, Chair
1410 High Street
Denver, CO 80218
303-436-1930
fax 303-322-2288

> *The ADR in Government subcommittee is focused on increasing the use of ADR, primarily mediation, in state government both internally and externally.*

Colorado Division of Administrative Hearings
Marshall Snider, Chief Administrative Law Judge
1120 Lincoln St., Suite 1400
Denver, CO 80203
303-894-2500
admin.hearings@state.co.us

> *Provides mediation and settlement conference services to parties in administrative proceedings, or potential proceedings, before the Colorado central panel administrative hearing agency.*

Colorado Judicial Department
Office of Dispute Resolution
Cynthia Savage, Director
1301 Pennsylvania St., Suite 110
Denver, CO 80203-2416
303-837-3672
fax 303-837-2340
cynthia.savage@judicial.state.co.us
http://www.courts.state.co.us/chs/court/mediation/odrindex.htm

> *Located in the Colorado Judicial Branch, the Office of Dispute Resolution was created by statute in 1983. The Colorado Dispute Resolution Act established ODR to assist Colorado's courts in ADR programs and in providing mediation and other dispute resolution services to the public. ODR is almost entirely cash-funded through the Dispute Resolution Fund established by the statute. Fees for ODR*

services are set by order of the supreme court to cover the program's expenses.

Colorado State Employees Mediation Program
Pat Romero,
1313 Sherman St., 1st Floor
Denver, CO 80203
303-866-4265
fax 303-866-2334
pat.romero@state.co.us
> *Provides Volunteer mediators for workplace disputes as well as training for mediators, both from within and outside state government. People who go through this training program are eligible to mediate employee disputes within Colorado State Government.*

Conflict Resolution Program
Tamra Pearson D'Estree, Henry R. Luce Professor
Graduate School of Social Work
Spruce Hall, Room 331
Denver, CO 80208
303-871-7685
tdestree@du.edu

Delaware

Attorney General's Office
Fraud and Consumer Protection Division
Ohla Rybakoff, Deputy Attorney General
820 N. French St., 5th Floor
Wilmington, DE 19801
302-577-8600
fax 302-577-6987
orybakoff@state.de.us
> *Provides landlord-tenant mediation.*

Superior Court of Delaware
Alternative Dispute Resolution
Margaret Derrickson, ADR Director
38 The Green
Dover, DE 19901
302-739-8431
fax 302-739-6193

Maggie.Derrickson@state.de.us

Court offers a multi-door ADR program of arbitration, media-tion and neutral assessment for cases involving less than $100,000. Arbitration, mediation or neutral assessment is selected mutually by the parties at case initiation, with arbitration being the default if there is no stipulation by the parties. There are over 200 trained attorneys who serve as mediators. There are also on-staff mediators (commissioners and other staff) at the court's disposal for court-or-dered mediation.

University of Delaware
Conflict Resolution Program
Kathy Wian, Coordinator
Institute for Public Administration
177 Graham Hall
Newark, DE 19716-7390
302-831-2927
fax 302-831-0450
kwian@udel.edu
http://www.ipa.udel.edu/crp/

Supports transformational and organizational change using democratic practices in non-profit, public, government, and educational settings. This is done primarily through the teaching and promotion of effective communication, collaborative problem solving, shared decision-making, and conflict resolution.

Florida

Florida Conflict Resolution Consortium
Institute of Government Partnership
Raphael Montalvo, Associate Director
University of Central Florida
36 West Pine St., Suite 201
Orlando, FL 32801
407-835-3444
fax 407-317-7815
rafaelm@mail.ucf.edu
http://consensus.fsu.edu/

Florida Conflict Resolution Consortium (Headquarters)
Florida State University
Robert Jones, Director
Shaw Building Suite 132
2031 E. Paul Dirac Drive
Tallahassee, FL 32310-4161
850-644-6320
fax 850-644-4968
rmjones@mailer.fsu.edu
http://consensus.fsu.edu/

> *The Consortiumbased at Florida State University in Tallahassee and University of Central Florida in Orlando, provides consensus building and conflict resolution services, education, training and research to build broader understanding of the value of collaborative approaches. The Consortium offers neutral technical assistance to a wide range of professionals, agency staff and private citizens and organizations engaged in public problems throughout Florida and helps to design and implement efforts for intergovernmental collaboration, community and public problem-solving, and land use and environmental dispute resolution.*

Florida Dispute Resolution Center
Sharon Press, Director
Supreme Court Building
500 South Duval Street
Tallahassee, FL 32399-1905
850-921-2910
fax 850-488-0156
presss@flcourts.org
http://www.flcourts.org/gen_public/adr/index.shtml

> *Provides assistance to the five state Supreme Court mediation boards and standing committees; certifies mediators and mediation training programs for the court; sponsors an annual conference for mediators and arbitrators; publishes quarterly newsletter; provides county court mediation training to volunteers; and assists the local state court systems as needed.*

Georgia

Consortium on Negotiation and Conflict Resolution
Georgia Institute of Technology
Michael Elliott, Director of Research
College of Architecture, City and Regional Planning Program
245 Fourth Street
Atlanta, GA 30332-0155
404-894-9841
fax 404-894-1628
michael.elliott@coa.gatech.edu
http://law.gsu.edu/cncr/index2.html
> *CNCR is an inter institutional, interdisciplinary program supporting theory building and practice in conflict prevention and resolution. Among the Consortium's goals is promoting the study of complex, multi-party, public policy disputes, particularly those involving the natural environment.*

Consortium on Negotiation and Conflict Resolution
Georgia State University College of Law
Carolyn Benne, Director
P.O. Box 4037
Atlanta, GA 30302-4037
404-651-1588
fax 404-651-4155
cbenne@gsu.edu
http://law.gsu.edu/cncr/index2.html
> *Provides conflict resolution and education, mediation, facilitation, dispute systems design, and consulting services within the university system of Georgia, and in community and private sector settings, domestic and international.*

Georgia Office of Dispute Resolution
Leila Taaffe, Director
244 Washington St. SW, Suite 423
Atlanta, GA 30334-5900
404-463-3788
fax 404-463-3790
taaffel@mindspring.com
http://www.ganet.org/gadr/
> *Provides expertise to new and existing court-connected ADR programs; trains neutrals; registers neutrals for court-connected ADR programs;*

implements the Dispute Resolution Commission's policies on qualification of neutrals and quality of programs; and collects statistics regarding ADR in court-connected programs.

Governor's Office of Georgia Human Relations
Cicley Breckenridge, Director of Policy and Mediation
2 Martin Luther King Jr. Dr.
Suite 1306, West Tower
Atlanta, GA 30334
404-463-2500
fax 404-463-2508
cicelyb@ghr.state.ga.us
   Works with state agencies, state lawmakers, and Georgia citizens to promote positive human relations and preserve civic harmony through mediation, negotiation, facilitation, and investigation/referrals.

Kennesaw State University
Conflict Management Program
Dr. Linda Johnson, Director
Dept. of Political Science & International Affairs
1000 Chastain Road
Kennesaw, GA 30144-5591
770-423-6299
fax 770-423-6880
ljohnst9@kennesaw.edu
http://www.kennesaw.edu/pols/mscm/index.shtml
   The Center for Conflict Management at Kennesaw State University provides conflict management services, including mediation, facilitation, and workshops to the campus and to other clients. The Center also serves at a home to the faculty, staff, and student ombuds at KSU.

Hawaii

Department of Commerce and Consumer Affairs
Medical Claims Conciliation Panel
Rod Miley
Medical Claims Conciliation Panel
250 South King St.
Honolulu, HI 96813
808-586-2823
oah_mccp@hotmail.com

The State Judiciary of Hawaii
Center for Alternative Dispute Resolution
Elizabeth Kent, Director
417 S. King Street, Room 207
Honolulu, HI 96813
808-539-4237
fax 808- 539-498
Elizabeth.R.Kent@courts.state.hi.us
> *Designs and builds dispute resolution programs for state and county government; facilitates and mediates a limited number of public policy disputes; manages the judiciary's contract with the community mediation centers; and promotes ADR through education, training, and research.*

University of Hawaii
Matsunaga Institute for Peace, Program on Conflict Resolution
Karen Cross, Manager
2424 Maile Way
Honolulu, HI 96822
808-956-6459
fax 808-956-5708
program@hawaii.edu
http://www.peaceinstitute.hawaii.edu/
> *Engages in research that furthers the understanding of disputing and dispute settlement practices. Encourages the practice and testing of a variety of dispute resolution procedures with an emphasis on Asia and the Pacific. Also offers training and workshops in conflict resolution, cross-cultural conflict, negotiation, and gender and conflict to individuals and organizations across the state. Provides training and services on conflict resolution for the University of Hawaii system.*

Idaho

Idaho Supreme Court
Patti Tobias, Administrative Director of the Courts
Supreme Court Building, 451 W. State St.
Boise, ID 83270-0101
208-334-2246
fax 208-334-2146
ptobias@isc.state.id.us
http://www2.state.id.us/cao/service.asp?service_id=3
> *Mediation of civil and family law disputes.*

Illinois

Center for Analysis of Alternative Dispute Resolution Systems
Susan M. Yates, Executive Director
11 East Adams, Suite 500
Chicago, IL 60603-6302
312-922-6475
fax 312-922-6763
caadrs@caadrs.org
http://www.caadrs.org
> *Assists courts in Illinois in making more effective use of ADR by providing research, analysis, resource center, program development and training services. Resource center includes a searchable database of resources on court-related ADR. CAADRS is affiliated with the Center for Conflict Resolution, a non-profit mediation organization.*

Illinois Judicial Conference Alternative Dispute Resolution Committee
Administrative Office of the Illinois Courts
Anthony F. Trapani, Program Coordinator
840 South Spring Street
Springfield, IL 62704
217-558-2114
fax 217-785-3793
ttrapani@court.state.il.us
> *Works with the circuit courts to coordinate the operations of arbitration programs throughout the state, assists in establishing new programs, provides support in drafting local rules, recruiting personnel, training new arbitrators, and in coordinating the collection of arbitration filing fees. AOIC staff also serve as liaison to the Illinois Judicial Conference Alternative Dispute Resolution Coordinating Committee.*

Indiana

Department of Environmental Management
Office of Legal Counsel
Mary Ann Habeeb
P.O. Box 6015
Indianapolis, IN 46206-6015
317-232-7696
MHABEEB@dem.state.in.us

Indiana Commission for Continuing Legal Education
Julia Orzeske, Executive Director
National City Center, Suite 1065 South Tower
115 W.Washington St.
Indianapolis, IN 46204-3417
317-232-1945
fax 317-233-1442
jorzeske@courts.state.in.us
http://www.courts.state.in.us/CourtMed.nsf
> *Maintains registry of court-approved mediators. Sets training standards for court-approved mediators.*

Indiana University
Indiana Conflict Resolution Institute
Lisa Bingham, Director
School of Public and Envirnomental Affairs # 322
1315 East 10th Street
Bloomington, IN 47405-2100
812-855-1618
fax 812-856-6031
lbingham@indiana.edu
http://www.spea.indiana.edu/icri
> *Provides information about conflict resolution to people throughout the state and to professionals in the field. Staff members are involved in research and investigations, which they add to the clearinghouse of information on conflict resolution programs used locally, nationally, and internationally.*

School of Public and Environmental Affairs
John L. Krauss, Director
Indiana University
342 North Senate Avenue
Indianapolis, IN 46204-1708
jkrauss@iupui.edu
http://www.urbancenter.iupui.edu/
> *The Center for Urban Policy and the Environment works in partnership with community leaders, business and civic organizations, nonprofits, and government. Using applied research, data analysis, and facilitation, Center analysts help leaders understand the critical choices facing them in public policy, healthcare, economic development, criminal justice, and land use. The Center supplies relevant, timely analysis to develop strategies that can*

strengthen organizations and improve the quality of life in communities. The Center was created by the Indiana University School of Public and Environmental Affairs in 1992.

Iowa

Department of Inspections and Appeals
Health Facilities Division
Marvin Tooman, Division Administrator
Lucas State Office Bldg.
3rd Floor
Des Moines, IA 50319
515-281-4233
fax 515-242-6863
mtooman@dia.state.ia.us

The DIA has received a $111,415 grant from the federal government to establish an Independent Informal Dispute Resolution (IDR) pilot project. The purpose of the project is to evaluate the benefits and disadvantages of an independent dispute resolution system involving nursing facilities that receive citations for deficiencies involving state and federal regulations.

Iowa Mediation Services
Mike Thompson, Executive Director
6200 Aurora Ave, Ste 608W
Urbandale, IA 50322
515-331-8081
mthmpsn@netins.net

Office of the Attorney General
Tam Ormiston, Deputy Attorney General
Hoover State Office Building
Des Moines, IA 50319
515-281-5166
fax 515-281-6771
tormist@ag.state.ia.us

Kansas

Office of Judicial Administration
Art Thompson, DR Coordinator
Office of Judicial Administration

301 W. 10th
Topeka, KS 66612-1507
785-291-3748
fax 785-296-1804
thompsona@kscourts.org
http://www.kscourts.org/adr
> *Provides expertise to court-related ADR programs. Provides no direct mediation services.*

Office of State Long-Term Care Ombudsman
Matthew Hickam, State Long-Term Care Ombudsman
610 SW 10th St., 2nd Floor
Topeka, KS 66612-1616
785-296-3017
fax 785-296-3916
LTCO@state.ku.us
http://www.da.state.ks.us/care
> *Investigate, resolve complaints, and mediate disputes for residents of long-term care facilities.*

University of Kansas
Public Management Center
Charles Jones, Director
715 SW Tenth St
Topeka, KS 66612-1617
785-296-2533
fax 785-296-2580
cfjones@ku.edu
> *Contracts to provide mediation training to state managers for handling conflict. At this time they provide six core mediation training seminars a year.*

Kentucky

Kentucky Department of Personnel
Division of Communication and Recognition, Kentucky Employee Mediation Program
Linda C. House, Personnel Mediation Mediator
200 Fair Oaks Lane, Suite 511
Frankfort, KY 40601
502-564-3433
fax 502-564-4311

ndaC.House@ky.gov
http://personnel.ky.gov/stemp/kemp/
> *The Kentucky Employee Mediation Program (KEMP) offers mediation to all Executive Branch employees to resolve conflicts between employees, employees and supervisors, harassment and discrimination issues, and workplace environment. The Personnel Board refers many of their appeals to KEMP.*

Natural Resources Environment and Public Protection Cabinet
Alan Wagers, Chief Hearing Officer
Office of Administrative Hearings
35-36 Fountain Place
Frankfort, KY 40601
502-564-7312
fax 502-564-4973
alan.wagers@mail.state.ky.us
http://www.eppc.ky.gov/
> *Responsible for administrative, adjudicatory hearings upon the filing of a petition or complaint, and to recommend to the Secretary the final action that should be taken. Mediation is offered as a non-binding, voluntary and confidential process for surface mining and environmental issues.*

Office of the Attorney General
Consumer Protection Division
Lori Farris, Branch Manager and Mediator
1024 Capitol Center Drive, Suite 200
Frankfort, KY 40601
502-696-5389
fax 502-696-5300

Maine

Bureau of Land and Water Quality
Division of Watershed Management
Donald T. Witherill, Director
Station #17
State House
Augusta, ME 04355
207-287-7725
fax 207-287-7191
donald.t.witherill@maine.gov

Program dealing with water quality issues at Maine DEP, the office convenes work groups from time to time for the purpose of finding solutions to water quality issues in Maine. Sometimes, these groups are served by outside (private) facilitators, and sometimes they are handled in-house.

Court ADR Service
Diane Kenty, Director of Court ADR
147 New Meadows Road
West Bath, ME 04530
207-442-0227
fax 207-422-0228
diane.kenty@maine.gov
> *Provides a mediation roster for Domestic Relations, Small Claims, Land Use and Environmental, and General Civil litigation.*

Division of Administrative Hearings
Allan Toubman, Chief Administrative Hearing Officer
2 Anthony Ave., Suite 1
Agusta, ME 04330-9477
207-624-5900
fax 207-624-5903
allan.a.toubman@state.me.us
> *Provides dispute resolution service to state agencies. It primarily hears appeals on Unemployment Compensation benefit issues for the Department of Labor.*

Office of the Attorney General
James McKenna, Assistant Attorney General
Station 6, State House
State House
Augusta, ME 04333
207-626-8800
fax 207-626-8865
jim.mckenna@state.me.us
> *The Attorney General's Consumer Mediation Service is a free service to Maine consumers who have a problem with a business. By offering this service, the Public Protection Division is able to monitor the types of problems consumers are having around the state. The Attorney General's Office is then in a better position to protect Maine consumers from unfair and deceptive business practices.*

Office of the Attorney General
Phyllis Gardiner, Assistant Attorney General
Station 6 State House
Augusta, ME 04333
207-626-8800
fax 207-626-8865
phyllis.gardiner@state.me.us

Maryland

Governor's Office of Smart Growth
Jessica Cogan, Chief of Staff
6 St. Paul Street
Baltimore, MD 21202
410-767-8710
fax 410-333-0719
jcogan@gov.state.md.us
> *As part of its mission, the Office promotes interagency consensus and cooperation on projects that are consistent with the State's Smart Growth policy.*

Maryland Department of the Environment
Bernard A. Penner, Enforcement and Compliance Coordinator
2500 Broening Hwy.
Baltimore, MD 21224
410-631-4405
fax 410-631-3888
bpenner@mde.state.md.us

Mediation and Conflict Resolution Office (MACRO)
Rachel Wohl, Executive Director
900 Commerce Road
Annapolis, MD 21401
410-841-2260
fax 410-841-2261
rachel.wohl@courts.state.md.us
http://www.courts.state.md.us/macro
> *Advances appropriate alternatives to litigation and alternatives to violence throughout Maryland's courts, neighborhoods, businesses, schools, government agencies, criminal and juvenile justice programs and businesses. Created in 1998 by the Chief Judge of Maryland's highest*

appellate court, this forty-member Commission includes judges, public officials, legislators, lawyers, ADR practitioners, community members, business representatives, educators and others. The Commission developed and is now implementing a practical action plan entitled "Join The Resolution."

Office of Administrative Hearings
Laurie Bennett, Administrative Law Judge
11101 Gilroy Road
Hunt Valley, MD 21031-1301
410-229-4100
fax 410-229-4111
lbennett@oah.state.md.us
Hears all contested state administrative law cases, mediates special education disputes, and encourages mediation where appropriate.

Office of the Attorney General
Donna Hill Staton, Esq., Deputy Attorney General
200 St. Paul Place
Baltimore, MD 21201
410-576-7051
fax 410-576-7036
dstaton@oag.state.md.us

University of Maryland
Institute for Governmental Service
Barbara Hawk, Director
4511 Knox Road, Suite 205
College Park, MD 20740
301-403-4610
fax 301-403-4222
bh34@umail.umd.edu
http://www.inform.umd.edu/EdRes/GradInfo/IGS/services/ind
Promotes excellence in governance by providing consulting, consensus building, and information services to governments and communities in the state, and by advancing the University's public service mission in a manner that warrants the highest degree of public confidence in its integrity, efficiency, and fairness.

University of Maryland School of Law
Program on Dispute Resolution
Roger Wolf, Director
500 W. Baltimore St.
Baltimore, MD 21201
410-706-3836
rwolf@law.umaryland.edu

> *Provides services to the courts, with plans to become a major service provider to state agencies. Produces a directory of Maryland ADR practitioners which is available to state agencies and other interested groups and individuals.*

Massachusetts

Massachusetts Office of Dispute Resolution
University of Massachusetts - Boston
Susan M. Jeghelian, Executive Director
100 Morrissey Boulevard
McCormack Building, Room 627
Boston, MA 02125
617-287-4047
fax 617-287-4094
susan.jeghelian@umb.edu

> *In partnership with the University of Massachusetts–Boston, MODR provides research opportunities for faculty, and practical training and internships for students on multi-party public policy disputes and the use of collaborative approaches in the public sector. It provides a variety of ADR services to all branches of state government and municipalities.*

Office of the Attorney General
Michelle Booth, Mediation Services Department Director
One Ashburton Place
Boston, MA 02108
617-727-2200   ext. 2916
fax 617-727-5762
michelle.booth@ago.state.ma.us

> *Funds community based and school mediation programs, and oversees a team of mediators who provide emergency services to schools in crisis.*

Michigan

Office of the Attorney General
Michael McDaniel, Litigation Coordinator
P.O. Box 30212
Lansing, MI 48909-0212
517-241-9137
fax 517-335-4253
mcdanielm@ag.state.mi.us
State Court Administrative Office
Office of Dispute Resolution
Douglas Van Epps, Director
Box 30048
Lansing, MI 48915
517-373-8922
fax 517-373-8922
vaneppsd@courts.mi.gov
http://www.courts.michigan.gov/scao/dispute/odr.htm
> *Develops dispute resolution practices and protocols for the state trial courts
> and provides training for judicial staff. The office also provides mediation
> services and technical assistance to state agencies.*

Minnesota

Department of Corrections
Community and Juvenile Services
Kay Pranis, Restorative Justice Planner
1450 Energy Park Drive, Suite 200
St. Paul, MN 55108
651-642-0329
fax 651-642-0457
kpranis@co.doc.state.mn.us
> *Provides training and some grants for restorative justice projects.*

Hamline University School of Law
Dispute Resolution Institute
David Larson, Director
1536 Hewitt Ave.
St. Paul, MN 55104-1237

651-523-2128
fax 651-523-2236
dlarson@gw.hamline.edu
http://web.hamline.edu/law/adr/
> *Offers DR training for lawyers, law students, and other professionals. Provides evaluation services for the Minnesota Supreme Court. Students in the program provide ADR services for the state Department of Human Resources as well as conciliation services for several county courts.*

Minnesota Office of Administrative Hearings
Phyllis Reha, Administrative Law Judge
100 Washington Square, Suite 1700
Minneapolis, MN 55401-2138
612-341-7602
fax 612-349-2665
phylllis.reha@state.mn.us
> *Provides low cost dispute resolution services to persons involved in disputes wherein at least one of the parties is a state agency or local unit of government. Also facilitates advisory groups formed to develop rules for various state agencies.*

Office of the Attorney General
Lori Swanson, Solicitor General
1100 NCL Tower
445 Minnesota Street
St. Paul, MN 55101
800-657-3787
fax 651-282-5833

Supreme Court ADR Review Board
Stacy Janke, ADR Assistant
140 Judicial Center
25 Constitution Ave.
St. Paul, MN 55155
651-297-7592
stacy.janke@courts.state.mn.us
> *Minnesota requires all parties to civil and family cases to consider ADR before getting a court date. ADR Review Board reviews claims against mediators and has compiled a code of ethics and a Code of Ethics Enforcement Procedure.*

University of Minnesota
Conflict and Change Center
Tom Fiutak, Director
252 Humphrey Institute
301 19th Ave. South
Minneapolis, MN 55455
612-625-3046
fax 612-625-3513
fiuta001@umn.edu
> *Provides seminars and workshops for organizations and departments in area of negotiating skills and conflict management advising. Also provides intervention service that facilitates specific organizational disputes.*

Mississippi

Office of the Attorney General
Hunt Cole, Head of Litigation
Department of Justice
P.O. Box 220
Jackson, MS 39205-0220
601-359-4209
fax 601-359-3441
hcole@ago.state.ms.us

Missouri

Office of State Courts Administrator
Juvenile and Adult Court Programs
Norma Rahm, Family Preservation Specialist
2121 Industrial Dr.
P.O. Box 104480
Jefferson City, MO 65110
573-751-4377
fax 573-522-8260
norma_rahm@osca.state.mo.us
> *Administers state funds from the Division of Child Support Enforcement and grants to courts for custody and visitation mediation services.*

Office of the Attorney General
Consumer Division
Laura Krasser, Assistant Attorney General

P.O. Box 899
Jefferson City, MO 65102
573-571-3321
fax 573-751-0774
attgen@mo.ago.org
Offers mediation is special cases.

Montana

Montana Consensus Council
Office of the Governor
Judy Edwards, Executive Director
1301 Lockey, Suite 301
Helena, MT 59620
406-444-9838
fax 406-444-5529
juedwards@state.mt.us
http://www.mcc.state.mt.us
Provides consensus building, training and education, research and publications for state and local government.

Public Policy Research Institute
University of Montana
Matthew McKinney, Director
516 N. Park Avenue
Helena, MT 59601
406-457-8475
matt@umtpri.org
http://www.umtpri.org/
The Institute serves as an impartial, non-partisan forum to exchange ideas, develop and analyze policy options, and solve public problems. We assist and equip people with diverse viewpoints to solve problems related to the integration of social, economic, and environmental interests. Created in 1987 by the Board of Regents, PPRI is supported by a partnership of the The University of Montana, the William and Flora Hewlett Foundation, and the Lincoln Institute of Land Policy.

Nebraska

Office of Dispute Resolution
Debora Brownyard, Director

521 South 14th Street, Suite 200
Lincoln, NE 68508
402-471-3148
fax 402-471-3071
> *Unique public/private partnership with 6 community-based mediation*
> *centers covering the entire state.*

Nevada

Nevada Supreme Court
Civil Settlement Conference Program
Ronetta S. Clark, Administrative Counsel
201 S. Carson St. Suite 201
Carson City, NV 89701-4702
775-684-1600
fax 775-684-1601
rclark@nvcourts.state.nv.us
> *Provides mandatory mediation program for civil appeals. All civil appeals*
> *are generally assigned automatically to the program, with the exception*
> *of 1) cases in which either party is not represented by counsel and 2) cases*
> *involving termination of parental rights.*

University of Nevada, Las Vegas, William S. Boyd School of Law
Saltman Center for Conflict Resolution
Jean R. Sternlight, Director
4505 Maryland Parkway, Box 451003
Las Vegas, NV 89154-1003
702-895-2358
fax 702-895-2482
Jean.Sternlight@ccmail.nevada.edu
> *The Center provides courses, symposia, and trainings related to conflict*
> *resolution while fostering scholarship and law reform work in the field.*

New Hampshire

New Hampshire Court ADR Program
Peter Wolfe, Chair
22 Main St.
Newport, NH 03773
603-863-3450
fax 603-863-3204

p_wolfe@conknet.com

Develops and provides ADR services to the different levels of courts. Superior Court requires all civil cases go to ADR. The parties elect which process they want to use, i.e. neutral evaluation, mediation, or arbitration. Court also has a program for neutral evaluation of marital cases in addition to a statute that suspends marital actions when the parties elect to go to marital mediation.

New Jersey

Administrative Office of the Courts
Thomas N. Farrell, Manager, CDR Programs
Hughes Justice Complex
P.O. Box 988
Trenton, NJ 08625
609-984-2337
fax 609-633-7142
thomas_farrell@judiciary.state.nj.us

Oversees Complementary Dispute Resolution (CDR) programs within the Special Programs Unit of the Administrative Office of the Courts. The Supreme Court Committee on CDR provides guidance in the development of CDR programs throughout the state judicial system.

Department of Law and Public Safety
Alternative Dispute Resolution Unit
Yakov M. Dombroff, Director
P.O. Box 45023
Newark, NJ 07101
973-504-6100
yakov.dombroff@lps.state.nj.us

Provides mediation for various types of consumer affairs cases; selection of cases decided upon solely by the referring agency.

Office of Administrative Law
Jeff Martin, Acting Director
Quaker Bridge Plaza, Bldg. 9
Quaker Bridge Road
P.O. Box 049
Trenton, NJ 08625-0049
609-588-6582

Handles environmental conflicts for the Department of Environ-

> *mental Protection. Conducts formal hearings on disputes, a success-*
> *ful settlement program prior to hearing, and arbitration involving*
> *toxic spills.*

Office of Dispute Settlement
Fran Snyder
25 Market Street
P.O. Box 850
Trenton, NJ 08625
609-292-7686
fax 609-292-6292
snyder_f@opd.state.nj.us
> *Provides mediation and other neutral DR services to the public and*
> *private sectors.*

Rutgers University
Center for Negotiation and Conflict Resolution
Sanford Jaffe, Director
Civic Square, Suite 104
33 Livingston Avenue
New Brunswick, NJ 08901-1958
732-932-2487
fax 732-932-2493
cncr@rci.rutgers.edu
http://www.policy.rutgers.edu/CNCR/
> *Serves as a resource both in and outside New Jersey for those interested*
> *in the theory and practice of conflict resolution. CNCR offers seminars,*
> *lectures, conferences and customized programs. It also works with groups*
> *that have a vital interest in improving the way disputes are managed,*
> *such as the judiciary, the Office of the Attorney-General, state government*
> *and bar associations.*

New Mexico

Consortium for Public Collaboration
Julia Hosford Barnes
NM Environment Department
200 W. De Vargas, Suite 2
Santa Fe, NM 87501
505-982-3993
jhb@nm.net

New Mexico ADR Advisory Council
NM Department of Health
Robert Horwitz
Department of Health
P.O. Box 26110
Santa Fe, NM 87502-6110
rhorwitz@health.state.nm.us

> *Established by Executive Order, the Council is made up of the head of each executive agency or their appointee and is responsible for insuring that agencies carry out the order to implement ADR.*

New York

Department of Environmental Conservation
Office of Hearings and Mediation Services
James T. McClymonds, Chief Administrative Law Judge
625 Broadway
Albany, NY 12233–1550
518-402-9003
fax 518-402-9037
http://www.dec.state.ny.us/website/ohms/index.html

> *The Office provides mediation services upon the mutual agreement of all parties in environmental permitting and enforcement cases. Mediation and facilitation is also offered in contested rule making proceedings.*

New York State Unified Court System
Division of Court Operations - Office of ADR Programs
Daniel Weitz
25 Beaver Street, Room 859B
New York, NY 10004
212-428-2863
fax 212-428-2696
dweitz@courts.state.ny.us

> *Oversees all ADR programs in the Unified Court System and provides technical assistance to all district administrative judges in developing and implementing ADR programs. Provides ADR services in the courts at every level for a variety of cases using mediation, arbitration, neutral evaluation and summary jury trials. Also provides educational programs and services for members of the judiciary, the bar, and court litigants. The*

> *Community Dispute Resolution Centers Program, in a joint local and state effort, provides community forums for the resolution of disputes as an alternative to criminal, civil, and family court litigation.*

New York University, Wagner Graduate School of Public Service
The Program on Negotiation and Conflict Resolution (PNCR)
Allen Zerkin J.D.
Robert F. Wagner Graduate School of Public Service
295 Lafayette St.
New York, NY 10012
212-998-7494
fax 212-995-3890
allen.zerkin@nyu.edu

> *The PNCR, often working in collaboration with other components of the university, serves as a convenor of consensus building processes and dialogues related to public policy and public affairs. Applications have included consensus development of legislation and regulations, sponsorship of fora for developing greater understanding of policy issues, mediation of local or organizational disputes, planning and implementation of public participation programs, and facilitation of meetings.*

Office of the Attorney General
Kermitt Brooks, Claims Bureau Chief
120 Broadway
New York, NY 10271
212-416-8492
fax 212-416-6033
kermitt.brooks@oag.state.ny.us

State of New York Public Service Commission
Department of Public Service
Judith A. Lee, Chief Administrative Law Judge
Three Empire State Plaza
Albany, NY 12233-1350
518-474-4520
judith_lee@dps.state.ny.us
http://www.dps.state.ny.us/directory.htm

> *The Office of Hearings and Alternative Dispute Resolution advances the public policy objectives of the New York Public Service Commission by providing an efficient forum for the conduct of its proceedings, through*

use of a variety of alternative dispute resolution processes, including mediation, arbitration, facilitation, collaboration, consensus building, negotiated rulemaking, and expedited dispute resolution. Administrative law judges are trained thoroughly and offer training in dispute resolution to other members of the agency and to the parties that appear in proceedings

North Carolina

North Carolina Dispute Resolution Commission
Leslie Ratliff, Executive Secretary
1100 Navaho Drive, Suite 126
PO Box 2448
Raleigh, NC 27602
919-981-5077
fax 919-981-5048
leslie.ratliff@aoc.state.nc.us
   Provides a roster of qualified neutrals to judiciary and to state agencies with ADR programs.

North Carolina State University Cooperative Extension
Natural Resources Leadership Institute
Steve Smutko, Director
Department of Agricultural and Resource Economics
Box 8109
Raleigh, NC 27695-8109
919-515-4683
fax 919-515-1824
steve_smutko@ncsu.edu
http://www.ces.ncsu.edu/depts/agecon/nrli/
   Provides training in public dispute resolution and participatory decision-making to extension educators, government agency staff, elected officials and citizens. Cooperative Extension also provides facilitation and mediation assistance to government organizations and others for managing conflict over environmental issues, and aiding collaborative decision-making. Offers a leadership development program with a focus on conflict resolution and collaborative problem solving.

University of North Carolina
John B. Stephens, Assistant Professor
Institute of Government

Campus Box 3330, Knapp Building
Chapel Hill, NC 27599-3330
919-962-5190
fax 919-962-2705
stephens@iogmail.iog.unc.edu
http://www.iog.unc.edu/programs/dispute/

North Dakota

The Consensus Council, Inc.
Rose Stoller, Executive Director
1003 Interstate Avenue, Suite 7
Bismarck, ND 58503-0500
701-224-0588
fax 701-224-0787
rstoller@agree.org
http://www.agree.org/
    Provides broad dispute resolution services at the state, regional and local levels.

University of North Dakota
Conflict Resolution Center
Kristine Paranica, Director
314 Cambridge
P.O. Box 8009
Grand Forks, ND 58202
701-777-3664
fax 701-777-6184
kristine_paranica@und.nodak.edu
http://www.und.nodak.edu/dept/crc/
    Provides conflict management training, mediation, and facilitation for state agencies, university community and others. Incorporates cutting-edge theory with emotional intelligence, learned optimism, dealing with change and other new theories.

Ohio

Commission on Dispute Resolution and Conflict Management
Maria Mone, Director
77 South High Street, 24th Floor
Columbus, OH 43266-0124
614-752-9595
fax 614-752-9682

MMone@cdr.state.oh.us
http://www.disputeresolution.ohio.gov/
> *Established in 1989, the Commission provides Ohioans with construc-*
> *tive, nonviolent forums, processes, and techniques for resolving disputes.*
> *Focused on four program areas – educational institutions, state and*
> *local government, courts, and communities – the Commission works*
> *to positively affect the lives of all Ohio citizens by providing dispute*
> *resolution and conflict management training, consultation and techni-*
> *cal assistance in designing dispute resolution programs, and facilitation*
> *and mediation services.*

Office of the Attorney General
D. Michael Grodhouse, First Assistant Attorney General
State Office Tower, 17th Floor
30 E. Broad St.
Columbus, OH 43215-5148
614-466-1339
fax 614-466-5087

Ohio Board of Tax Appeals
Tom Wang, Attorney Examiner
Rhodes Office Tower 24th Floor
30 E. Broad St
Columbus, OH 43266-0422
614-466-6700
fax 614-644-5196
http://www.bta.ohio.gov/rules2002.htm
> *The Board has a mediation program that utilizes ALJs to provide media-*
> *tion and settlement negotiation in real property tax evaluations, sales tax,*
> *income tax, and franchise tax cases.*

Ohio Civil Rights Commission
Mediation and Civil Rights Complaints
Matthew D. Miko
1111 E. Broad St., Suite 301
Columbus, OH 43205-1370
614-466-9261
fax 614-644-8776
mikom@ocrc.state.oh.us

Mediation of Discrimination Complaints.
Ohio Department of Mental Health
Mental Health Complaints Mediation
Ellen Deacon
30 E. Broad St. 8th Floor
Columbus, OH 43266
614-466-2333
deacone@mhmail.mh.state.oh.us

Ohio School Facilities Commission
Construction Contract Partnering
Crystal Canan, Chief of Projects
88 E. Broad St. Suite 1400
Columbus, OH 43215
614-466-6290
crystal.canan@osfc.state.oh.us

Public Utilities Commission of Ohio
Utility Complaints Mediation and Arbitration
Russ Gooden
180 E. Broad St. 12th Floor
Columbus, OH 43215
614-466-0114

Supreme Court of Ohio, Judicial and Court Services Division
Dispute Resolution Section
Bruce Heckman, Section Manager
65 S. Front Street, 6th Floor
Columbus, OH 43215-3431
614-387-9420
fax 614-387-9409
heckmanb@sconet.state.oh.us
http://www.sconet.state.oh.us/dispute_resolution/
Provides funding and technical assistance to trial and appellate court mediation services. Staff works to provide mediation training, program monitoring and administration of policies and procedures developed by the Supreme Court Advisory Committee on Dispute Resolution, a committee appointed by Thomas J. Moyer, Chief Justice.

Oklahoma

Administrative Office of the Courts
Sue Darst Tate, Director
1915 N. Stiles, Suite 305
Oklahoma City, OK 73105
405-521-2450
fax 405-521-6815
tates@OSCN.net
> *Seeks to develop community-based ADR services and support state agencies.*

Appellate Settlement Conference Program
Administrative Office of the Courts
Honorable Don Barnes, Program Administrator
1915 N. Stiles, Suite 218
Oklahoma City, OK 73105
405-521-2450
janice.naghavian@oscn.net
> *Statewide settlement conferences for cases appealed to the Oklahoma Supreme Court.*

Department of Human Services Employee Mediation Program
Personnel Resources Division, Employee Relations Unit
Clarese Amadi, Mediation Program Manager
P.O. Box 25352
Oklahoma City, OK 73125
405-521-3646
clarese.amadi@okdhs.org
http://clarese.amadi@okdhs.org
> *Statewide in-house program for Department Of Human Services Employees.*

Oklahoma Department of Corrections
Post Conviction Mediation Program
Michael T. Oakley, Assistant General Counsel
3400 Martin Luther King Ave.
Oklahoma City, OK 73136
405-425-2666
mike.oakley@doc.state.ok.us
> *Statewide in-house program for victims and offenders.*

Oklahoma Department of Corrections
Workplace Conflict Management Group
Samuel Terry, Mediation Program Manager
3400 Martin Luther King Ave.
Oklahoma City, OK 73136-0400
405-425-2583
fax 405-425-2886
samuel.terry@doc.state.ok.us
   Statewide in-house program for Department of Corrections employees.

Oklahoma Merit Protection Commission
Melanie Cherry, ADRP Coordinator
201 N. E. 38th Terrace, Ste.5
Oklahoma City, OK 73105
405-525-9144
fax 405-528-6245
   Statewide services limited to state government employers and employees.

Oklahoma State University
Institute for Issue Management and Alternative Dispute Resolution
Andrea Braeutigam, J.D., LL.M., Program Manager
Seretean Wellness Center
1514 West Hall of Fame Avenue
Stillwater, OK 74078
405-744-3305
fax 405-744-3050
andrea.braeutigam@okstate.edu
http://iimadr.okstate.edu/
   Delivers public-sector ADR services, training, education, research and
   design for Oklahoma and the region for topics in agriculture, rural living,
   the environment, and government. Certified by both USDA and the State
   Administrative Office of the Courts.

Oklahoma Victim Restitution/Juvenile Offender Responsibility Program
Jerry Davis, Program Director
P.O. Box 268812
3814 N. Santa Fe
Oklahoma City, OK 73126-8812
405-530-2867
fax 405-530-2800
   Statewide Program for juvenile offenders and community victims.

State Agency Workplace Mediation Program
Gas Gathering ADR Program
Larry Fiddler, Manager of Technical Services
P.O. Box 52000-2000
Oklahoma City, OK 73152-2000
405-521-2489
l.fiddler@occmail.occ.state.ok.us
> *Statewide mediation services for disputes between producers and gatherers of natural gas during contract negotiations.*

Oregon

Department of Justice
General Counsel Division
Nicole Waldner, Contact
1162 Court Street NE
Salem, OR 97310
503-378-4620
fax 503-378-3784
nichole.waldner@doj.state.or.us
http://www.doj.state.or.us/ADR/

Oregon Consensus Program
Elaine Hallmark, Director
Hatfield School of Government - Portland State University
P.O. Box 751
Portland, OR 97207-0751
503-725-9070
fax 503-725-9099
consensus@pdx.edu
http://www.orconsensus.pdx.edu
> *Provides neutral conflict resolution service to state and federal agencies, the Oregon Legislature, the Oregon Courts, tribal governments, local governments and a variety of stakeholders involved in issues related to development and application of public policies in Oregon. The Program incorporates components of the former Oregon Public Policy Dispute Resolution Program of the Oregon Dispute Resolution Commission, which were transferred to the Hatfield School by the 2003 Legislature.*

Oregon Judicial Department
Court Community Justice Services Division

Alice Phalan, Director
Office of the State Court Administrator
1163 State Street
Salem, OR 97310
503-986-5935
fax 503-986-6419
alice.phalan@ojd.state.or.us
> *Assists courts in establishing programs, policies, and procedures for appropriate dispute resolution, including mediation, community justice, and integrated family and drug courts. Oversees research and evaluation of innovative ADR programs and integrated family and drug courts. Provides technical assistance and training to local state courts, ADR/mediation commissions, and family law advisory committees.*

Pennsylvania

Commonwealth Court of Pennsylvania
John Gordon, Esq., Program Director
Widener Building, Ste. 980
1339 Chestnut St.
Philadelphia, PA 19107
215-560-5730
fax 215-560-3252
john.gordon@commonwealth.court.state.pa.us
> *Court of original jurisdiction hears state cases. Senior judges serve as mediators.*

Office of the Attorney General
Bureau of Consmer Protection
Frank Donaghue, Esq., Director, Chief Deputy Attorney General
Strawberry Square
Harrisburg, PA 17120
717-787-9707
fax 717-787-1190
fdonaghue@attorneygeneral.gov

Pennsylvania Deparment of Corrections
Office of the Victim Advocate Mediation Program for Victims of Violent
Jeffery Beard, Secretary, Department of Corrections
P.O. Box 598
Camp Hill, PA 17001-0598
717-731-7060
jbeard@state.pa.us

Pennsylvania Department of Environmental Protection
Center for Collaboration and Environmental Dispute Resolution
Jennifer Handke, Director, CEDR
400 Market St., 15th Floor RCSOB
Harrisburg, PA 17105-2063
717-783-1653
fax 717-787-2938
JHandke@state.pa.us

> *To further improve and expand their problem solving capabilities, the DEP has created the Center for Collaboration and Environmental Dispute Resolution. CEDR provides ADR services including facilitation, mediation, stakeholder negotiation (i.e., of regulations, policy, or multi-party dispute), and hybrids of each. CEDR provides facilitation and mediation services to guide participants in collaborative decision-making/problem-solving.*

Pennsylvania Department of Labor and Industry
Bureau of Mediation
William D. Gross,
419 Labor and Industry Building
Harrisburg, PA 17120
717-787-2803
fax 717-705-6329
wigross@state.pa.us

> *Provides free mediation service to employers and employees in Pennsylvania.*

Pennsylvania Public Utility Commission
Office of Administrative Law Judge
Herbert Nurick, Mediation Coordinator
P.O. Box 3265
Harrisburg, PA 17105-3265
717-783-5428
fax 717-787-0481
hnurick@state.pa.us

> *The Commission's mediation policy accords all utilities, under the jurisdiction of the PUC, and their customers, the opportunity to mediate disputes. The Office of Administrative Law Judge manages the mediation program, which allows parties to request mediation prior to or during a proceeding.*

Pennsylvania State University
Center for Research in Conflict Negotiation
Barbara Gray, Director
313 Beam Business Administration Building

University Park, PA 16802-1913
814-865-3822
fax 814-865-0123
B9G@psu.edu
http://www.smeal.psu.edu/crcn/index.html

Conducts research on conflict, negotiation, coalition formation, and multiparty collaboration. Also provides DR services including training, facilitation, mediation, conflict assessment and organizational development to a variety of academic and administrative units across the university as well as to public and private organizations within Pennsylvania and throughout the world.

Pennsylvania State University, The Dickinson Law School
The Center for Dispute Resolution
Nancy Welsh, Associate Director
150 S. College St.
Carlisle, PA 17013-2899
717-241-3508
fax 717-240-5126
nxw10@psu.edu

The Center provides dispute resolution services such as mediation, facilitation and systems design and engages in a variety of scholarly and outreach activities that examine the latest theory and innovations in dispute resolution. These activities include faculty scholarship, a certificate program in dispute resolution and advocacy for law students, an annual dispute resolution symposium, and training in mediation and other conflict resolution skills.

Rhode Island

Department of Environmental Management
Administrative Adjudication Department
Kathleen Lanphear, Program Administrator
235 Promenade Street, 3rd Floor
Providence, RI 02908
401-222-1357   ext. 4800
fax 401-222-1398
kathleen.lanphear@dem.ri.gov
http://www.dem.ri.gov/

The Department of Environmental Management offers a voluntary, non-binding mediation program to help parties resolve disputes with the Department, better utilize the department's limited resources and improve the service and manner in which the DEM serves the regulated community.

South Carolina

Office of Human Resources
State Employee Grievance Procedure
Samuel Wilkins, Assistant Director
1201 Main St., Ste. 1000
Columbia, SC 29201
803-737-0900
swilkins@ohr.state.sc.us
> *Mediation and Arbitration of state employment disputes under the State Employee Grievance Procedure Act (mandatory).*

Supreme Court Commission on ADR
South Carolina Bar
Andrew M. Walsh Esq., Dispute Resolution Director
P.O. Box 608
Columbia, SC 29202-0608
803-799-6653
fax 803-799-5290
andrew.walsh@scbar.org
http://www.scbar.org/adr/
> *Establishes rules and certifies neutrals for mediation/arbitration in the South Caroling state courts.*

Texas

Center for Public Policy Dispute Resolution
University of Texas Law School
E. Janice Summer, Executive Director
727 E. Dean Keeton
Austin, TX 78705
512-471-3507
fax 512-232-1191
jsummer@mail.law.utexas.edu
http://www.utexas.edu/law/academics/centers/cppdr/
> *Provides conflict resolution services, including education and training. The Center is a not-for-profit organization of professionals who focus on state and local government and are dedicated to the stewardship of conflict resolution in state and local government, the UT community, and the public.*

Utah

Office of the Attorney General
Consumer Complaints
Mailei Bucher
160 E. 300 S., 5th Floor
Salt Lake City, UT 84114-0872
801-366-0310
fax 801-366-0315
atmain.mbucher@state.ut.us

Office of the Property Rights Ombudsman
Department of Natural Resources
Craig Call
1594 West North Temple, Suite 3710
PO 145610
Salt Lake City, UT 84114-5610
801-859-22
fax 1-801-538-73
craigcall@utah.gov
http://www.utahpropertyrights.com/

State ADR Council
Utah State Tax Commission
Palmer DePaulis, Chair
210 North, 1950 West
Salt Lake City, UT 84134
801-297-3906
fax 801-297-3919
palmer@utah.gov
http://www.tax.utah.gov/adr/

> *Created in 2001 by Utah Governor Michael Leavitt, acting on legislation passed by the State Legislature. The Council is comprised of a representative from each agency of government whose mission is to change the culture of interaction between government and citizens by reducing conflicts and disputes through the use of ADR techniques, specifically mediation. The Council also seeks to promote collaboration and consensus building among state policy makers to achieve efficiencies, reduce the cost of government, and promote better outcomes.*

Utah Intergovernmental Roundtable
Center for Public Policy and Administration
Dr. David Patton, Director
University of Utah
260 S. Central Campus Drive, Room 214
Salt Lake City, UT 84112-9154
801-581-6781
fax 801-585-5489
david.patton@cppa.utah.edu
http://www.cppa.utah.edu/uir/

> *The mission of the Utah Intergovernmental Roundtable is to facilitate discussion and promote understanding of intergovernmental issues to enhance the cooperation and interaction of governmental entities. The Roundtable is administered by the Center for Public Policy and Administration at the University of Utah.*

Utah Intergovernmental Roundtable
Center for Public Policy and Administration
David Patton, Ph.D., Director
University of Utah
260 S. Central Campus Drive, Room 214
·Salt Lake City, UT 84112-9154
801-581-6781
fax 801-585-5489
david.patton@cppa.utah.edu
http://www.cppa.utah.edu/uir/

> *The mission of the Utah Intergovernmental Roundtable is to facilitate discussion and promote understanding of intergovernmental issues to enhance the cooperation and interaction of governmental entities. The Roundtable is administered by the Center for Public Policy and Administration at the University of Utah.*

Utah State Tax Commission
Palmer DePaulis, Director of the Tax Commission's Appeals Unit
210 North 1950 West
Salt Lake City, UT 84134
801-297-3813
palmer@utah.gov

> *The Commission provides Administrative Law Judges to mediate property tax disputes in an attempt to resolve issues prior to formal hearings, at no charge.*

Vermont

Department of Public Service
Consumer Affairs and Public Information
Deena Frankel, Director
112 State St., Drawer 20
Montpelier, VT 05620-2601
802-828-4021
fax 802-828-2342
frankel@psd.state.vt.us

Human Rights Commission
Robert Appel, Executive Director
135 State St., Drawer 33
Montpelier, VT 05633-6301
802-828-2480
fax 802-828-2481
robert.appel@state.vt.us
http://www.hrc.state.vt.us/mediation.htm
> *Provides conciliation and mediation services, at no cost to the parties, in cases falling within the Commission's jurisdiction. These include cases charging discrimination in housing and state employment and in the provision of services by businesses and government.*

Office of the Attorney General
Tim Tomasi
109 State St.
Montpelier, VT 05609-1001
802-828-3173
fax 802-828-3187
ttomasi@atg.state.vt.us

Vermont Family Court Mediation Program
Susan Fay, Director
32 Cherry St., Suite 400
Burlington, VT 05401
802-951-4049
VFCMP@mail.state.vt.us

Vermont Supreme Court
Office of the Court Administrator
Lee Suskin, Court Administrator

109 State Street
Montpelier, VT 05609-0701
802-828-3278
fax 802-828-3457
lee@supreme.crt.state.vt.us
> *Oversees court-related ADR, including family and civil court.*

Woodbury College
Dispute Resolution Center
Neal Rodar, Director
660 Elm St.
Montpelier, VT 05602
800-820-0442
nealr@woodbury-college.edu
http://www.woodbury-college.edu/drc/
> *In addition to mediation services, the Woodbury Dispute Resolution Center also offers meeting facilitation, program consultation, training and workshops.*

Virginia

Department of Employment Dispute Resolution
Claudia T. Farr, Director
One Capitol Square
830 E. Main St., Ste. 400
Richmond, VA 23219
804-786-7994
fax 804-786-0100
administrator@edr.virginia.gov
http://www.edr.state.va.us/
> *Provides comprehensive conflict resolution services to state agencies and their employees. Administers the state's workplace mediation program and employee grievance procedure, conducts training in conflict resolution, mediation, and the grievance procedure, and provides one-to-one consultations with agency managers and employees in managing and resolving employment issues.*

Supreme Court of Virginia
Department of Dispute Resolution
Geetha Ravindra, Director
Office of the Secretary
100 North Ninth Street
Richmond, VA 23219

804-786-6455
fax 804-786-4760
GRavindra@courts.state.va.us

Responsible for developing court-annexed alternative dispute resolution processes and programs. Oversee the training, certification, and recertification of certified mediators and mediation training programs. Educate the Judiciary and Bar on the value of ADR and provide technical assistance to courts implementing new programs. Seek and administer funding for court-annexed mediation programs.

University of Virginia
Institute for Environmental Negotiation
Frank Dukes, Director
164 Rugby Road
Charlottesville, VA 22903
434-924-1970
ed7k@unix.mail.virginia.edu
http://www.virginia.edu/~envneg/IEN_home.htm

Works with localities, state and federal agencies, citizen organizations, and businesses to resolve conflicts and build consensus for complex policy choices involving land use and the natural and built environment. IEN is affiliated with the Department of Urban and Environmental Planning in the University of Virginia School of Architecture.

Virginia Interagency ADR Advisory Council
The Honorable Sandra D. Bowen,
Secretary of Administration (Council Chair)
Patrick Henry Building, Third Floor
1111 East Broad Street
Richmond, VA 23219
804-786-1201
fax 804-371-0038
secadmin@governor.virginia.gov
http://www.vadra.virginia.gov

As charged by the Virginia Administrative Dispute Resolution Act, provides guidance and training to state agencies in using collaborative practices and ADR across a broad range of governmental functions. Composed of private sector members appointed by the Governor, agency representatives appointed by each Cabinet Secretary, and liaison representatives from the Office of the Attorney General.

Virginia Office of the Attorney General
Richard Campbell, Solicitor General
900 Main St.
Richmond, VA 23219
804-786-0083
fax 804-371-0200
Rcampbell@oag.state.va.us

Washington

Central Puget Sound Growth Management Hearings Board
900 4th Ave, Suite 2470
Seattle, WA 98161
206-389-2625
fax 206-389-2588
central@cps.gmhb.wa.gov
> *Mediation services are provided to parties before the boards concerning land use planning disputes. Each board serves a geographic area of the state. The mediation service is provided by board members in three geographic areas.*

Department of Health
Office of Professional Standards
Eric Schmidt Sr., Health Law Judge
P.O. Box 47879
Olympia, WA 98504-7879
206-389-2600
fax 360-236-4677
pam.mena@doh.wa.gov
> *Provides mediation services to health profession licensees concerning disciplinary and licensing hearings. These mediators are also used for workplace disputes within the agency. Mediation is provided by hearing officers.*

Department of Social and Health Services
Interagency Mediation Project
Jack W. Lien, Contracts Consultant, Liaison
P.O. Box 45811
Olympia, WA 98504-5811
360-664-6056
lienjw@dshs.wa.gov

Eastern Growth Management Hearings Board
15 West Yakima, Suite 102
Yakima, WA 98901
509-574-6960
fax 509-574-6964
aandreas476@ew.gmhb.wa.gov

> *Mediation services are provided to parties before the boards concerning land use planning disputes. Each board serves a geographic area of the state. The mediation service is provided by board members in three geographic areas.*

Environmental Hearings Office
Phyllis MacLeod, Administrative Appeals Judge
P.O. Box 40903
Olympia, WA 98504-0903
360-493-9223
eho@eho.wa.gov
http://www.eho.wa.gov

> *Mediation available for environmental disputes within the Board's jurisdiction. Mediation provided by hearing officers.*

Natural Resources Leadership Academy
Washington State University
Michael Gaffney, Associate Director
Cooperative Extension Program
P.O. Box 644870
Pullman, WA 99164
509-335-3329
fax 509-335-2362
mjgaffney@wsu.edu

> *The Pacific Northwest Natural Resources Leadership Academy provides training in collaborative leadership skills to state and federal resource protection and program/policy professionals involving interest based problem solving, collaboration, group facilitation, community oriented resource protection modeling and advanced communication skills.*

Office of Community Development
Growth Management Division
Ike Nwankwo, Interim Managing Director
P.O. Box 48300
Olympia, WA 98504-8300

360-725-3056
Iken@cted.wa.gov
> *Provides mediation services to state agencies, communities and local governments in disputes concerning comprehensive growth plans, county-wide planning and urban growth areas. Mediation is also available through referral.*

Office of the Attorney General
Mary Barrett, Senior Assistant Attorney General
P.O. Box 40100
Olympia, WA 98504-0100
360-664-2475
fax 360-586-7671
maryb@atg.wa.gov
> *Participates in interagency mediation project that provides mediation services for workplace disputes by using a shared mediator pool comprised of trained mediators from participating state agencies. Informal resolution services for "lemon law" complaints through statewide network of Consumer Resource Centers. Early Resolution Project authorizes expedited resolution of tort claims/cases through direct negotiation and ADR bypassing the litigation track.*

Personnel Appeals Board
Don Bennett, Executive Secretary
P.O. Box 40911
Olympia, WA 98504-0911
360-664-0373
info-pab@pab.state.wa.us
http://www.wa.gov/pab/process.htm
> *Mediation is required for state civil service employee appeals. Mediators provide services under contract.*

Western Washington Growth Management Hearings Board
Les Eldridge, Board Member
905 24th Way SW, Suite B-2
P.O. Box 40953
Olympia, WA 98504-0953
360-664-8966
fax 360-664-8975
western@ww.gmhb.wa.gov/
http://www.gmhb.wa.gov

> *Mediation services are provided to parties before the boards concerning land use planning disputes. Each board serves a geographic area of the state. The mediation service is provided by board members in three geographic areas.*

WSU-UW Policy Consensus Center
Washington State University
Rob McDaniel, Co-Director
Hulbert Hall 215
PO Box 646230
Pullman, WA 99164-6230
509-335-2937
fax 509-335-2959
mcdaniel@wsu.edu
http://depts.washington.edu/wsuuwpcc/
> *A service and research program housed within the Daniel J. Evans School of Public Affairs at the University of Washington.*

WSU-UW Policy Consensus Center
University of Washington
Jon Brock, Co-Director
406 Parrington Hall, Box 353055
Seattle, WA 98195-3055
206-543-7958
fax 206-543-1096
jbrock@u.washington.edu
http://depts.washington.edu/wsuuwpcc/
> *As a joint effort of Washington State University and the University of Washington, the Center's mission is to act as a neutral resource for collaborative problem solving in the region. The Center provides expertise that improves the availability and quality of voluntary collaborative approaches to policy development and multi-party dispute resolution. Center services include conflict assessment and neutral forums; capacity building activities such as training and systems design; and research that frames issues and advances the effectiveness of collaborative processes.*

Wisconsin

Wisconsin Department of Natural Resources
101 S. Webster Street
Madison, WI 53707
608-267-7151

The Department has a staff specialist on collaborative-based problem solving, facilitation, and conflict resolution. ADR clients are internal staff teams or groups, as well as committees made up of stakeholders from the private, non-profit, and state/local government sectors.

Wisconsin Waste Facility Siting Board
Patti Cronin, Executive Director
201 W. Washington Ave
Madison, WI 53703
608-267-7854
fax 608-267-3770
patti.cronin@wfs.state.wi.us

By law, the Board oversees mandatory negotiation for every new and expanded solid and hazardous facility in the state. The Board negotiates/mediates/arbitrates social and economic issues while regulatory issues, which are not negotiable, are handled by the Department of Natural Resources.

Wyoming

University of Wyoming
Institute for Environment and Natural Resources
Harold Bergman, Director
P.O. Box 3971
Laramie, WY 82071-3971
307-766-5080
fax 307-766-5099
ienr@uwyo.edu
http://www.uwyo.edu/enr/ienr/Projects/collab.asp

The Institute for Environment and Natural Resources (IENR) helps to assure informed decision-making on environmental and natural resource issues affecting the West by promoting collaborative approaches that sustain both the economy and the environment.

Conclusion

Thus, one may conclude that mediation is becoming extremely important, and the role of this profession will increase. In such a situation, it is quite easy to enter this profession with the correct training and knowledge. To achieve respect and high earnings, a mediator needs to get trained, work hard, seek coaching/mentoring, constantly progress and constantly learn much about the field of mediation. When these conditions mentioned above are fulfilled, a mediator can count for a well-paid profession.

So You Want To Be
an Arbitrator

Objective
To explore the requirements for becoming an
arbitrator and identify immediate avenues for
entering the arbitration profession.

Introduction

Law is a valuable career with various sides and aspects. Arbitration is a very important area of law. Arbitrators are neutral third parties in hearing cases where a dispute takes place, whether it occurred between employers and employees or between relatives, friends, and neighbors. Arbitrators are chosen to settle issues between parties engaged in a dispute. Under such circumstances, firms, couples searching for a divorce, and other disputing parties are able to resolve their disputes out of court. This is one of the main advantages of arbitration. The arbitration service reduces the quantity of cases in the court system. Besides, it is far cheaper than the services of a litigator or trial attorney to handle the case in court.

Today, many companies fully understand the value of arbitrators' services and, accordingly, are constantly searching for highly qualified and experienced people. Thus, arbitration is perceived to be a faster and less expensive service in comparison to litigation. The other advantage of arbitration is that people who cannot afford to pay a litigator to get their case heard may use the services of an arbitrator. Arbitration allows getting a day in court for everyone who is involved in arbitration. There are two types of arbitration—binding and non-binding—but usually the decision is binding, which means that an appeal is impossible. In general, the disputing parties involved in the case allow arbitrators to decide the fate of their case (Marshall, n. d.).

The task of this chapter is to identify the role of an arbitrator, describe the needed skills and education, identify organizations that provide arbitration training programs, and state the advantages of arbitration over litigation. This chapter also discusses likely income and career outlook.

What Is an Arbitrator?

Arbitration is perhaps the most widespread field applying Alternative Dispute Resolution (ADR) techniques. It has been stated, "For an arbitrator goes by the equity of a case, a judge by the law, and arbitration was invented with the express purpose of securing full power for equity" (Smith, 1998). Today, arbitration "typically contains the essential elements of court adjudication: proofs and arguments are submitted to a neutral third party who has the power to issue a binding decision" (Goldberg, Sander, and Rogers, 1992).

In the process of arbitration, disputing parties submit their dispute to one or more impartial persons, known as arbitrators, who will make a final and binding decision to solve the dispute (Marshall, n. d.). The arbitrators are able to resolve conflicts outside of the court system. The arbitrator helps opposing parties find a mutual decision to handle their disputes. Arbitrators develop knowledge in a certain field—such as contract law, divorce and other relationship disputes, residential problems, and others. They hear both sides of the dispute and make a decision after carefully weighing the evidence.

There are two types of arbitration—binding or non-binding. Binding arbitration is similar to an order in court. Binding arbitration is almost always voluntary and private. It is usually used by private parties to commercial disputes. During the process of binding arbitration, a judgment is made by a third party to settle a dispute between two other parties, and the judgment is obligatory (both parties agree in advance to abide by the result). In non-binding arbitration, parties or their representatives present a dispute to an impartial, or neutral, individual for issuance of an advisory, or non-binding, decision (i.e., the parties do not have to accept the opinion). The parties have the ability to choose an arbitrator or panel with some expertise and knowledge in the disputed issues.

What Are the Different Career Choices For Prospective Arbitrators?

Dispute resolution methods can be applied to solve all dispute types. Any individual, company, organization, corporation, agency, government, or country can solve any dispute by making the choice of arbitration to decide the problem. The following are the most common types of disputes decided through the process of arbitration, which provide various career choices for prospective arbitrators: business disputes, property disputes, entertainment disputes, debt problems, financial disputes, investment services, corporate problems, international disputes, discrimination, construction claims, and architect problems (*Overview of Dispute Resolution Methods*, n. d.).

Why Do People Prefer Arbitration Over Litigation?

Arbitration offers some important advantages over litigation. First of all, arbitration is less expensive than litigation. Ordinary arbitration costs include reasonable filing and hearing fees. Businesses generally pay for all—or the biggest part—of the arbitration expenditures for consumers, employees, and patients. Besides, the whole process of arbitration is simpler and can be more effective than litigation since arbitration provides parties with a unique possibility for civil justice.

The most evident difference between an arbitrator and a litigator is that litigators are attorneys who practice law in the courtroom. As it was already mentioned, arbitrators work outside the courtroom. Litigation can involve years and many thousands of dollars to resolve disputes, and even then appeals may take more court time and money. For instance, "the average civil lawsuit takes two years or more to conclude in court, while arbitrations average eight to nine months" (*Fair Play*, 2003).

It is known that arbitration is private and, thus, the participants must pay the expenses. A person looking for justice is far better off paying $2,000 in forum expenses and $10,000 in legal fees for arbitration than paying almost nothing in forum expenses but paying $20,000 in legal fees (*Fair Play*, 2003). Most business clients prefer arbitration over litigation for the same reasons—it is fast, cheap, and confidential (*Arbitration of Business Disputes*, n. d.).

All this proves that arbitration is a wonderful alternative—it eliminates litigation, expensive fees, and the waste of valuable time. Arbitrators work to facilitate the problems resulting from litigation and the court system. Additionally, many people do not trust for the court system because so many injustices which they believe have arisen in the court system. Arbitration gives both sides an option to have their day in court and obtain the justice they deserve.

Advantages of Arbitration

To summarize, arbitrations are quicker and more cost-effective than court trials, usually taking less than six months from the beginning to the end of the process, and costing probably half as much as a civil trial (*Arbitration of Business Disputes*, n. d.). Besides, these are private forums—so competitors and the public cannot access information and testimony that the parties may not want to make public (Choong, 2004). Arbitration allows both sides to get their day in court (Chou, 2002). It "offers affordable, substantial, measurable, due process" (*Fair Play*, 2003). It requires limited exchanges of documentation and information. Arbitration may allow people who are not financially able to hire a litigator to get justice. After the end of the arbitration process, all parties preserve business relationships.

How Much Do Arbitrators Earn?

In 2002, arbitrators earned an average of $47,320 (*Judges, Magistrates, and Other Judicial Workers*, 2004). For example, hearing arbitration cases with a disputed amount of $1,000 warrants a $2,500 fee for the arbitrator. In a case where the dispute sum is $20,000, the arbitrator who took that case will receive at least $2,500 and no more than $3,400, and even if the disputed sum is as little as $50 the arbitrator is guaranteed to get $2,500 (Marshall, n. d.). Thus, the disputed sum defines how much an arbitrator can charge, according to the International Court of Arbitration. In the Nationla Association of Securities Dealers (NASD), for instance, arbitrators are not employees but they get an honorarium at the rate of $200 per single-session hearing and))400 per double session, where a single session hearing lasts up to four hours and a double-session lasts for more than four hours, with hearings averaging about two-and-a-half days (*Become an Arbitrator*, 2005). Compensation for services on cases resolved without an in-person hearing is $125 per case.

What Is the Career Outlook for an Arbitrator?

According to the U.S. Department of Labor's *Occupational Outlook Handbook* (2004), "employment of arbitrators is expected to grow as fast as the average for all occupations through 2012." Many individuals and businesses intend to reduce litigation, which can cause many delays, expensive costs, and unwelcome publicity. Arbitration and other alternatives to litigation generally are quicker, less expensive, and more final, encouraging the demand for the arbitrators' services. In the year 1999, arbitrators accounted for about 6,260 jobs in the USA (*Judges, Magistrates, and Other Judicial Workers*, 2004).

The rising cost of litigation connected with labor-management disputes may encourage a demand for labor relations workers who can assist in solving these disputes out of court (*Job Profile*, 2005). Besides, legal arbitrator training is useful in many other professions, such as lawyer, patent agent, journalist, legislative assistant, title examiner, and lobbyist. Other workers with expertise and skills in interpersonal relations—including counselors, sociologists, psychologists, social workers, teachers, and public relations specialists—are also in demand as arbitrators.

What Skills and Education Does One Need to Become an Arbitrator?

In general, there are no definite qualifications to become a private arbitrator. Most people in this area have a bachelor's degree. The educational requirements for lawyers include "a four-year college degree, three years in law school, and successful completion of a written bar examination" (*Job Profile*, 2005). Degrees in similar fields, such as public policy and law, can provide a background for prospective arbitrators. For example, an evident background in law and industrial relations is highly desirable. A prospective arbitrator must be able to "cope with conflicting points of view, function under pressure, and demonstrate discretion, integrity, fair-mindedness, and a persuasive, congenial personality" (*Job Profile*, 2005). In addition, an arbitrator must have research and writing skills and be able to speak easily and with authority. The ability to analyze and think logically are also required.

Many U.S. states demand that arbitrators have at least five years active experience in the state bar, with a focus on civil litigation. Retired judges are often qualified for the position of an arbitrator. But some states demand potential arbitrators, lawyers, and judges take part in training and orientation programs.

What Organizations Provide Arbitration Training Programs?

No definite statement can be made in regard to the requisite credentials or experience of arbitrators, but some jurisdictions have developed standards for arbitrators in definite fields. There are special training programs for becoming an arbitrator, available through independent arbitration programs, national and local arbitration membership organizations, and postsecondary schools. One of the most popular arbitrator training programs is offered by the American Arbitration Association. The American Arbitration Association (AAA) demands that people seeking an AAA certification finish an AAA training course, obtain recommendations from trainers, and complete an apprenticeship.

In 2002, 16 colleges or universities in the USA offered master's degrees in dispute resolution or conflict management, and 8two of them offered doctoral degrees (*Judges, Magistrates, and Other Judicial Workers*, 2004). Other schools offered conflict management specializations within other degree programs. Degrees in law, public policy, and related areas are an advantage for prospective arbitrators.

NASD, Inc. (formerly known as the National Association of Securities Dealers) is the primary Self Regulatory Organization (SRO) responsible for the regulation of persons and companies involved in the securities industry in the United States, with delegated authority from the Securities and Exchange Commission. NASD Dispute Resolution also conducts several advanced arbitrator training courses online at http://www.nasd.com/. Other arbitrator training programs include Settlement Now and Entry and Fellowship Level Training, Chartered Institute of Arbitrators (London). Other ADR programs are sponsored by the American Bar Association (http://www.abanet.org/), the King County Bar Association, the Washington State Bar Association, and the Society of Professionals in Dispute Resolution (SPIDR) (http://www.spidr.org/). NFA (National Futures Association) also provides arbitrator training programs in many U.S. cities.

The New York Stock Exchange (NYSE), nicknamed the "Big Board," is a New York City-based, privately-owned stock exchange. It is the largest stock exchange in the world by dollar volume and the second largest by number of companies listed. The New York Stock Exchange (NYSE) is another forum offering arbitrator training seminars.

Contact Information for Arbitration Training Courses

ADR **Works**
4 Cannon Court
Whitby ON, L1N 5V8
Phone: 905-430-8880
Fax: 905-430-0772
AJAX line: 905-428-8000
Toronto: 416-492-0989
http://www.adrworks.com/

> *There is no specific pre-requisite for taking this course. Usually almost half of the students are lawyers with most of the rest being professionals or business people. Many students are accountants, engineers, architects or real estate brokers and appraisers. Many students are people who have retired or hope to retire but still earn good income from occasional work where they can apply the skills and experiences developed in their careers. Some of our students have been able to obtain jobs and even judicial appointments with this course being a qualifying factor. Please call directly to Murray Miskin at 905-428-8000 to discuss whether the course is right for you. The course is also of great assistance as a skill and confidence builder for non-lawyer Mediators who require more legal training.*

Arbitration Certification Program
1625 North Market Blvd. Ste. N112
Sacramento, CA 95834
916-574-7350 or 800-952-5210
acp@dca.ca.gov

> *The Department of Consumer Affairs' Arbitration Certification Program (ACP) certifies and monitors third-party arbitration programs of participating automobile manufacturers to ensure compliance with California laws and regulations governing resolution of warranty disputes involving new/ used vehicles purchased with the manufacturer's new-car warranty.*

Arbitration/Mediation Section
(Condominiums, Cooperatives, and Homeowners' Associations)
1940 N. Monroe Street
Northwood Centre, Suite 16
Tallahassee, FL 32399-1029
Karl M. Scheuerman, Lead Attorney
Condominium/Cooperative Inquiries—Phone: 850-414-6867
Homeowner Association Inquiries—Phone: 850-488-1122 Fax: 850-487-0870

Mediator and Arbitrator Certification Programs
Under the new law, the Department is required to establish mediator and arbitrator certification programs for use in the new mediation and arbitration programs administered by the Division.

Certification requirements. The current certification requirements are contained in section 720.311(2)(c), Florida Statutes, as amended by Section 23 of Chapter 2004-345, Laws of Florida.

In order to be certified as an arbitrator or mediator a person must:
1. *Attend 20 hours of training in mediation or arbitration;*
2. *Have mediated or arbitrated at least 10 disputes involving community associations within 5 years of applying for certification; or*
3. *Have mediated or arbitrated at least 10 disputes in any area within 5 years prior to the date of application; and*
4. *Have completed 20 hours of training in community association disputes.*

Arbitration Forums
3350 Buschwood Park Drive
Bldg. 3 Suite 295
Tampa, FL 33618
888-272-3453
Fax: 813-931-4618
Betty Jo Shaw, Special Product Manager, 864-878-3523
Rob Reynolds, Special Product Sales Manager, 859-523-2725
http://www.arbfile.org/webapp/pgStatic/content/pgBecomeArbitrator.jsp

Better Business Bureau
AUTOLINE
4200 Wilson Blvd., Suite 800
Arlington, VA 22203-1804
800-955-5100
> *AM General (Hummer), General Motors (includes Buick, Cadillac, Chevrolet, GMC, Geo, Pontiac, Oldsmobile), Honda/Acura, Hyundai, Isuzu, Kia, Land Rover, Nissan/Infiniti, Peugeot, Porsche, Rolls Royce/Bentley, Saab, Saturn, Volkswagen/Audi.*

Customer Arbitration Board
Northern California
DaimlerChrysler
Customer Arbitration
P.O. Box 280400
San Francisco, CA 94128-0400
800-279-5343

Southern California
P.O. Box 885
La Mirada, CA 90637
800-279-5343
Chrysler (includes Dodge, Eagle, Jeep, Plymouth)

Construction Dispute Resolution Training Institute
Email: cdrs@cdrsllc.com
Office Phone: 505-474-9050
toll free 888-930-0011
Phone/Fax: 505-474-9061
http://www.constructiondisputes-cdrs.com/index.htm

Course Content: The history of arbitration, all of the procedures involved in the arbitration process including, but not limited to: claims and counterclaims, pleadings and opening statements, discovery, witnesses and depositions, examinations and cross examinations, motions, closing statements, post-hearing briefs, arbitration award, appeals and award enforcement, arbitration administration, pre-hearing conferences, ex parte communications, the New Mexico Arbitration Act and the Federal Arbitration Act, confidentiality and neutrality, challenges to the arbitration, arbitration disclosure and disqualification, arbitration ethics, legal and professional standards that apply to arbitrations, how to decide matters based on impartiality and on the evidence provided, mediation-arbitration-litigation will be discussed as to their proper application to the dispute resolution process, power imbalance, the role of attorneys, fairness to the parties, the Construction Dispute Resolution Services, LLC "Arbitration Rules and Procedures" will be thoroughly reviewed along with other procedural and legal issues related to the arbitration process, and much, much more.

Arbitrain Training Systems
1325 Airmotive Way
Reno, NV 89502
Phone/Fax: 775-562-8067
answers@arbitrain.com
http://www.arbitrain.com

Certification Training For Debt Arbitration Professionals

Arbitrain Training Systems provides this industry standard in Professional Debt Settlement Training to associates in all parts of the U.S. and Canada. The training is based on proven methods and techniques used everyday by graduates of Arbitrain training program and Associates of leading Debt Management firms. Professional Debt Arbitration is a multi-billion dollar industry. There are literally tens of thousands of unresolved Debt disputes. Until now, the parties involved had no option, other than to be dragged into the process of litigation (court) to try and salvage whatever possible. Professional Debt Arbitration is the alternative.

NASD **Dispute Resolution, A Division of** NASD
One Liberty Plaza
165 Broadway, 27th Floor
New York, NY 10006
http://www.nasd.com/
Margaret Duzant at 212-858-4310

Arbitrator Recruitment

Serving as an NASD Dispute Resolution Arbitrator

The success of securities arbitration depends on the quality of the arbitrators who hear and decide the disputes presented by the parties. If you qualify, you will join a group of dedicated individuals serving the investing public and the securities industry.

Members of NASD's Dispute Resolution arbitrator roster come from a broad cross-section of people, diverse in culture, profession and background. Our goal is to recruit arbitrators from different backgrounds, such as educators, accountants, medical professionals and others, as well as lawyers and securities professionals. If you have at least five years of business or professional experience, you may qualify to serve on our roster. Please note that all applications are subject to approval to determine if your credentials match our needs. We require all approved applicants to successfully complete our mandatory training.

Applying to the Roster

You may download the Arbitrator Application Kit using the link below. NASD Dispute Resolution staff will conduct a preliminary review of your completed application before forwarding it to a subcommittee of the National Arbitration and Mediation Committee for final approval. The screening process generally takes 60 days. The tuition for our mandatory, basic arbitrator training program is $125.

FMCS **Institute for Conflict Management**
202-606-3627 or 206-553-2773

National Office
Federal Mediation and Conciliation Service
2100 K Street, NW
Washington, DC 20427
Phone: 202-606-8100 Fax: 202-606-4251

Eastern Region
Regional Director: Jack Buettner, jbuettner@fmcs.gov
6161 Oak Tree Boulevard, Suite 120
Independence, OH 44131
Phone: 216-520-4800 Fax: 216-520-4815
Field Station Responsibility:
Jack Sweeney, DMS, jsweeney@fmcs.gov, 732-726-3120
D. Scott Blake, DMS, sblake@fmcs.gov, 215-861-3355

Western Region
Regional Director: Dan O'Leary (Acting), doleary@fmcs.gov
908 North Elm Street, Suite 203
Hinsdale, IL 60521
Phone: 630-887-4750 Fax: 630-887-7183

Criteria for Being an Arbitrator on the FMCS Roster
Applicants for the FMCS Roster must demonstrate experience, competence, and acceptability in decision-making roles in the resolution of disputes arising from collective bargaining agreements. The Arbitrator Review Board, which is appointed by the Director of FMCS, reviews the qualifications of all applicants for listing on the Roster and recommends to the Director the acceptance or rejection of applicants for the Roster.

National Futures Association
200 W. Madison Street, Suite 1600
Chicago, IL 60606
http://www.nfa.futures.org/index.asp
Toll Free: 800-621-3570
Phone: 312-781-1410 Fax: 312-781-1467

Become an NFA Arbitrator
Arbitration is a popular dispute resolution alternative to time consuming and costly litigation. The success of NFA's arbitration program is directly tied to the quality of the individuals who serve as arbitrators. There are

currently over 2,400 individuals on the NFA roster. They come from various professions and walks of life, but the skills they share are integrity, impartiality and sound judgment. NFA also considers an individual's educational background and business experience. However, technical expertise in the commodity futures markets is not a requirement.

New York Stock Exchange
20 Broad Street
New York, NY 10005

All new arbitrators are required to attend an arbitrator training seminar. This requirement may be satisfied by attendance at a training program sponsored by another organization, subject to Exchange approval. The training program must include instruction in ethical considerations, arbitrator conduct and arbitration procedures. A certificate of attendance from the program is required. All arbitrators are expected to attend a training program every four years to keep current on the rules, procedures and other important changes.

Persons appointed to the Exchange's panel of arbitrators may be asked serve in an area near to where they live or work. Arbitrators receive an honorarium* of $400.00 per day ($475.00 for the Chair of the panel). The Exchange does not reimburse arbitrators for commuting expenses or overnight travel unless it requests the travel. Many cases are concluded in two days, but others may require several days of hearings.

Arbitrators are generally asked to serve once or twice each year depending on the geographic area and caseload. Arbitrators should not contact NYSE staff to obtain appointments. Arbitrators may decline to serve on any case if they are unavailable, cannot devote sufficient time, or if serving would constitute a conflict of interest.

* The honorarium is intended to cover arbitrators' incidental expenses.

Applying to be An Arbitrator
The New York Stock Exchange now allows potential arbitrator candidates to enter their biographical information via the secure Arbitrator/Mediator Profile Portal.

The portal will allow you to enter all information, including your address, education, employment history, background, brokerage accounts, and securities affiliations, directly into an electronic profile form. To access the portal, please forward to Tiwana Braddox, New York Stock Exchange, 20 Broad Street, New York, NY 10005, a cover letter with your name, address, social security number and e-mail address, two letters of recommendation, and copies of certificates of all securities related arbitration training courses you have taken.

Upon receipt of this information, the Exchange will send you a letter with your ID and password which will enable you to access the on-line portal. After the Exchange receives your electronic profile, you will be notified if your name has been added to the list of neutral arbitrators. We look forward to hearing from you and thank you for your interest in serving as a New York Stock Exchange arbitrator.

Who Hires Arbitrators?

Today, many employers fully understand the value of arbitration for the workplace in their companies. Various companies are currently searching for arbitrators—from retail to construction and insurance to medical firms.

Usually, an arbitrator works in private offices or meeting rooms and out of court. As mentioned above, arbitrators held 6,260 jobs in 1999. About half of them were employed by state and local governments. The rest worked for labor organizations, insurance carriers, law offices, other private firms, and organizations that specialize in offering dispute resolution services.

So, to become a private arbitrator or to work for a certain company, such as private organizations, public organizations or governmental agencies is quite possible. Besides, in most U.S. states, individuals who provide private mediation services are not required to get a license, certification, or specific course work. But those private arbitrators who seek to increase their market and the majority of those affiliated with such large arbitration organizations as the American Arbitration Association (AAA) or the International Chamber of Commerce Arbitration (http://www.iccwbo.org/), Judicial Arbitration and Mediation Services, Inc. (JAMS), or Arts Arbitration and Mediation Services, have completed arbitration training courses and agreed to fulfill certain ethical requirements.

Arbitration is a procedure that can be helpful between private individuals, states, and private individuals. In the case of arbitration between states, or between states and individuals, the Permanent Court of Arbitration and the International Center for the Settlement of Investment Disputes (ICSID) are the predominant organizations (*Arbitration,* 2005). It would be useful to try to become the arbitrator of such reputable organizations.

The National Arbitration Forum is another leading arbitration provider in the USA, and it is a potential employer. Arbitration also takes place in international sport through the Court of Arbitration for Sport, also a possible choice for the prospective arbitrator.

An increasing tendency among employers whose employees are not represented by a labor union is to organize an internal problem-solving process, the final stage of which includes arbitration of the problem completed by an independent arbitrator. These internal processes employ arbitrators to resolve different employee grievances in regard to "application of employer policies or claims of employee misconduct" (*Arbitration,* 2005).

Some labor unions and employers are often called to employ arbitration specialists to resolve employee complaints appearing under a collective bargaining agreement.

Generally, the majority of standard customer agreements determine which forums will be allowable for arbitration of customer grievances. There are several brokerage firms which belong to determine the American Arbitration Association (AAA) as an allowable forum for the arbitration process of customer complaints grievances.

Among these forums are the prestigious NASD and the NYSE, which hire independent arbitrators. NASD Dispute Resolution is the largest forum for dispute resolution in the U.S. securities industry and handles over 90% of all securities arbitration claims filed by customers of brokerage companies, as well as brokerage companies and their employees (*Become an Arbitrator,* 2005). NASD Dispute Resolution offers assistance with the help of neutral and highly qualified arbitrators to assist in keeping its fair, impartial, and effective dispute resolution system. NASD arbitrators are attentively chosen among many people, different in profession, background and culture. Disputes with the participation of an investor demands that most of the arbitrators did not belong to the securities sphere. The purpose of the company is to employ arbitrators from various backgrounds. This can be accountants, educators, lawyers, business and securities professionals, and many others.

Conclusion

The career of an arbitrator can be prestigious and highly paid—especially if a candidate is a person interested in the field of alternative dispute resolution. Arbitration is a process for those who cannot spend the time or money on litigation to obtain justice. Moreover, there is not just one winner in this process, and each person is still able to receive their day in court. As more companies appreciate the value of arbitrators, the demand for arbitrators will increase. Many colleges, universities, and law schools—seeing the potential in the arbitration profession—have introduced special arbitrator courses and programs that will help train future arbitrators.

Finding an ADR Job

Objective
This chapter will explore other opportunities available
that primarily require conflict resolution skills.

Introduction

If the thought of going it alone or working for yourself as an ADR practitioner makes you nervous, there is another avenue. Everyday, there are countless job opportunities within the field. This chapter will help you to uncover these hidden opportunities to participate in the wonderful world of ADR by working for someone else.

There are nine steps to finding an Alternative Dispute Resolution job, which will be explored in detail throughout this chapter. The steps are as follows:

1. Explore career options
2. Find current job opportunities
3. Network
4. Write a resume or curriculum vitae (CV)
5. Write cover letters
6. Research potential employers
7. Interview

8. Follow up
9. Get hired

Explore Career Options

There are several other career choices in the dispute resolution field to consider. In this section we will explore the job titles of various opportunities within the ADR field. Below are thirty representative job titles in the field of ADR, along with a brief job description, experience required, and income. You should select several from this list that appear to be of interest to you before moving on through the rest of this chapter. The list follows:

Alternative Dispute Resolution Specialist

These individuals develop agency ADR programs; develop innovative dispute resolution models and techniques; conduct and/or acquire mediation and negotiation training for agency officials as well as outside participants.

Experience: Varies.
Income: Varies.

Customer Service Dispute Representative

Position is responsible to handle incoming phone calls from cardholders with questions regarding potential disputes with their credit or debit card. The position is responsible for the cardholder dispute process as outlined according to Visa and MasterCard rules and according to Federal Regulations.

Experience: High School education or equivalent, 1+ years customer service experience.
Income: Varies.

Dispute Relationship Manager

Assist the Customer with billing inquiries by communicating with external banks, processing charge-backs, contacting merchants and reviewing general ledger accounts.

Experience: High School education or equivalent, 2–5+ years customer service experience.
Income: Varies.

Administrative Judge

Sometimes called hearing officers or adjudicators, are employed by government agencies to make determinations for administrative agencies. These judges make decisions, for example, on a person's eligibility for various Social Security or workers' compensation benefits, on protection of the environment, on the enforcement of health and safety regulations, on employment discrimination, and on compliance with economic regulatory requirements.

Experience: A minimally-qualified applicant must have at least 7–10 years of work experience in a field or fields directly related.

Income: $95,500–$135,000 per year.

Immigration Judge

The Immigration Judge presides in formal, quasi-judicial hearings. Proceedings before Immigration Judges include but are not limited to deportation, exclusion, removal, rescission, and bond. The Immigration Judge makes decisions, which are final unless formally appealed.

Experience: Applicants must have an LL.B. or a J.D. degree and be duly licensed and authorized to practice law as an attorney under the laws of a state, territory, or the District of Columbia (include date of admission to bar). Applicants must be U.S. citizens and have a minimum of 7 years of relevant post-bar admission legal experience at the time the application is submitted.

Income: $109,720–$149,200 per year.

Arbitrator

Conduct hearings that are private and confidential, and the processes are less formal than a court trial.

Experience: Minimum qualifications would be a high school diploma.

Income: Median income of $54,760 per year.

Asylum Officer

These individuals make final determinations on application for both asylum and withholding of deportation. They serve as the final Immigration and Naturalization Service signatory authority for the adjudication of asylum applications.

Experience: Varies.

Income: Varies.

Consultant

A specialist in their particular profession that advises others.

Experience: Varies.

Income: Varies.

Industrial Relations Specialist

Industrial relations officers aim to encourage employees and employers to work toward effective organizational practices. They may represent industrial, commercial, union, employer or other organizations in industrial negotiations.

Experience: Varies.

Income: $50,000+ per year.

Convenor/Facilitator

A neutral called a convenor studies regulatory issues, attempts to identify the potentially affected interests, and then advises the agency concerning the feasibility of convening representatives of these interests to negotiate a proposed rule.

A neutral called a facilitator manages the meetings and coordinates discussions among the parties.

Experience: Varies.

Income: Varies.

Mediation Program Specialist

Provides a wide range of administrative specialist support duties for the mediator cadre, including preparing training material to educate customers regarding alternative dispute resolution principles and practices.

Experience: One year of experience which must have equipped the applicant with the particular knowledge, skills, and abilities to successfully perform the duties of the position.

Income: $36,671.00–$56,822.00 per year.

Housing Referral Assistant

The primary purpose of this position is to obtain community support for off-base housing; mediate landlord/tenant complaints; provide relocation assistance; and investigate reports of alleged discrimination in off-base housing.

Experience: One year of experience which must have equipped the applicant with the particular knowledge, skills, and abilities to successfully perform the duties of the position.

Income: $31,209 per year–$40,569 per year.

Equal Employment Specialist

This position involves nurturing employer-employee relations that contribute to satisfactory productivity, motivation, morale, and discipline. They provide guidance, consultation and assistance to management and employees on employees relations matters and advise on grievances and appeals, adverse actions, employee discipline and related matters.

Experience: One year of experience which must have equipped the applicant with the particular knowledge, skills, and abilities to successfully perform the duties of the position.

Income: $43,336.00–$56,342.00 per year.

Administrative Assistant, Manhattan Mediation Center

Assist the director in the daily activities of the mediation center. Ordering, distributing and keeping inventory of all supplies for main site and community site. Assisting Director in coordinating services for mediators to include coverage for all types of cases, maintaining an updating directory of mediators and trainees.

Experience: High school diploma/GED and three years of related experience or Associate Degree and two years of related experience.

Income: Mid to high $20k's.

Human Resources Assistant (Labor Relations)

Conducts technical and administrative research for and assists the negotiations team, on special projects and in resolving a variety of issues relating to grievances.

Experience: One year of specialized experience at a level close to the work of this job that has given you the particular knowledge, skills, and abilities required to successfully perform.

Income: $40,612.00–$52,794.00 per year.

Executive Director

The Executive Director is responsible for the overall direction and management of the organization's programs, services, resource development, finances, personnel, contracts, and assets in accordance with the organizational mission and operational policies. The Executive Director will spend the majority of his/her time on business strategy and external relations, relying on highly skilled programmatic staff to focus on day-to-day program delivery.

Experience: The ideal candidate will have a track record of successful and progressively responsible experience in management, strategy, relationship building, marketing, and resource development.

Income: $30,000+ per year.

Labor Relations Specialist

Advises on collective bargaining and negotiation processes; dealings with National Labor Relations Board, Bureau of Mediation Services and other agencies. Participate in the development of bargaining strategy including research, salary and benefit analysis. Draw up or assist in drawing up labor agreements. Advise on the administration of labor agreements Create appropriate procedures for, and participates in, the grievance process. Conduct research; prepare briefs and other documents for arbitration cases and conduct presentations at arbitration or mediation proceedings.

Experience: Bachelor's degree in Industrial Relations, Business Administration, Human Resources Administration, Public Administration or related field. Four or more years of professional human resources experience, two of which must be in labor relations.

Income: $54,600–$81,900 per year.

Hearing and Appeals Officer

This position requires the adjudication of cases arising under Federal statutes or regulations or involve the conduct of appellate reviews of prior decisions.

Experience: Varies.

Income: $50,000+ per year.

Senior Paralegal/PIP Arbitration Specialist

Responsible for actively handling a caseload of PIP arbitration files from assignment to conclusion. This will include, but will not be limited to: preparing submissions and summaries to support defense of PIP hearings; preparing the case (witnesses, experts, and doctors, and submit documents for arbitration hearings) and making court appearances; appearing and arguing before PIP arbitrators. Perform/or appeals to the arbitrator; perform file reviews with the claims department prior to the assignment and/or will provide guidance and direction for handling the file.

Experience: Solid knowledge of PIP and procedural law combined with knowledge of medical terminology. Previous experience in preparing and attending PIP arbitration hearings and knowledge of arbitration procedures related to the insurance industry is required.

Income: $50,000+ per year.

Labor-Management Relations Examiner

These individuals supervise or perform investigations, evaluations and the resolution of cases involving charges of unfair labor practices collective-bargaining representation issues or disputes.

Experience: 3–5 years relevant experience.

Income: $47,000+ per year.

Mediator (Working for a Court System)

A neutral, third-party facilitator of negotiations. This is highly responsible work mediating cases referred by the court. The Mediator advises parties of the mediation process, assists parties in resolving disputes, and prepares settlement agreements for review by the Court and incorporation into orders, as appropriate. The Mediator is also responsible for maintaining required statistical data.

Experience: Minimum qualifications include proof of training certificate providing evidence of at least 52 hours of training.

Income: $45,000+ per year.

Professor of Conflict Studies

Specialist in conflict studies who has both analytical and practical skills, demonstrated by a record of excellence in academic publications and teaching, as well as international field experience.

Experience: The successful candidate must have a scholarly and teaching record sufficiently strong to gain tenure in the department of appointment. Applicants at the assistant professor level should demonstrate promise of building such a record.

Income: $27,000–$99,000 per year.

Ombudsman

A person who acts as an intermediary on behalf of a citizen complainant , assuring that complaints are acted upon or investigated in a timely fashion and provides information on complaint status to the citizen. Ombudsmen often become involved in negotiations to resolve citizen grievances against government agencies or other organizations that employ them (e.g., universities, healthcare organizations, auto manufacturers, etc.).

Experience: A bachelor's degree and they must have a history of positive and effective interactions with those at all levels of a corporation. In addition, they must possess an established reputation for integrity and for dealing fairly, comfortably, and responsibly with individuals in sensitive situations.

Income: $65,000+ per year.

Structured Settlements Professional

An expert consultant in the diverse means of structuring settlements, who typically is called upon to work with a neutral in assisting this disposition of a dispute. The Structure Settlements Professional is often brought in to offer creative options and help reestablish a dialogue when there is an impasse in the ADR proceeding.

Experience: Varies.

Income: Varies.

Full-Time Trainer

A person professionally trained in an area of alternative dispute resolution.

Experience: Minimum 2 years of experience in ADR.

Income: $75,000+ per year.

Assistant Conflict Specialist

Assistant Conflict Specialist will serve as a Project Assistant who will work collaboratively with other members of the team on complex, long- term conflict management projects.

Experience: An entry-level position for someone who has one to two years work experience and a master's degree in conflict resolution, environmental policy, psychology, communications, or organizational development or related field.

Income: $50,000+ per year.

Child Welfare/Permanency Planning Mediation

Part time/private contractors with masters level or higher in social work, psychology or related field.

Experience: Three years of full-time supervised work experience in the field of child welfare having direct experience with multi-problem, high-risk families involving issues related to child abuse, domestic violence and substance abuse and one year experience providing adoption-planning services for children in the foster care system.

Income: $70–$85 per hour.

Mediation Program Coordinator: Juvenile

Conduct case development of juvenile dependency cases and spearhead the development and coordination of an innovative "victim-offender" juvenile delinquency mediation program.

Experience: Possess an organized, efficient, and collaborative work style; strong verbal/written skills; proven administrative ability;

training in mediation/conflict resolution; experience in nonprofit or community services organizations; experience in the area of juvenile justice, youth and/or mediation programs; and word processing and database experience.

Income: $4,011–$5,015 per month.

Assistant/Associate Professor Dispute Resolution

Faculty teach a range of dispute resolution courses, conduct research, and usually engage in some form of conflict resolution intervention.

Experience: Have a doctorate or other terminal degree.

Income: $24,000–$104,000 per year.

No-Fault Arbitration & Litigation Adjusters

Knowledge of No-Fault Regulations, as well as familiarity of common court and/or arbitration decisions. Excellent written and verbal communication skills to effectively and professionally negotiate with attorneys and defend Company views in litigated matters.

Experience: Certified adjusters with 2–5 years experience.

Income: $23,000–$65,000.

Training & Facilitation Specialist

Key responsibilities in this position include moderating ongoing manager peer group meetings to aid clients in making business improvements and presenting workshops.

Experience: 7–10 years in education.

Income: $60,000+ per year.

The next step in finding an ADR job is to find current job opportunities within the field. Many sites will allow you to search for jobs and post your resume online, and they will alert you with an email when a job matches your skills. The following is a comprehensive list of online employment search engines.

National Job Search Engines

Monster.com is one of the best-known job search sites.

CareerBuilder.com is one of the largest job search, employment, and career sites.

HotJobs.com is Yahoo!'s popular job search site.

Idealist (http://www.idealist.org/) has connected millions of people with thousands of organizations around the world.

Craigslist.org is a great place to find jobs and you can also advertise your services for free.

America's Job Bank, at http://www.jobsearch.com/, also includes "Career Tools" to help you learn more about available jobs and the money you could earn in different occupations.

OPM.gov can help you find government positions.

Job Search Sites for Bilingual Speakers

Hispanic-Jobs.com will connect you with employers who are searching for bilingual and Spanish-speaking job seekers.

HireDiversity.com has resources for minority job seekers.

LatPro.org is a job board for Hispanic and bilingual job seekers, featuring employers who are dedicated to diversity.

Temporary, Part-Time, and Hourly Jobs

SnagAJob.com is for part-time and hourly positions.

Nettemps.com has postings for temporary jobs.

When using any of these search engines, use key words such as mediation, arbitration, conflict resolution, trainer, EEO, dispute resolution, mediator, arbitrator, alternative dispute resolution, facilitation, consultant, or any other words relevant to the ADR field.

Also, check with your local chamber of commerce to ask about career/job fairs that may be planned for the near future. Search the Chamber of Commerce International Directory for contact information at http://www.clickcity.com/.

Networking

Thirty years ago, the average professional remained with his or her company for a lifetime or changed jobs only once before retirement. Networking once consisted of trading business cards at cocktail parties, sporting events, or anywhere professionals gathered for social activities. Today, networking is a way of life. Companies estimate that they fill more than 25% of their open positions by networking.

Networking is defined in *Merriam Webster's Collegiate Dictionary (Tenth Edition)* as "the exchange of information or services among individuals, groups, or institutions." The prospect of changing jobs can be daunting, even for the most intrepid professionals. However, networking is not about gaining the confidence to call strangers and ask for a job. Networking is about collecting information, educating yourself about employment opportunities, increasing your list of professional contacts (who may be aware of employment opportunities), and informing them of your potential availability.

It is also a numbers game, and it is one you can win. The more people you contact, the higher the odds that you will gain access and exposure to a new career opportunity. But, to network successfully, you must communicate clearly and effectively to leave a good impression with every contact you make. Your success depends on personal commitment, dedication, and thorough follow-up. You must be prepared to devote at least one hour every day to your personal business task of finding a new job.

How to Network

Open your contact management system, Rolodex, or stack of business cards. Make a list of people to call—friends, professional colleagues, former supervisors, vendors, and social contacts. Everyone is a potential source of information or additional contacts. Do not be biased—use them all.

If you do not belong to a professional organization relevant to your field, consider joining one. These colleagues can be excellent sources for leads, contacts, and moral support. Another great source for leads and contacts can be found through employee-referral programs. Many companies offer their employees cash and other incentives for referring job candidates. These programs create win-win situations for you, your contact, and your contact's company.

The first call to a contact is your opportunity to introduce yourself and announce your availability. If you do not know the person you are calling, explain how you got their name and why you are calling. If the contact is too busy to talk to you, try to schedule another time to call. If the contact is resistant, do not pressure him. Thank the contact for his time, even if you believe the contact cannot help you in your present situation. The busy contact of today may be your ally tomorrow.

If the contact is willing to talk to you, thank them again and deliver your short speech about your background and interests.

A Sample Script for a First Call

Hello Bob, I am Mary Smith, former Senior Customer Service Specialist with ABC Company. I appreciate your taking the time to speak with me. John Doe gave me your name and indicated that you would be a good contact in my networking activities.

Is this a good time for us to talk or would you prefer that I call at a more convenient time?

By the way, John Doe has been very helpful to me. How did you come to know John? Well, let me get to the point of my call today. Due to a recent downsizing, I am taking this opportunity to evaluate other career opportunities. While at ABC Company, I supervised twelve junior specialists, successfully implemented a Total Quality Management process for the customer service department and developed and launched the customer dispute resolution program. I have 5 years of customer service experience and have spent three of those years as a proven leader and manager. I am searching for a career opportunity that will allow me to bring my business and dispute resolution approach to customer service and share my knowledge of mediation and management. I am open-minded about relocation, but would prefer to stay in the Northwest. Since I have direct experience working in both large and small companies, the size of the organization is not critical. Since my career is focused on management, I would like to continue in a management role.

Bob, what specific opportunities within your organization are you aware of that might fit my background and desires?

Record the information from your call in your contact management system. Contact all referrals gained from the first call. Be sure to leave clear personal or voice mail messages.

Follow-Up on Calls
Send the initial contact a typed letter that contains specific results from contacting each lead the contact provided. The letter might be written as follows:

Reference: Telephone Call of [Date] [Time]

Dear [Contact]:

Thank you for speaking with me the other day. The information you shared with me was both helpful and informative. I was able to call [ ], who sends his (her) regards to you. [ ] referred me to two more people and suggested that I contact ABC Company.

I left messages for both referrals and sent a resume to [ ], vice president of engineering at ABC Company.

I have taken the liberty of enclosing a copy of my resume. Please feel free to share it with any colleagues who may have an interest in my background.

If you are like most of my contacts, you probably thought of additional names or companies for me to contact. Therefore, I will call you in a few days to see whether you would be willing to share the information with me.

Once again, thank you for speaking to me. I look forward to our continued contact.

Sincerely,

Do not stop networking until you find the position that is right for you. When you find a new position, send a thank-you note to each person in your network and give each one your new contact information.

After you find the right position, continue networking. You may not be looking for a job, but others may be in the same position you were in only a short time ago. Take time out of your busy day to answer a networking call made to you. Networking depends on the courtesy and reciprocity given by busy professionals like you every day.

The next step is to prepare your resume and cover letter. Knowing what to include, what not to include, what to highlight, and what to de-emphasize is extremely important. Human resource professionals and hiring managers receive hundreds of resumés for any given position and, on average, they will spend about 10–30 seconds on yours. Organizing information incorrectly could cost you a shot at an interview.

Review job postings online and in the newspapers for positions that interest you, which you identified in the previous step. Each listing will almost always have a brief blurb about the company and the position available. Read the job description closely, and use the key words listed in these ads, matching them to the bullet points in your resumé. Chances are that you have some of these as key points already; however, if you have missed any, be sure to add them to your resumé. It sounds obvious, but it's worth mentioning that using a custom resumé instead of a generic one will greatly increase your chances of an interview, as you will be a better match in the eyes of the reader.

The accepted standard for a resumé is no more than two pages containing your professional experience in reverse chronological order. Deviations from this format may not be well received by human resource professionals.

Sample Resume

Name	E-mail: address@abc.com
Street Address	Office phone: (XXX) XXX-XXXX
City, State, Zip+4	Fax number: (XXX) XXX-XXXX

Objective
Note: Choose your words carefully. Be sure that your objective doesn't limit your prospects or contain jargon.

Education
Degree (spelled out), Institution, City, State.
Major and honors, if any.

Career Experience
Note: Present your experience in reverse chronological order. Describe your last ten years of experience in detail, even if it takes up to one and one-half pages to do so.

Company Name, City, State   *(19XX to present)*
Title   *(Dates in the position)*
Responsibilities include: primary and secondary responsibilities, title of the person you report to, number of direct and indirect reports, matrix management responsibility, budget responsibility, and external and internal interfaces.

Note: The reader should be able to determine the scope of your responsibilities in no more than four or five sentences.

Key Accomplishments
Note: For your most recent job title, include three to five bullet points outlining your key accomplishments. Your accomplishments should be as quantitative as possible. Don't forget to use power words such as "met, achieved, exceeded" and phrases such as "successfully developed and implemented."

♦ Saved the company $X in X months

Note: Continue with sections for each job title, but use fewer bullet points in the section on key accomplishments. When you reach the last third or quarter of page two, change to the following format:

Other Career Experience
Company Name, City, State   *(19XX to present)*
Title   *(Dates in the position)*

As for the cover letter, keep in mind that the reviewer is only interested in one thing—the facts. Do not think of your cover letter as an autobiography; it should be brief and to the point. The purpose of the cover letter and resumé should be one thing—it should demonstrate that you meet or exceed the requirements listed in the job description. It should demonstrate that you're interested in the position, and that you are available to accept the position, if offered. Additional information beyond this can be counterproductive, as it diminishes the purpose of the cover letter and resume.

When writing the cover letter, avoid negatives. A cover letter is not the place to explain why you left or are leaving an employer, why there are gaps in your employment dates, etc. These negatives are best delivered in person during the interview so that your personality can counter them.

Once you have been called to schedule an interview, you must do everything you can to research the organization that granted the interview. Know everything you can about the ADR industry. Find out as much as you can about the position and the company and its needs. Knowing these facts will enable you to prove how your background meets those needs. Research the company on the Internet and at your local library. Employers are as interested in your questions as they are in your answers. It is a huge plus if you ask intelligent questions about the position, the company, and the industry.

The Interview

This next step is your time to shine—you have an interview! The first few minutes are critical and will set the tone for the interview. To succeed, you must project enthusiasm about the position and show confidence and competence. Your goal is to convince the interviewer that you would be an asset to the company. You must sell yourself.

Dress appropriately for the position you are seeking. Your attire must fit well within the office and be immaculate. If you don't know what the typical attire at the company is, ask when setting up the interview. Your shoes should be polished with pants/skirts and shirts pressed. Clean hair and fingernails are essential. Avoid excessive cologne, jewelry, or make-up.

Be on time! Allow extra time for traffic, parking, and slow elevators. Do whatever it takes to arrive a few minutes early. If necessary, drive to the company the night before and time yourself. Late arrival for a job interview is never excusable.

The eighth step is follow-up. Often overlooked, the follow-up is the final step in the interview process. It's essential that you send a thank-you note to every person you met at the organization (remember to ask for business cards). In your letter, summarize your conversation and re-emphasize the skills you would bring to the position. If you are interested in the position, avoid sending a generic thank-you letter—besides the general "thank you for your time," note some reasons why you are the perfect candidate for the job. Chances are that hundreds of people are interviewing for the same position. You want to note something that will make you stand out and be remembered.

Outline of Thank-You Letter

Thank the interviewer for taking the time to meet with you and remind him of the position for which you interviewed.

Reiterate your sincere interest in the position and company. Be sure to mention something you learned from the interview, or comment on something of importance that you discussed. This will make you stand out from the other applicants. Emphasize your strengths, experiences, skills, and accomplishments, and as noted previously, tweak them towards the points that the interviewer considered the most important for the position.

End by thanking the interviewer for his time and consideration. If you feel it is appropriate, close with a suggestion for next steps (a second interview perhaps), or mention that you plan to follow-up with a phone call in a few days.

The last step is to get hired. You have done all the hard work—now sit back and wait for the call offering you the job. Another great resource, Get Hired NOW! (http://www.gethired.com/), is a complete job search system for the job-seeker in any field. It has everything you need to get your job search unstuck, make the best use of your time and energy, stay motivated in the face of rejection, and land the job you want.

Conclusion

Finding an ADR job can be simple if you use a system for success. This chapter provides such a system in order to propel you into opportunities within the field. Each step is a prerequisite for the former step; therefore, it important not only to avoid skipping steps but also to follow them chronologically.

Grant Money Available
for ADR Professionals

Objective
This chapter explores simple strategies
for successful grant procurement.

What Is Grant Money?

A grant is a type of financial assistance the benefit of which is that it is absolutely non-repayable (*What is a Grant?* n.d.). This assistance is provided by one organization to for support to start or continue activity that it would not or could not undertake without help. On the other side, a grant may be given to convince the organization to abstain from some activity. According to the Association of Fundraising Professionals, a grant is "a financial donation given to support a person, organization, project, or program," which is "typically awarded to a nonprofit organization from a foundation, corporation, or government" (*Social Science and History* 2005). Grants are given to an agency for a distinct purpose or program and, therefore, a grantmaker usually gives priority to

- ♦ a specific population, such as children, or organizations in some region or country
- ♦ definite forms of nonprofits such as environmental groups or churches

♦ certain kinds of support such as financing for equipment or seed money

It is worthwhile to note that many people perceive grants as free money to obtain. However, despite the fact that the grant is not paid back, it is necessary for a grant-seeker to invest a significant amount of time, effort, thought, and money to win a grant. After obtaining a grant, the recipient will have to monitor income and expenditures, observe the successes and failures of the project, and report the detailed information back to the funder. Thus, before searching for grant funding and asking for support, it is important to be certain of possessing the expertise and knowledge to fulfill a project.

How Much Grant Money Is Available?

Every year billions of dollars in grant money are provided by government agencies and more than 30,000 grant-making foundations in the USA through about 1,500 grant programs. Grant money is not a bank loan and, therefore, these grant-making foundations and government agencies don't have to act according to the strict requirements required by banks. The grant-seeker decides how much money is necessary. If it's lawful and coincides with the foundation's main criteria, the money is kept by the grant-seeker and never paid back to the funder. Grant money is non-taxable and interest-free. It is possible to apply for an indefinite number of grants. The grant programs do not demand credit checks, collateral, security deposits, or cosigners. Even in the case of the grant-seeker having a bankruptcy or bad credit, as a taxpayer and U.S. citizen he is eligible to ask for grant money. Usually, grant amounts for American citizens or residents range from $500 to $250,000 but, in some cases, grants may reach up to $5,000,000 (*Free Money from the Government*, n.d.). The amount depends on the nature and purpose of the programs for which the grant-seeker applies. This year over $900 billion dollars in grant money are intended to be awarded by private foundations and government grant programs (*Grant Money for Business and Personal Use*, n.d.).

Who Qualifies to Receive Grant Money?

Currently, any U.S. citizen who is 18 years or older is entitled to apply for United States government and private foundation grant programs. Some programs may have their own requirements. The application also depends on the needs of the grant-seeker. There are many grant programs that depend on the personal need or the need of the grant-seeker's community or organization—nonprofit and community groups, state and local governments, health care organizations, educational institutions, small businesses, women, minorities, entrepreneurs, individuals, and others (*Frequently Asked Questions,* n.d.).

Additionally, the following programs can qualify for grants: community development, drug prevention/treatment, housing programs (housing for the needy, not personal houses), job training, small businesses, education/scholarships, education resources, health care, AIDS assistance, food programs, women in business, and many others (*Frequently Asked Questions* n.d.).

According to U.S. law, a foundation can only provide funds for charitable goals, and Section 501(c)(3) of the Internal Revenue Code identifies these tax-free organizations as "organized and operated exclusively for religious, charitable, scientific, testing for public safety, literary, or educational purposes," and they are entitled to get tax-deductible contributions (Schladweiler, n.d.). An organization described in Section 501(c)(3) is further measured according to Section 509(a) of the Internal Revenue Code, which states that a 501(c)(3) organization is supposed to be a private foundation unless it can prove that it belongs to one of the following four organizations categories (Schladweiler, n.d.):

a. organizations described in Section 170(b)(1)(A) of the Internal Revenue Code, which consist of churches, schools, colleges, medical research institutes, hospitals, governmental organizations, support organizations to educational institutions, publicly supported organizations, and community foundations, etc.
b. organizations that usually receive more than one-third of their support from grants, gifts, fees, and gross receipts from admissions, sales, etc., and usually receive not more than one-third of their investment income support
c. supporting organizations, which coordinate and operate similar to public charities but are not publicly supported
d. organizations working specifically for testing for public safety

Accordingly, nonprofits are generally presented as social service organizations (such as Habitat for Humanity and the Red Gross), private educational or religious organizations, or cultural, historical, arts, and community educational organizations such as symphonies, museums, etc. Additionally, there are nonprofit organizations like health organizations (hospitals and clinics), political and advocacy groups (Greenpeace and National Association for the Advancement of Colored People [NAACP]), professional, trade and business organizations (the American Medical Association and the U.S. Chamber of Commerce). Other nonprofit organizations include research and scientific institutions, philanthropic foundations, community development organizations, youth leadership and development organizations (the Girl Scouts of America), and cooperative utility companies in rural areas (Wallis, n.d.).Grants are usually, but not always, given to nonprofit organizations for programs and services that bring benefits and advantages for the public or the community at large.

How Does a Nonprofit Organization Apply for Grant Money?

As it is already known, a nonprofit organization is any organization that does not take part in profit-making, commercial operations and has been given tax-exempt status by the Internal Revenue Service (IRS). To be successful in winning a grant, there are some essential steps for nonprofits to undertake. Receiving grant funds takes a certain amount of time. Thus, it is necessary to start working on the requests as soon as possible and go step-by-step.

First, you must determine what organizations are able to grant funds to your organization by searching for funding sources that meet the interests and mission of your organization (*Writing a Grant Proposal*, n.d.). It is worthwhile to remember that it may be more beneficial receiving a grant from a local organization, rather than a national one or one in another part of the country.

Secondly, it is absolutely required to understand the purpose of the grant program (*Writing a Grant Proposal*, n.d.). If possible, it would be useful to visit the funding organization and discuss all details of the grant program, especially because most funding organizations will ask the grant-seeker to present a specific proposal format.

And finally, there are possibly one to three documents that must be completed—such as an application, a letter of appeal and/or a grant proposal—to request a grant (*Frequently Asked Questions* 2005).

An application is generally a form requested by and received from a potential funder, which must be filled out by the grant-seeker. In the case where a small amount of money (up to $2,500) is requested, only an application is sent. The application usually comes with certain guidelines from the funder; therefore, the grant-seeker mainly fills in the blanks.

A letter of appeal is a summarized version of the grant proposal. It includes a brief but concise outline summarizing the grant-seeker's needs and requirements. For instance, if you are asking for money for a school project which will decrease school violence, here is a sample request for grant: "We would like to request a Grant in the sum of $25,000 to assist in the costs associated with the after-school program we have just developed to reduce crime within our community" (*Frequently Asked Questions,* 2005). Additionally, it is required to add a brief summary of the grant-seeker's program. It is also worthwhile to examine the average amount of grant money usually given by the foundation to whom the grant-seeker is applying. If the foundation only gives money from $3,000 to $20,000 and the grant-seeker requires $25,000, he is allowed to request only the limit set by the foundation. For example, someone may apply for $20,000 from one foundation and then apply to another foundation for the remaining $5,000.

A proposal is a document for requesting $5,000 to $50,000 or more which shows in more detail the grant-seeker's project and need for granting funds.. First, you need to send a letter of appeal to the potential funder. After receiving the guidelines and application, you must follow the given instructions, submit the application, and then submit the proposal.

A successful application or grant proposal must be well-prepared and should thoughtfully outline a project. Various grant programs have different waiting periods, but usually the grant money is provided to the grant-seeker within 30 to 90 days after the application is submitted and processed. If the funding organization denies the application, you should determine the reason in order to be successful next time when writing an application or grant proposal.

Sample Successful Grant Application

This chapter presents the winning nonprofit grant application submitted by Arlene Schwartz of Pomona Middle School to East Ramapo Teachers' Center (http://www.ertconline.org/), which provides funds to supplement financing from the District for attendance at a professional conference (*Writing a Good Grant,* n.d.). This is a real sample for writing a successful mini-grant. It follows all guidelines for preparing a winning, complete, and professional-looking proposal for a grant. The grant is organized into relevant sections. This application is straight-forward and focused; therefore, anyone could follow its directions.

East Ramapo Teachers' Center
Innovator/Developer Mini-Grant

Title:	A-B-C's of Cooking
Writer:	Arlene Schwartz
Date:	October 10, 2001
School:	Pomona Middle School
Phone:	577-6200
Initiative Addressed:	English Learning Standards 1–3

I. Statement of Purpose

The purpose of this program is for children to experience re-searching and preparing recipes with an alphabet slant to it. It is an interdisciplinary program in which students gain insight into preparations of food, shopping for foods, and creating their own unique class cookbook. A-B-C's of COOKING rein-forces oral language, written language, alphabetizing. and vocabulary expansion. It encourages sequencing, predicting, problem solving and following directions. Reading, mathematics, nutrition, and computer skills are developed through practical applications. It also gives my E.S.L. students an opportunity to improve their language skills using their 5 senses. Students also learn how to budget, shop, read newspaper ads and develop life skills as well.

II. Description of Project

The students each create their own A-B-C cookbook by being given one or more letters of the alphabet. It is then their job to research through magazines, cookbooks and family members for a recipe beginning with that letter. e.g. A- Apple Streudel, B- Banana Nutcake etc. Each child is then given $7.00 a piece to shop for the necessary food. They then make a shopping list, study newspaper ads for prices, shop for the ingredients, follow directions and prepare the recipe at home. The student then serves the dish for the class to enjoy. They then explain how the dish was prepared and write the recipe on the board. The rest of the class copies this into their notebook and goes to the computer room and creates the A-B-C COOKBOOK using all these recipes. These cookbooks can be shared with other classes and their families. Adjustments can be made according to the ages of the students.

III. Goals and Expected Outcomes
1) increase oral English ability
2) increase written English ability
3) bolster self image
4) gain computer skills related to word processing
5) increased math ability
6) following directions increased

IV.ENGLISH LEARNING STANDARDS
1) Students will read, write, listen, and speak for information and understanding
2) Students will read, write, listen, and speak for social interaction
3) Students will read, write listen and speak for critical analysis and evaluation

V. Evaluation
1) L.A.B. test will be administered to determine increase in English ability
2) Teacher evaluation
3) Teacher made rubric will be used to assess speaking and writing projects

VI. Budget
paper plates, napkins, plastic silverware etc.	$30.00
$7.00 per child for food supplies	$140.00
magazines for recipes	$30.00
TOTAL	$200.00

List of Resources for Nonprofit Organizations to Apply for Grant Money Nationwide

After establishing the nonprofit organization and defining the project's purposes and funding needs, the next step for a grant-seeker is to find the best grant opportunities. Foundations and private grant-making organizations award grants to many different nonprofit organizations. For a grant-seeker, there are two ways to receive grant money. The first source is the public sector—money which is controlled by the local, state and federal levels of government. The second source is the private sector, granting non-governmental funding for charitable or philanthropic goals. Two major sectors—such as grants from foundations and corporations, and grants from federal, state, and local government agencies—will be researched to present the list of necessary resources for nonprofits to apply for grants (*How to Find Grants for Your Nonprofit Organization*, 2005).

Foundation and Corporate Funding

Foundations are established by an individual, a group of individuals (such as a family), an organization, a community, or a corporation (Chess, 2004). A foundation is a form of nonprofit organization that exists in order to grant money for charitable goals. These foundations, as well as corporate giving, are the first funding resources to be reviewed here. Unless the grant-seeker's organization is not of large size, there is no need for him to buy the directories or databases with information about foundations funding. The Internet and public library are the best sources for searching.

So, the first and the most important resource for grant programs is the Foundation Center's Guide to Grantseeking on the Web, a convenient directory of online resources available at http://www.foundationcenter.org/. Through the Foundation Center's Grantmaker website page (http://www. foundationcenter.org/funders/grantmaker/index.html), it is possible to find the organizations if you know the name of a particular foundation, and through Foundation Finder page (http://lnp.fdncenter.org/finder.html) it is possible to find the foundation's website, contact information, brief description, and a link to a recent 990-PF form (the information return that foundations file with the IRS).

If the grant-seeker does not know the names of foundations, such information is available on the Foundation Center's Foundation Directory Online at http://fdncenter.org/learn/classroom/fdoguidedtour/. Foundation Directory Online contains about 80,000 foundations and corporate giving programs in the USA.

To find the latest funding opportunities, it is useful to visit the Foundation Center's Philanthropy News Digest/RFP Bulletin (http://fdncenter.org/pnd/) and the Philanthropy News Network (PNN) (http://www.pnnonline.org/)—a free online resource.

Another helpful resource is GuideStar (http://www.guidestar.org/)—a directory of more than 850,000 nonprofit organizations in the USA—and registration is free.

Again, if the grant-seeker does not know the names of foundations and corporations that grant funds, it is useful to visit the public library or its website if such exists. For example, in the Baltimore area, there is the Enoch Pratt Free Library's Central Library/State Library Resource Center (400 Cathedral Street, Baltimore, MD). Its website is http://www.epfl.net/. In turn, the Pratt Library subscribes to GrantsDirect.com (http://www .grantdirect.com/), a database that contains data specifically on Maryland, D.C., and Northern Virginia. GrantsDirect.com is mainly useful for pinpointing foundations that grant small (less than $10,000) amounts.

The Pratt Library Grants Collection offers the Grants Collection Subject Guide (http://www.pratt.lib.md.us/slrc/ssh/grantscoll.html), and the library subscribes to directories of foundations and the grants they donate:

♦ *Big Book of Library Grant Money.* Chicago: Taft. (SSH GRANTS COLL XZ683.2.U6B54Q)
♦ *Corporate Giving Directory.* Rockville, MD: Taft Group. (SSH GRANTS COLL XHV97.A3T32Q)
♦ *Operating Grants for Nonprofit Organizations.* Phoenix: Oryx Press. (SSH GRANTS COLL XHV41.2.O46Q)

If your library doesn't have subscriptions to any of these databases, it is possible to use Foundation Center products, which are published yearly:

♦ *The Foundation Directory* (SSH GRANTS COLL XAS911.A23. A97Q)
♦ *The Foundation Directory, Part 2* (SSH GRANTS COLL XAS911.A23F681Q)
♦ *Guide to U.S. Foundations, Their Trustees, Officers, and Donors* (SSH GRANTS COLL XAS911.A23G85Q)

The Foundation Center publishes different "National Guides" to grants by subject:

♦ *National Guide to Funding in Arts and Culture* (SSH GRANTS COLL XNX711.U5N37Q)
♦ *National Guide to Funding in Health* (SSH GRANTS COLL XHV687.N3N37Q)
♦ *National Guide to Funding in Religion* (SSH GRANTS COLL XHV89.N28Q)

Another possibility is to make certain whether some grant-makers' association, or an association for nonprofit organizations, exists in the grant-seeker's region. From time to time these organizations print directories and other information regarding their members, or about grant-makers who grant funds to them. Another possibility is to find out whether a government agency in the grant-seeker's state keeps records on such foundations.

Additionally, there are some funding organizations for definite types of interests, such as Grantmakers in the Arts (http://www.giarts.org/) and Funders Concerned about AIDS (http://www.fcaaids.org/).

Trade magazines and journals for fundraisers are another wonderful solution to find necessary information. Some magazines have online versions, but usually it is necessary to visit a library. For instance, Pratt's Periodicals Department subscribes to

- *Chronicle of Philanthropy*—http://philanthropy.com/
- *Foundation News and Commentary*—http://www.foundation news.org/
- *Grassroots Fundraising Journal*—http://www.grassrootsfund raising.org/
- *Nonprofit Times*—http://www.nptimes.com/

It is worthwhile to note that these magazines are only some of many other useful periodicals for nonprofit management and fundraising. The Foundation Center's Washington, D.C., library provides a larger database of magazines and newsletters at http://fdncenter .org/washington/dc_periodicals.html, and it is possible to read articles online at no cost or to visit their location.

There are many other very helpful, free Internet databases for nonprofit grant-seekers. Here is a sample list of these Internet resources:

- A Look at the Private Sector: Institutions and Individuals—http:// www.cnmsocal.org/grant-seekers/chapter8.html
- An Internet Virtual Library of Government, Foundation, and Corporate Grants and Grant Writing Support Material (nonprofit grants)—http://dgriesmann.blogspot.com/
- Arts and Humanities Grants—http://www.fundsnetservices.com/
- Center for Nonprofit Management: The Grant Seeker's Handbook—http://www.cnmsocal.org/
- Community Foundations by State—http://www.tgci.com/funding/federal.asp

- Connecting Nonprofit Professionals Worldwide—http://charitychannel.com/
- Grantmakers and Grantseeking Resources for Non-profits—http://npguides.org/links.htm
- Grant Money for Nonprofits—http://www.veripic.com/solutions/grants.htm
- Grant-making Organizations and Foundations—http://www.proposalwriter.com/grants.html
- Grant Programs and Deadlines 2006—http://www.neh.gov/grants/grants.html
- Grant Opportunities—http://www.proposalwriter.com/grant-opps.php
- Education Grants and New Funding Opportunities for Non-Profit Organizations, Schools, Districts, Consortia and State Education Agencies—http://www.grantsalert.com/
- Links and Books for Nonprofit Organizations Seeking Grants and Funding Opportunities Related to Many Spheres—http://www.lib.msu.edu/harris23/grants/2sgalpha.htm
- Nationwide Grants for K-12 Schools, Educators, and Students—http://www.schoolgrants.org/
- Nonprofit Funding Web Links—http://www.compasspoint.org/
- The Nonprofit Resource Center—http://www.not-for-profit.org/
- The Nonprofit Resource Library—http://www.cnmsocal .org/Library/

U.S. Government Funding

If the grant-seeker is looking for government funding for his organization or project, it is required to research the federal, state, and local agencies. Most federal funding is donated to state, county, or city governments, who then make decisions which local charities will get the grants.

It is actually easier to find free information about federal grants on the Internet. The federal government has some websites and publications to inform the public about grant-funding opportunities:

Federal Register—http://www.gpoaccess.gov/fr/index.html

The Catalog of Federal Domestic Assistance contains all the U.S. Government's grants, loans, and benefits programs with possibilities for nonprofits, businesses, state and local governments, families, and individuals. It can be found online at http://www.cfda.gov/ or in print.

Grants.gov—http://www.grants.gov/—a one-stop shopping center for grantees

The websites for grant-seekers of some federal agencies include:

♦ Department of Education—http://www.ed.gov/about/inits/
list/fbci/
♦ Department of Health and Human Services—http://www
.hhs.gov/fbci/
♦ Department of Justice—http://www.ojp.usdoj.gov/fbci/
♦ Department of Labor—http://www.dol.gov/cfbci/
♦ U.S. Federal Grants Websites for Nonprofits—http://
www.nonprofits.org/if/idealist/en/FAQ/QuestionViewer/
default?category-id=111&item=63&section=19&sid=3867
9097-60-jrXgx

There are also some websites that lead nonprofits through the process of applying for federal resources, filing necessary paperwork, and fulfilling a federally-funded program. For example:

♦ GrantsNet (http://www.hhs.gov/grantsnet/roadmap/) established
by the U.S. Department of Health and Human Services
♦ FirstGov for Nonprofits (http://www.firstgov.gov/Business/
Nonprofit.shtml) established by the U.S. General Services
Administration

Other Funding Options

The grant-seeker should remember that grants are only part of the whole fundraising strategy. There are many other options to obtain grant funding. These are donations from the common public through direct mail, the Internet, telemarketing, membership programs, major gift campaigns, partnering or receiving sponsorship from a larger non-profit organization, marketing cooperation with corporations, selling products and services, special events, etc, (*How to Find Grants for Your Nonprofit Organization*, 2005).

Conclusion

The main focus of this chapter has been grant-seeking by non-profit organizations. The resources presented herein are intended for nonprofit organizations, because the largest portion of the grant money available from funders is awarded to such organizations.

Professional Organizations

Here is a list of professional associations that will help you get involved quickly in the ADR field. You should use these resources as a means to contribute to the profession, network, and—most importantly—to attend important events within the field of Alternative Dispute Resolution.

Association for Conflict Resolution

Based in Washington, D.C., the Association for Conflict Resolution represents more than 6,000 mediators, arbitrators, and educators in the field of conflict resolution. Here is the contact information:

Association for Conflict Resolution
1015 18th Street, NW, Suite 1150
Washington, D.C. 20036

Phone: 202-464-9700
Fax: 202-464-9720

E-mail:

General Inquiries:	acr@ACRnet.org
Chapters:	chapters@ACRnet.org
Conferences:	conferences@ACRnet.org
Membership:	membership@ACRnet.org
Publications:	publications@ACRnet.org
Professional Interest Sections:	sections@ACRnet.org
Website:	web@ACRnet.org

National Institute for Advanced Conflict Resolution

Founded to advance the field of conflict resolution, the National Institute for Conflict Resolution provides information and resources to practicing mediators and members of the public. Here is the contact information: http://www.niacr.org /.

Association for Dispute Resolution of Northern California

A chapter of the Association for Conflict Resolution, the Association for Dispute Resolution of Northern California provides education and training to locally based conflict resolution professionals. Here is the contact information:

Association for Dispute Resolution of Northern California

601 Van Ness Ave. #E3-102
San Francisco, CA 94102-6300

Phone:	650-745-3842
Fax:	650-745-3842
Email:	ADR@ADRnc.net

American Bar Association's Section of Dispute Resolution

This section of the ABA provides information and assistance to its members, to legislators, and to the general public on all aspects of dispute resolution. Here is the contact information:

American Bar Association

740 15th Street, N.W.
Washington, D.C. 20005-1019

Phone:	202-662-1000

Association of Family and Conciliation Courts

The AFCC is an association of judges, mediators, psychologists, attorneys, custody evaluators, and social workers dedicated to the resolution of family conflict. Here is the contact information:

Association of Family and Conciliation Courts
6525 Grand Teton Plaza
Madison, WI 53719

Phone:	608-664-3750
Fax:	608-664-3751
Email:	afcc@afccnet.org
Website:	http://www.afccnet.org/

California Dispute Resolution Council

A statewide, non-profit organization of mediators and arbitrators that exists to develop and influence legislation and public policies for effective conflict resolution in California. Here is the contact information:

California Dispute Resolution Council
P. O. Box 177
La Jolla, CA 92038
Phone: 866-216-CDRC

Fax:	858-454-1021
Email:	cdrc@mediate.com

International Peace Research Association (IPRA)

Membership in IPRA will benefit scholars, practitioners and students of peace research conflict transformation and peace building. Here is the contact information:

Faculty of Social Sciences
University of Leuven
Van Evenstraat 2B
B3000 Leuven, Belgium

Phone:	32-16-323241
Fax:	32-16-323088
E-Mail:	sgipra@soc.kuleuven.be.
Website:	http://www.ipraweb.org/

Peace History Society

Annual dues are currently $40 per year, (or a special rate of $25 for students, retirees, and people unemployed). In addition to receiving regular issues of *Peace & Change* and the PHS newsletter, members are encouraged to organize PHS-sponsored sessions at an array of conferences as well as nominating and electing colleagues to the Board of Directors and the Executive Committee.

Membership forms and dues should be directed to:

Christy Snider
  Department of History
  5010 Mt. Berry Station
  Berry College
  Mt. Berry, GA 30149

  Phone: 706-368-5652

For institutional subscribers, please contact:

Malcolm Crystal, Journals Editor
  Blackwell Publishers
  350 Main Street
  Malden, MA 02148

  Phone: 781-388-0438

All other membership queries or questions should be directed to

Joyce Blackwell-Johnson, Chair
  Department of History and Political Science
  Saint Augustine's College
  1315 Oakwood Avenue
  Raleigh, NC 27610

  Phone: 919-516-4280

The Peace and Justice Studies Association (PJSA)

This is a nonprofit organization that was formed in 2001 as a result of a merger of the Consortium on Peace research, Education and Development (COPRED) and the Peace Studies Association (PSA). Both organizations provided leadership in the broadly defined field of peace, conflict and justice studies.

This organization is dedicated to bringing together academics, K-12 teachers and grassroots activists to explore alternatives to violence and share visions and strategies for peace building, social justice, and social change.

PJSA also serves as a professional association for scholars in the field of peace and conflict resolution studies. Here is the contact information:

Peace & Justice Studies Assoc.
5th Floor University Center
2130 Fulton Street
San Francisco, CA 94117-1080

Phone: 415-422-5238

Peace, War, and Social Conflict
The purpose of the Section on Peace, War, and Social Conflict is to encourage the application of sociological methods, theories, and perspectives to the study of peace and war. Here is the contact information:

American Sociological Association
1307 New York Avenue NW, Suite 700
Washington, D.C. 20005-4701

Website: http://www.peacewarconflict.org/

Conclusion

As you can see, whether you're an amateur or a pro, this book has provided information that is not found in any other single source. This book should help you prosper and advance in the field of Alternative Dispute Resolution. Hence, this book, through the completion of the success checklist on page 9, should assist you in finding a true secret of happiness in life and in business. This profession is all about being a servant-leader and providing a light on the path for others. I wish you much success in your pursuit of this field and would be delighted to hear from you about your triumphs.

ADR Glossary

The following are some commonly used definitions of ADR terms. Agencies may differ in the manner in which they define such terms. Also, some of these terms may be used differently in other contexts.

Arbitration—A dispute resolution process whereby a neutral third party is empowered by agreement of the parties to issue a decision on the controversy, following the conduct of a trial-like hearing. An arbitrator's decision is generally binding and not reversible, absent fraud or misconduct on the part of the arbitrator. Arbitrators often are asked to attempt to mediate (see below) a settlement first, and to impose a decision on the parties only as a last resort. This hybrid process is frequently referred to as med-arb.

Conciliation—Efforts by a neutral third party to assist in the resolution of an issue in controversy, including holding meetings with individual parties to discuss the controversy and potential solutions, contacting individual parties by telephone or mail, and serving as a conduit for information between them.

Early Neutral Evaluation—The process by which a neutral third party imparts to the parties his views as to the strengths and weaknesses of their respective positions relating to an issue in controversy. This process frequently is combined with conciliation or mediation.

Fact Finding—A process in which a neutral third party assists the parties to determine, in an objective manner, the facts relating to an issue in controversy. Frequently, fact finding will be engaged in as a prelude to mediation.

Mediation—An effort by a neutral third party to resolve an issue in controversy through the conduct of face-to-face meetings between the disputing parties. The third party is not authorized to impose a settlement upon the parties, but rather seeks to assist the parties in fashioning a mutually satisfactory solution to the issue in controversy. Mediation can take two forms: (1) facilitative mediation, in which the mediator simply facilitates discussions between or among the parties and does not provide any form of evaluation of the merits of their respective positions; and (2) evaluative mediation, in which the mediator provides the parties, either individually or jointly, with early neutral evaluation (see above)—i.e., his views as to the strengths and weaknesses of their respective positions—in conjunction with the mediator's efforts to help the parties fashion an amicable resolution to their controversy.

Mini-Trial—A procedure where the parties make abbreviated presentations to a neutral third party who sits with the parties' designated principal representatives as a mini-trial panel to hear and evaluate evidence relating to an issue in controversy. The neutral may thereafter meet with the principal representatives to attempt to mediate a settlement. The mini-trial process may also be a prelude either to the neutral's issuance of a formal, written, non-binding advisory opinion or to the neutral's rendering of a binding arbitration award.

Ombudsman—An individual who has been designated as a confidential and informal information resource, communications channel, complaint-handler, and dispute-resolver. The ombudsman role was intended to be an antidote to abuses of governmental and bureaucratic authority and administration, and ombudsmen may serve as effective intervenors in cases of arbitrary decision-making.

Summary Trial with Binding Decision—A binding ADR procedure utilized by a Board of Contract Appeals wherein the parties make abbreviated evidentiary presentations concerning an issue in controversy, and the Board's judge renders a summary binding and non-appealable decision. The decision, frequently rendered from the bench, may not be used as precedent in the future.

Mediator—A neutral, third-party volunteer who has been trained to mediate. The mediator assists the parties in reaching a consensus by facilitating their communication, but it is the parties themselves who shape their agreement.

Neutral—Not aligned or taking sides with a particular group.

Chapter Resources

Chapter 1

ADR Options. http://www.directionservice.org/cadre/other.cfm (accessed September 17, 2006).

Alternative Dispute Resolution. http://www.opm.gov/er/adrguide/Section1-a.asp (accessed September 17, 2006).

Arbitration. http://www.mediate.ca/arbitration.htm (accessed September 17, 2006).

Centre for Effective Dispute Resolution (CEDR). http://www.cedr.co.uk/index.php?location=/library/glossary.htm (accessed September 17, 2006).

Information About Expert Determination. http://www.iama.org.au/expert.htm (accessed September 17, 2006).

Mackie, Karl J. *A Handbook of Dispute Resolution: ADR in Action.* Routledge, 1991.

Maclaury, Judson. "Alternative Dispute Resolution." *Monthly Labor Review*, Vol. 128 (2005).

Ombudsmen. http://www.adrnow.org.uk/go/SubSection_15.html (accessed September 17, 2006).

Reasons to Use ADR. http://www.mediate.ca/reasonstouse.htm (accessed September 17, 2006).

Spangler, Brad. 2003. *Adjudication.* http://www.beyondintractability .org/essay/adjudication/ (accessed September 17, 2006).

Chapter 3

Buscher, Ranae. *Establish Yourself as an Expert.* http://www.workz .com/content/view_content.html?section_id=465&content_id=5675 (accessed September 18, 2006)

Business plan. http://www.myownbusiness.org/s2/ (accessed September 18, 2006)

Career Outlook. http://www.acinet.org/acinet/select_educ.asp?next =oview1&optstatus=&id=&nodeid=&soccode=&stfips=00&jobfam (accessed September18, 2006)

Career Portfolio. http://careerservices.uvic.ca/tutorials/career-portfolio .html (accessed September 18, 2006)

Creating portfolio. http://www.careermag.com/ (accessed September 18, 2006)

How to Become a Consultant. http://www.coker.com.au/~russell/ consultant/how-do-i.html (accessed September 18, 2006)

Sample Contract Form. http://www.managementhelp.org/misc/smplcntr .htm (accessed September 18, 2006)

Starting a consulting business. http://www.cbsc.org/servlet/Content Server?cid=1106739780776&pagename=CBSC_FE%2Fdisplay &lang=en&c=GuideHowto (accessed September 18, 2006)

Starting a Consulting Business. http://www.entrepreneur.com/ startingabusiness/businessideas/startupkits/article41384.html (accessed September 18, 2006)

Starting Consulting Company. http://www.gaebler.com/Starting-Consulting-Company.htm (accessed September 18, 2006)

Chapter 4

Cool, Lisa Collier. *How to Write Irresistible Query Letters.* Writer's Digest Books, 2002.

Harper, Timothy (editor). *The ASJA Guide to Freelance Writing: A Professional Guide to the Business, for Nonfiction Writers of All Experience Levels.* St. Martin's, 2003

Herman, Jeff, and Deborah Levine Herman. *Write the Perfect Book Proposal: 10 That Sold and Why.* Wiley, 2001.

Hill, Bonnie Hearn. *The Freelancer's Rulebook: A Guide to Understanding, Working With and Winning Over Editors.* Story Line Press, 2001.

Horowitz, Shel. *Grassroots Marketing: Getting Noticed in a Noisy World.* Chelsea Green, 2000.

Kipfer, Barbara Ann (editor). *Roget's International Thesaurus.* 6th ed. Harper Collins, 2001.

Kremer, John. *1001 Ways to Market Your Books for Authors and Publishers.* Open Horizons, 2006.

Larsen, Michael. *How to Write a Book Proposal.* Writer's Digest Books, 2004.

Laufenberg, Cynthia. *Formatting and Submitting Your Manuscript.* Writer's Digest Books, 2004.

Levinson, Jay Conrad, Rick Frishman, and Michael Larsen. *Guerrilla Marketing for Writers.* Writer's Digest Books, 2001.

Masterson, Pete. *Book Design and Production.* Aeonix, 2006.

Merriam-Webster's Collegiate Dictionary. 11th ed. Merriam-Webster, 2006.

Plotnik, Plotnik. *Spunk & Bite: A Writer's Guide to Punchier, More Engaging Language & Style.* Random House, 2005.

Poynter, Dan. *Self-Publishing Manual: How to Write, Print and Sell Your Own Book.* Para Publishing, 2006.

Reiss, Fern. *The Publishing Game: Publish a Book in 30 Days.* Peanut Butter and Jelly Press, 2003.

Ruberg, Michelle (editor). *Writer's Digest Handbook of Magazine Article Writing.* Writer's Digest Books, 2005.

Strunk, William, Jr., and E. B. White. *The Elements of Style.* 4rd ed. Longman, 1999.

Chapter 5

Average Sales Training Manager Salary. http://swz.salary.com/salarywizard/layouthtmls/swzl_compresult_national_SM1500016.html (accessed November 23, 2005).

Fripp, Patricia. 2005. *Business leader, what do you charge for talks? Appropriate fees for business executives seeking engagements?* http://www.fripp.com/art.charge.html (accessed November 23, 2005).

National Speakers Association. 2003. *National Speakers Association 2003 Member Survey.* http://www.nsaspeaker.org/2003_survey_results.shtml (accessed November 23, 2005).

Walters, Lilly. 2002. *Speaking Industry Report 2002.* http://www.paidpublicspeaking.com/speakingindustryreport.html (accessed November 23, 2005).

Women's Calendar. Speech Terms. www.womenscalendar.org/SpeakerSpot/SearchTerms.asp (accessed November 23, 2005).

Chapter 6

Benfari, R. C. *Understanding and Changing Your Management Style.* Jossey-Bass, 1999.

Gitlow, H. S. *The Deming Guide to Quality and Competitive Position.* Prentice-Hall, 1997.

Howard, F. *Recent Economic Trends.* Routledge, 2000.

Mohrman, S. A. *Tomorrow's Organization: Crafting Winning Capabilities in a Dynamic World.* Jossey-Bass, 1998.

Newel, D. *Gaining a Holistic View of the Customer.* LA: Printword, 2001.

Peters, T. J. *In Search of Excellence: Lessons From America's Best-Run Companies.* Harper & Row, 2002.

Schein, E. H. *Organizational Culture and Leadership.* Jossey-Bass, 1999.

Schmitt, B. *Mediation.* The Free Press, 2001.

Stewart, J. *Mediation: Future Perspectives.* New Publishers, 2001.

Wilkins, A. L. *Developing Corporate Character: How to Successfully Change an Organization Without Destroying It.* Jossey-Bass, 1999.

Chapter 7

"Arbitration of Business Disputes". 2000. http://www.stimmel-law.com/articles/arbit_dis.html (accessed November 30, 2005).

"Arbitration". 2005. From Wikipedia, the free encyclopedia, November 22. http://en.wikipedia.org/wiki/Arbitration (accessed November 30, 2005).

"Ashley Marshall's Report on the Ins and Outs of an Arbitrator". n. d. http://student.elon.edu/amarshall/report/TMPp8bed7e731.htm (accessed November 30, 2005).

"Become An Arbitrator". 2005. http://www.nasd.com/web/idcplg?IdcService=SS_GET_PAGE&nodeId=864 (accessed November 30, 2005).

Choong, Vikki. 2004. "City & Country: The advantages of arbitration." *The Edge Malaysia*, Lexis-Nexis, November 03

Chou, Timmy. 2002. "Arbitration/Mediation: Arbitration Reports?" September 17, http://experts.about.com/q/908/2554408.htm (accessed November 30, 2005).

Edition. Bureau of Labor Statistics, U.S. Department of Labor. http://www.bls.gov/oco/ocos272.htm (accessed November 30, 2005).

"Fair Play: Perspectives from American Arbitration Association on Consumer and Employment Arbitration." American Arbitration Association, 2003. http://www.adr.org/ (accessed November 30, 2005).

Goldberg, Sander, and Rogers. *Dispute Resolution: Negotiation, Mediation, and Other Processes.* 2nd ed. Little, Brown, 1992

"Job Profile: Arbitrator, Mediator and Conciliator". 2005. http://legal .monster.com/articles/arbitrator/ (accessed November 30, 2005).

"Judges, Magistrates, and Other Judicial Workers". 2004. In: *Occupational Outlook Handbook, 2004-05*

"Overview of Dispute Resolution Methods." n. d. Advanced Dispute Resolution Institute at the William Mitchell college of Law. http://www .adrinstitute.org/basics_0.htm#arb (accessed November 30, 2005).

Smith, Robert M. *ADR for Financial Institutions.* West Group, 1998

Chapter 8

Bermont, Todd. *10 Insider Secrets To Job Hunting Success! Everything You Need To Get The Job You Want In 24 Hours—Or Less!* 10 Step Corporation, 2001

Cinocca, Tracy A. *Careers in the Law: Success Without College.* Barrons, 2001.

Creative Job Search. Minnesota Department of Economic Security; 2003.

Darling, Diane C. *The Networking Survival Guide: Get the Success You Want By Tapping Into the People You Know.* McGraw-Hill, 2003.

Deluca, Matthew J. *Best Answers to the 201 Most Frequently Asked Interview Questions.* McGraw-Hill, 1996.

Dikel, Margaret, and Roehm, Frances E. *Guide to Internet Job Searching, 2002-2003.* 1st ed. McGraw-Hill, 2002

Erickson, Stephen K., and McKnight, Marilyn S. *The Practitioner's Guide to Mediation: A Client-Centered Approach.* 1st ed. Wiley, 2000.

Farr, J. Michael. *The Very Quick Job Search: Get a Better Job in Half the Time.* 2nd ed. Jist Works, 1995.

Graber, Steven, and Littmann, Barry. *The Everything Online Job Search Book: Find the Jobs, Send Your Resume, and Land the Career of Your Dreams-All Online!* Adams Media; 2000

Krannich, Ronald L., Krannich, Caryl Rae, and Krannich, Ron. *201 Dynamite Job Search Letters.* 4th ed. Impact Publications; 2001

Lovenheim, Peter. *Becoming a Mediator : An Insider's Guide to Exploring Careers in Mediation.* Jossey-Bass; 2002.

Lowstuter, Clyde C., and Robertson, David P. *In Search Of the Perfect Job.* McGraw-Hill, 1992.

McCarty, Martha, and Jensen, Jill (editor). *Don't Stop With the Want Ads: Conducting a Successful Job Search.* Provant Media, 1998.

Melançon, Robert M. *The Secrets of Executive Search: Professional Strategies for Managing Your Personal Job Search.* 1st ed. Wiley: 2002.

Mosten, Forrest S. *Complete Guide Mediation: Cutting Edge Approach to Family Law Practice.* American Bar Association; 1997.

———*Mediation Career Guide: A Strategic Approach to Building a Successful Practice.* 1st ed. Jossey-Bass; 2001.

Studner, Peter K. *Super Job Search: The Complete Manual for Job-Seekers & Career-Changers.* 3rd ed. Jamenair, 1998.

Warters, William C. *Mediation in the Campus Community: Designing and Managing Effective Programs.* Jossey-Bass; 1999.

Chapter 9

Chess, Harvey. *The Grant Seeker's Handbook: A Guide to Finding Funds.* Edited by Lauren Kay and the Center for Nonprofit Management. August, 2004. http://www.cnmsocal.org/Grantseekers/intro.html (accessed November 16, 2005).

Free Money from the Government. http://www.government-free-money .com/Grants.htm (accessed November 16, 2005).

Frequently Asked Questions: Proposal Writing & Nonprofit Services Since 1988. 2005. http://www.grantproposalservices.com/html/faqs.html (accessed November 16, 2005).

Grant Money for Business and Personal Use. http://www.government-free-money.com/Grant.htm (accessed November 16, 2005).

How to Find Grants for Your Nonprofit Organization. Social Science and History. In Central Library/ State Library Resource Center, Enoch Pratt Free Library, Baltimore, Maryland. July 29, 2005. http://www.pratt.lib.md.us/slrc/ssh/ewg_grants.html (accessed November 16, 2005).

Schladweiler, Kief. *Foundation Fundamentals: A Guide for Grantseekers.* 7th ed. http://fdncenter.org/learn/bookshelf/ff/text.html (accessed November 16, 2005).

Wallis, T.J. *Do Good And Make Money In A Nonprofit Organization?* http://www.findarticles.com/p/articles/mi_m0HUV/is_3_29/ai_67160958/print (accessed November 16, 2005).

What is a Grant? http://www.grant-4-you.com/what_is_a_grant.html (accessed November 16, 2005).

Writing a Good Grant. http://www.ertconline.org/grants/MG/MiniGrant_Innovator.htm (accessed November 16, 2005).

Writing a Grant Proposal. http://www.scoreknox.org/printlib/grantprint .htm (accessed November 16, 2005).